as Teachers

Reinventing Ourselves
as Teachers:
Beyond Nostalgia

Claudia Mitchell and Sandra Weber

UK   Falmer Press, 1 Gunpowder Square, London, EC4A 3DE

USA   Falmer Press, Taylor & Francis Inc., 325 Chestnut Street, 8th Floor,
Philadelphia, PA 19106

© C. Mitchell and S. Weber 1999

First published in 1999

**A catalogue record for this book is available from the British
Library**

ISBN 0 7507 0625 2 cased
ISBN 0 7507 0626 0 paper

**Library of Congress Cataloging-in-Publication Data are
available on request**

Jacket design by Caroline Archer
Cover photo by Stéphanie Anne Weber Biron

Typeset in 10/12 pt Garamond by
Graphicraft Limited, Hong Kong

*Printed in Great Britain by Biddles Ltd., Guildford and King's Lynn
on paper which has a specified pH value on final paper manufacture
of not less than 7.5 and is therefore 'acid free'.*

*Every effort has been made to contact copyright holders for their
permission to reprint material in this book. The publishers would
be grateful to hear from any copyright holder who is not here
acknowledged and will undertake to rectify any errors or omissions
in future editions of this book.*

Contents

List of Figures

List of Boxes

Acknowledgments

Along the way, there have been many people who have contributed to this book — starting with all the former teachers, former students, and school friends who play significant roles in our own memory work around learning and teaching.

The original research on memory work and the use of photographs, film and video in teacher education received support from several granting agencies: the Social Science Research Council of Canada (SSHRCC); Fonds pour la Formation de Chercheurs et l'Aide à la Recherche (FCAR) and the British Council. We gratefully acknowledge their financial support.

We thank the many teachers in our undergraduate and graduate courses who enthusiastically participated in workshop activities around 'playing school', 'teachers in film', 'photo day' and 'self-video', and who gave us permission to use their accounts for the book. Their material also served to generate even more stories from other students and colleagues. We acknowledge, too, the valuable insights offered by our masters and doctoral students who are themselves engaged in studies of memory, autobiography, self-study and teacher education.

We thank the following individuals: our research assistants, Rita Hamel and Faith Butler whose enthusiasm for the project, and whose unwavering dedication to 'getting the job done' has been an inspiration throughout; Vanessa Nicolai who lent her insightful comments and editing skills; Sophie Grossman who assisted us in the conceptualization of the research; all those who read and in some cases contributed a story to particular chapters: Valerie Free, Paul McAdams, Jacqueline Reid-Walsh, Carolyn Sturge Sparkes, Chris Tromp and Jo Visser and Robert Sutherland who assisted with data collection.

We are grateful to Anna Clarkson of Falmer Press both for her support of the book and for her timely 'nudges' to finish.

Our families have played no small role in the life of this book: Sarah Mitchell listened, offered suggestions and has generally contributed to the shape of the book in so many ways, both tangible and intangible; Stephanie Anne Weber Biron contributed her photography skills and enthusiastic support; Matthew Fogel lent his computer skills to our project; Rebecca Mitchell, Dorian Mitchell, Marcus Peterli and Zachariah Campbell at various points have offered their own memory accounts of school.

Finally, there are two people who in addition to having read every word of the book several times over and to having offered so many valuable suggestions, continue to provide spiritual and intellectual support. Thank you Ann Smith and Michel Boyer.

Claudia: To my mother, Elsie Brown Skinner who continues to be the best teacher ever of the significance of memory work.

Sandra: For Stephanie, in loving memory of her father, Serge Biron.

Studying Ourselves as Teachers: An Introduction

Look, I spend hours at home, preparing my lessons. The children keep me on the go all day, I barely have time to breathe, let alone reflect. The last thing I need is to spend yet more time at my job doing some kind of study no-one but me is going to see. (Reaction of a primary school teacher attending a professional development seminar)

It's all so new to us, you know, planning lessons, trying to figure out what our supervisors want, keeping the kids in line. It's exhausting. There is so much pressure on us and so much work. And now you want us to study ourselves too? (Excerpt from a teaching log kept by a pre-service high school teacher)

I just can't hack it anymore. I've changed — I've seen it all and I can't take it one second longer. I can't teach the same old stuff the same old way — that's not who I am anymore. There's got to be a better way, one that lets me be me . . . maybe I should just quit teaching altogether . . . (Comments made at a professional development seminar by a primary teacher)

These teachers have a point. In contrast to those who remember their good old school days and wonderful teachers through a veil of nostalgia, only current practitioners know just how time-consuming, difficult, under-valued, and emotionally draining teaching often is. Too often our work can be frustrating, boring, or even dangerous. There may even be times when we question why we ever chose teaching to begin with (if indeed we did choose it!), times when we don't *feel* like teaching, or times when we wonder if 'teacher' is an increasingly cumbersome mask that hides who we really are. These darker moments make the occasions when we feel quietly satisfied or even delighted by our work and students, the mornings we wake up eager to get into the classroom, or the times we feel pride and a sense of belonging in calling ourselves 'teacher' seem all the more significant.

How might we better understand and use both the darker and lighter aspects of our work? Throughout this book we explore the use of a variety of forms (for example, photography, written memoirs, movies and video) to focus on specific aspects of the teaching self. The emphasis is on reflective, inventive, even playful action. Much of our work explores using the creative power of images, memories, everyday details, technology, and nostalgia in unexpected or unconventional ways. Through stories about our own and other teachers' struggles for self-knowledge and identity, we suggest ways to investigate and reinvent teacher identity and practice.

School as a Nostalgia Factory

The ad below, inviting former students and teachers back to their country school for a reunion, appeared in a small town newspaper in Canada's mid-West. The ad taps into what might be called 'back to school' nostalgia, evoking the special place that school occupies in people's thoughts, fantasies and memories. In North America, for example, the one-room school-house is a powerful and romantic symbol of the past, a veritable 'nostalgia factory' that churns out images hearkening to scenes from popular fiction like *Little House on the Prairie, How Green was My Valley*, or *Anne of Green Gables*. It conjures up the rural life and pioneer days of yesteryear, as well as many other images: national flags, portraits of heads of state, wooden benches, chalk dust, pointers, maps, globes and slates. These images are often seen and exploited as wistful symbols of a more innocent and noble past, of childhood pleasure and laughter, or of almost proud recollections of childhood pain and endurance ('We had to walk 15 miles in deep mud or snow to get to school each day'). As Mary Phillips Manke (1994) points out, the one-room country school in American history is remembered through a veil of nostalgia — 'home to happy, well-behaved children' and an ideal teacher (p. 243). Similarly, Isobel Quigly (1982) notes that in Britain, the very word 'school' is an emotive one that provokes immediate interest and deep feelings of nostalgia.

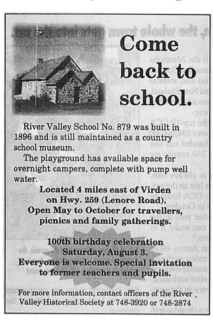

Come back to school.

River Valley School No. 879 was built in 1896 and is still maintained as a country school museum.
The playground has available space for overnight campers, complete with pump well water.

Located 4 miles east of Virden on Hwy. 259 (Lenore Road).
Open May to October for travellers, picnics and family gatherings.

100th birthday celebration
Saturday, August 3.
Everyone is welcome. Special invitation to former teachers and pupils.

For more information, contact officers of the River Valley Historical Society at 748-3920 or 748-2874

Figure 1.1   School-house advertisement

Consider the kinds of artefacts or 'prompts' that trigger images and memories, taking us back to school. Merely the accidental glimpse of a school desk, a blackboard, or a particular textbook can bring back long-forgotten memories of school. As we shall see in great detail later on in the book, photographs, too, are richly evocative. So are smells — copying fluid, cleaning materials, or the sweat of a gymnasium. The sound of children playing in a school yard or the school bell ringing can have the same effect. Think of all the memories associated with the school readers that were shared by so many students. The *Dick and Jane* reading series, for example, will probably be clearly remembered by people schooled in North American classrooms between 1940 and the late 1960s.

So potent are some of these images in evoking memory, that even people who were not taught with this particular series may be convinced that they were, unwittingly allowing a dominant image to 'overwrite' their memories of their own experiences! To evoke nostalgia or other strong feelings, artefacts do not have to be very old. Even teenagers can wax nostalgic when they come across their early copybooks, drawings or yearbooks.

Making the Past Usable: Returning to School

Come back to school? School? My school? Not on your life.

Come back to school? I've always been in school. First it was kindergarten, followed by elementary school, high school, university, getting a job teaching in a school . . . Come back? I've never left! (Teachers)

This last statement probably has more truth to it than the speaker ever imagined. Leave school? It would be hard to leave it totally behind, even if we wanted to. We may physically leave the school building that we work or learn in, but once outside, school is ever-present, whether we notice it or not. We are immersed in a *school outside of school*. Look around and listen: School yard chants and radio songs taunt or praise teachers, back-to-school fliers and advertisements arrive unbidden in the post, scores of popular television programs for children and adults are set in school environments or involve teachers. In newspaper and magazine stores, Miss Grundy stares out from the *Archie* comics in the racks. Available in many languages and countries, school novel series such as *Sweet Valley High* or the many British boarding school series line the shelves of the children's sections of book stores. And as for cinema — if it isn't *The Prime of Miss Jean Brodie* or *To Sir With Love*, it's *The Substitute, Sarafina, Mathilda, Clueless, Dangerous Minds, Kindergarten Cop, Mr. Holland's Opus, Waterland, In & Out*, and so on. A never-ending parade of celluloid teachers keeps us omnipresent in the public eye and in our own. Want to buy a toy? You can choose from Teacher Barbie, or chalkboards or magnetic letters, or Playskool toys or the Little Professor calculator or Arthur's Terrible Teacher Troubles CD ROM to mention just a few. Reading the newspaper, it's hard to escape editorials, cartoons and letters about education. It seems everyone has an opinion.

The photograph on the cover of this book shows an empty classroom, a kind of 'blank slate' that invites viewers to choose their own memories and time. Some of us might look at the image and think of classrooms in which we have taught, or are currently teaching, or remember classrooms in which we ourselves were students. We might focus on the classroom clock, remembering how often we stared up at it from our desks, hoping against hope that the day or period was almost over. Maybe we imagine a teacher preparing to teach class, gathering materials together. Gazing at the chairs, we might even find ourselves fidgeting in sympathy with the imagined students or reminiscing with fondness about favourite teachers we had. The wooden chair might evoke a particular kind of classroom, the metal chairs another. In short, the image may take us back to school both as a teacher and a student, helping us visualize what was or could be.

The fact that we all have had extensive experience in classrooms as students informs a great deal of our work as teachers. How does our past experience play into who we are and how we teach today? How can we revisit or use that past to study and reinvent ourselves as teachers?

A memoir called *A Life in School: What the Teacher Learned* written by Jane Tompkins (1996) provides a good example of the kind of remembering that can be useful for professional growth. Now an English professor at Duke University, Tompkins looks back on her school life as a student. She uses a self-reflective or critical style of writing to assess the importance, not only of the past she remembers, but also of the past she now realizes she missed out on, the one she didn't have but wishes she had. For example, she notices with regret that she recalls almost no instances where teachers told the students anything about their own lives:

> *The only instance that stands out was in third grade, when Mrs. Higgins, my favorite teacher, told us, for reasons I shall never know, that that morning her son, John, had brought her a glass of orange juice while she was in the shower. It had something to do with her having a cold. The feeling that accompanied this tiny anecdote was abundantly clear: proud pleasure. Mrs. Higgins was boasting and enjoying her boast, and I enjoyed it almost as much as she did. I saw the steamy bathroom, felt the heat and moisture in the air, saw the orange of the glass of orange juice held out toward the shower stall by the hand of the mysterious John (in my mind a tall youth with brown hair). And behind the clouded glass door was the naked body of Mrs. Higgins, enjoying itself.*
>
> *What I remember thinking at the time had nothing to do with Freudian relationships. Rather, I was amazed and pleased to learn that Mrs. Higgins had a family life just as I did. I pictured her bathroom being very much like my own, her apartment another version of ours. And her relationship to John — that was what was so interesting. I knew she had told us this little story to show us that her son cared for her, that she was loved within the bosom of her family, that she, Mrs. Higgins, despite her cold, was the luckiest person in the whole world.*
>
> *I dwell on this incident because it symbolizes something that was missing from education as I knew it: the reality of private life. Taking showers, having a naked body, drinking orange juice, being a member of a family, needing to know that you are loved, needing to tell about it. It was the sense of life itself that was missing, of sensory and emotional experience not divided up into 'subjects' — hygiene, psychology, nutrition, family relations*

— but embedded in a narrative, part of a lived history, a history I could relate to my history and the histories of the people around me, how we felt, what we really thought about, what it was like for us to be alive and going through the world. (pp. xiv–xv)

Tompkins wrote her memoir at a point in her career when she was questioning the value and purpose of an education that does not address the personal life of teachers and students. While the focus of her memoir is, of course, her own experience, the reader gets a clear sense that she is concerned, not only with herself, but also with education in general and life as a 'teacher' — now and in the future. Tompkins' narrative also reinforces the significance of the personal in teaching, not only to students and teachers in their daily classroom lives, but also to professional self-knowledge. Writing the memoir makes her past usable not only to herself, but to others. It speaks to teachers of her generation by tapping into some of the commonalities of their schooling and teaching experience that are seldom discussed in professional discourse.

But dwelling on the past is not always useful in and of itself — indeed, it can become obsessive or self-destructive. It is possible to take refuge in the past, living in memory in order to forget the present. When remembering slides into what bell hooks (1989) describes as a type of *useless longing*, the sort that makes us even more reluctant to face the present and shape the future, we know we are off track. We agree with hooks's contention that the objective of memory work is to make the past usable, so that remembering serves to 'illuminate and transform the present' (p. 17). Such is the approach we adopt in this book.

Individual Memory and Collective Study

To situate our interest in studying the professional self, we offer the following episode, which is based on a letter one of the authors received from a school friend, Alison, a former teacher who is now in her late forties. In one passage of the lengthy, self-reflective letter, Alison recalls how the behaviour of her grade 3 teacher represented a turning point in her sense of self as a learner and knower:

I remember that I was very scared of her [the grade 3 teacher] as she was very handy with the yardstick. Different times I received a rap on the shoulder when I wrote a wrong answer on the blackboard. One day she grabbed the neck of my sweater and I thought she was going to choke me. Another time she kept me in after school and the bus driver chewed me out. I went home crying. She was always mean towards me. By the end of grade 3, I was a nervous wreck. She definitely had a negative effect on me as a child. From that point on I was afraid of teachers, afraid to answer a question for fear I was wrong, and I thought I was dumb. My self-esteem was damaged. Mom was telling me recently that she and I went to a retirement tea for Miss R. but I don't remember it.

For Alison, writing the letter was a way of working back through the past in order to better understand herself in the present. But her letter was not only useful to herself — it was also very helpful to us in our own work as teacher educators, although not necessarily in the ways we had anticipated.

The first occasion we had to refer to this letter (with Alison's permission) was during a workshop with beginning teachers. Their responses were telling, revealing two different perspectives within the group about the value of writing memories. After hearing the above excerpt read aloud, one male high school teacher, Ben, asked,

> *Why doesn't she just get over it? We can't spend our lives living in the past or blaming one particular incident or teacher!*

According to Ben, there is too great a tendency to wallow in the past, blaming parents, teachers and society for our own failures in life. Others who shared his view voiced suspicions about the authenticity of memories. Even days later, another teacher was still shaking his head over the fact that anyone could have even written such a thing — it was just 'not normal' for a 48-year-old woman to still be carrying around the scars of schooling. To him, she sounded very self-absorbed.

Many teachers in the group, however, reacted very differently. Some of them nodded their heads knowingly, as if they understood exactly what Alison was talking about. Lisa, for one, spoke up, saying the letter was power-ful because it provoked her own memories:

> *It reminds me of my secondary math teacher. God, I used to hate him. He made fun of me in front of the whole class and I didn't really appreciate what he used to say to me: 'If Lisa can solve the problem, surely anybody can solve it.' He was the only teacher who humiliated me and I still have bad feelings about this teacher. He made me feel dumb. In a way I am still scarred by this comment.*

Like Lisa, many of the women in the class thought that Alison's account was extremely valuable, not only for Alison, but for them as well. Several others, however, shared the 'get over it' position initially expressed by some of the male teachers. One woman for example, said, '*Sure some teachers were awful, but you just got on with things*'.

A few men commented on the sheer pain they experienced in looking back at their own schooling. One teacher recalled being strapped by a female teacher. In his recollection, the experience seemed worse because it had been a woman who had administered the punishment. Others remem-bered being picked on because they were short or not very good at sports. Another teacher referred to his size, remembering that he was always being called 'fatty' in school and affirming that he still bore the emotional scars. While these latter stories say more about humiliation at the hands of peers or teachers, they nonetheless point to the ways that the scars of school experience remain. Moreover, they show how the divisions of opinion within the group did not neatly follow gender lines.

In short, the teachers in our workshop did not respond to our introduction to memory work in any sort of unified way: some were very comfortable reading aloud or telling their memories within the group setting, others were only willing to commit their memories to paper (in private), but liked listening to other people's accounts. Some teachers tended initially to dismiss other people's uncomfortable memories ('get over it'), while others simply claimed to have no memories of schooling at all. Each of these responses and the reasons for the differences among them are important for us to address individually and collectively.

During the workshop, we came to recognize the pedagogical significance of the discovery that other people's memories are quite different from one's own. We also recognized the need for approaches to memory that could take us beyond the telling of stories or recounting of memories in impressionistic, idiosyncratic and unchallenged ways: *'This is what I remember . . .', 'This is how it was for me . . .', 'That's not how I remember it . . .'*

We ended the workshop with a number of questions: Whose pasts were being represented? Why and how? What accounts for the kinds of memories we have, and even more significantly, what accounts for the different ways we interpret and react to what we and others remember? What is important about both pleasant and painful memories? What about suppressed memories or invented memories? What is the significance of what is forgotten or omitted in the telling? How does memory work take us into the future? These sorts of questions provide the impetus for our experimentation with different modes of self-study.

Revisiting Images of Teachers

In our previous book, *That's Funny, You Don't Look Like a Teacher!* (Weber and Mitchell, 1995), we explored the ways in which images of 'school' and 'teacher' are firmly entrenched in popular culture. We realized it was time that teachers, the insiders, began to take seriously these various images and representations of teachers and school. We concluded the book with the suggestion that what is needed is *a teacher gaze* through which to examine critically what's out there in the general culture as well as what's hidden within ourselves:

> Critical interrogations of the popular images of teaching may lead in surprising directions. For one, we may discover images of hope that please in the most unlikely of places . . . By clarifying and displaying those images that we do like, by articulating and sharing those that resonate deeply, we breathe new life into them, and their power increases. The project that grows out of a close reading is to imagine and realize other possibilities, ways to get beneath the stereotypes, sometimes, paradoxically, by embracing them. The *post-reading project* [italics added] becomes a writing project, one that creates new images . . . (ibid, pp. 139–140)

This project we call a *pedagogy of reinvention*. Creating new images is an active process that transforms the creator. As teachers, we want to study and recreate ourselves, rather than become the objects of someone else's study or reform plans, be they film producers or politicians. We use the term 'pedagogy of reinvention' to describe the process of making both the immediate and distant pasts usable. It is a process of going back over something in different ways and with new perspectives, of studying one's own experience with the insight and awareness of the present for the purposes of acting on the future. As Mavor Moore (1994), Canadian cultural critic, playwright and theatre producer, puts it:

> Reliving one's life is not an exercise I recommend. But reinventing it is another story. (p. x)

The idea of reinvention is relevant to both beginning and experienced teachers because it implies an approach to professional identity that is ongoing — we are perpetually becoming teachers, so to speak. The term also connotes playfulness, pleasure, and fantasy — things we may not usually associate with professional identity but that are essential to it in a rather serious way, as we shall see in later chapters.

Voices of the Selves: Writing/Reading This Book

From the outset we acknowledge that the term 'selves' in the title is a highly contested one. Which self (selves) are we looking at? The private self? The personal self? The public self? The social self? The political self? The embodied self? The individual self? The collective self? How do we not sound overly psychological and individualistic when we mean to address the social and political contexts within which we live? We struggle with these questions by recasting them in terms of the evolving teaching self, and by demonstrating very practically throughout the book that as teachers we have multiple selves.

In reading this book, you may also notice that we use multiple voices: our voices as practitioners, teacher educators and researchers, former school teachers, writers, feminists, friends, parents, daughters, and so on. We also include the voices of many others, especially those of our students, teaching colleagues, family members, friends, and the scholars whose work inspires us. Occasionally, we try to alert the reader to specific voices, for example, by writing our suggestions for practical activities in boxes, by listing certain key theoretical points, or by italicizing personal stories and viewpoints. But most of the time, our voices are too intermingled to signpost, because, as we shall explain more clearly, we wrote this book through our 'whole' (multiple and ever in flux) selves. We encourage our readers, too, to read and discuss the various chapters (in whatever order they wish) with their multiple voices and 'whole selves'.

As for the 'researcher self', we encourage readers to think about how the various protocols and subsequent analyses offer a particular 'take' on the research process itself, regardless of whether such activities are done as part of a classroom project, as part of a collective of teachers in a school, district or virtual network, or within a framework of qualitative study. Studying ourselves is a form of research, and our own accounts of 'how we got here' can contribute to a body of knowledge about teaching, learning, and adult identity. Studying ourselves might be regarded as research-in-action.

Finally, as a reminder to the reader (and ourselves), we regard reinvention as a cumulative process. We do not imagine anyone proceeding through all of the approaches offered here in one short block of time, maybe not even in one lifetime! We do, however, imagine that readers will invent their own ways of looking at some of these ideas, extending them into new methodologies and so on. Start with any chapter that catches your eye. Look at the pictures, read the stories, or focus on the boxes. Try things out. Take pleasure in the process, in the uncertainty. Reinvent.

Chapter 1

Childhood as a Memory Space: Teachers (Re)play School

> After school I used to go to Poppy's place to play school in her wash-house, where we lined up her father's empty beer bottles and made them breathe in and out, and do dry land swim with chest elevator, arms bend upward stretch, running on the spot with high knee raising. We also gave them tables and asked them to name and draw the clouds, cirrus, numbus [sic], stratus, cumulus, while we chanted the names, cirrus, nimbus, stratus, cumulus . . . We made them learn the mountains in the mountain chains, too — Rimutaka, Tararua, Ruahine, Kaimanawa . . . And we strapped them, saying sharply, 'Pay attention. Come out here.' The beer bottles stood in a row on the bench facing northwest, lit golden by the rays of the setting sun shining through the dusty little window. Sometimes if we broke a bottle, we looked through a piece of glass at the golden world. (Frame, 1991, pp. 42–43)

This memory of playing school is, taken from the first volume of the auto-biography of the New Zealand novelist, Janet Frame. It operates as a type of signposting for events to come. In the course of the autobiography, we follow Frame from her childhood days through to her experiences in secondary school and teachers' college where she, like the beer bottle student, also 'breaks'. The reader becomes aware of her imminent breakdown during a scene from her probationary year of teaching. In the midst of a visit to her classroom by a school inspector who is supervising her, Frame simply walks out of the class-room and out of the school — never to return. Immediately thereafter she has a complete breakdown and is hospitalized. In the film *An Angel at My Table*, based on this autobiography, you can hear the fading sounds of the school — children singing and chanting, a teacher's voice — as Janet walks, shoes in hand, across the playground and out on to the street, her bare feet a further act of transgression. In the film the beer bottle teaching scene vividly depicts and foreshadows the idea of breaking and fragmentation. As we see in the following excerpt from the screen play, teachers and schools are associated with this breaking.

POPPY: Faster, faster! Up on your toes, Dot Mather!
They stop running on the spot.

JANET: We might see if they know their New Zealand mountains, Miss Evans.
Poppy and Janet look sternly at their pupils.

JANET: Excuse me, Miss Evans. Sally Oates! Pay attention!
Janet lifts the Sally Oates bottle out in front of the other bottles.

POPPY: You'll have to stay in at playtime, Sally Oates, and write out the mountain chain.

POPPY: I think we should have geography now, Miss Frame.

JANET: One hundred times!

POPPY: Smack her!
Janet lifts the Sally Oates bottle and smacks it. She drops the bottle. It smashes on the floor. Whoops! Poppy claps her hands, and Janet makes a bell's ding-a-ling noise.

POPPY: Class dismissed! (Jones, 1990, p. 12)

We have included this scene of playing school for its symbolic significance, as well as for its more literal suggestion that memories of childhood play can relate to adult work. Frame's return, in her autobiography, to the beer bottle scene from her childhood highlights the significance of re-playing school — playing it again — in the same way that we might re-play a scene from a film or a 'play' from the Super Bowl or a World Cup match. When we play it again, we better understand what comes later. Or we understand what led up to something; or we see a particular detail or event differently in hindsight.

For Frame, there is a symbolic value attached to the inventiveness of playing school with beer bottles. Although the image of a piece of broken glass one of her 'students' held up to the setting sun seems to foreshadow the shattering of her world, it also becomes a golden lens through which imagining a better life becomes possible. Indeed, it is not that long after she has been hospitalized that word is received from Britain that she has won a prestigious award for her collection of short stories, *The Lagoon and Other Stories* (Frame, 1961).

At a more literal level, the scene of young Frame and her friend Poppy playing school depicts an activity that many teachers (and non-teachers) remember doing as children. The ways that children play at work — be it as a nurse, doctor, teacher, librarian, or business executive — tell us something about how they are socialized into certain occupational roles. Such memories also provide insights into how childhood experience contributes to adult identity. For our purposes, Frame's account serves to highlight the potential significance of childhood as a *memory space* within which to engage in studying ourselves as teachers.

Retrieving and Recounting Childhood Memories of School

It is a poor sort of memory that only works backward. (Lewis Carroll)

What can we learn about ourselves as teachers by going 'way back'? How can the raw material of school-related memories become central to studying our work as teachers?

Throughout this chapter and the ones that follow, we advocate remembering as a social activity to be done through individual and group work. Some of the prompts we use might loosely be called 'other people's memories'. We use other people's memories of teachers and school as an approach to doing memory work for several reasons. First, because there are many people who claim not to have any early memories, the memories of others can act as a type of memory jog for them. We are also interested in the ways in which memories of school can be seen to run beyond the personal to include the social. Other people's memories can take us out of our own idiosyncratic remembering, and into broader issues.

Working with childhood memories of school, however, is also about *not* remembering, *not* recording particular events in the first place and so on. Working with what we remember and what we have forgotten speaks to the present as much as it does to the past. When it comes to teachers' memories of school, the raw materials are abundant. We focus in this chapter on three types of memories:

- memories of playing school;
- painful memories of learning something;
- memories of teachers.

We will treat each set of prompts separately, but begin with a general reading guide for looking at childhood memories of school (box 1.1) to provide a context for reading personal memories.

Contextualizing Memory Construction

Recounting memories in a social context may contribute to constructing these memories a particular way. Indeed, the very purpose of and audience for the retellings may colour what is told in the memory account. For example, an adult might retell a particular memory from his or her early school days as a way to reassure a young child who is going to school for the first time. The memory may not have otherwise been that important, but it is told for its relevance to the moment. As another example, we might cavalierly dismiss a memory of a childhood crush as 'childish', or pretend not to remember it simply because it isn't 'cool' to own up to that sort of memory.

Sutherland (1997) cautions about 'the well-used anecdote' — the memories that we tell about ourselves over and over again:

Box 1.1

Guide For Reading Childhood Memories of School

1   Age in relation to remembering school
- from what time period are your earliest memories of school-related episodes?
- what is the relationship between the age of the rememberer and the time remembered? (Do older people remember situations from an earlier period more readily? Do males and females differ in your group in terms of how far back they go with memories?)

2   Recounting memories
- who is recounting the memory?
- to whom and for what reason?
- which memories do you tell over and over again? Why might that be?

3   Memory as mediated by the accounts of others
- which memories are stories you have heard over and over again?
- what are the conditions under which you hear these memories repeated?
- how do you feel about hearing these memories repeated?

4   Forgetting
- are there incidents from school that you remember but which your friends or family members don't remember?
- are there incidents that others remember but of which you have no memory? Why might this be?

5   Vicarious experience (witnessing) and memory
- are there incidents that happened to someone else in school but which are vivid in your memory?

6   Emotion
- what emotions are attached to the memory?
- how do you feel about other people's memories of school?

7   Gaps and absences
- what's missing from the memories in the group?

One begins to recognize those items that have become part of a person's regular lore, told to amuse, or to make a point about the 'good old days', or to emphasize to today's youngsters 'did I ever have it tough as a kid.' Each has been told many times to its narrator's family and friends. These stories are perhaps true in essence, but the fine honing that comes from constant recon-structing, retelling, and polishing also removes them farther and farther away from the reality that they are supposedly portraying. (p. 21)

As an example, we know a retired school teacher who is now greatly in demand as an archivist and raconteur of school stories in her local community. Certain of her anecdotes have become official history, and as such, are practically cast in stone. Similarly, there are less public anecdotes — family stories, for example — which also have a type of 'official' status. How have some stories come to be such well-used anecdotes? What is the story of our school days that we tell most frequently? Why this one? How do the multiple retellings contribute to our official history of ourselves as learners and as teachers? These can be important questions for self-study. What does their retelling contribute to our sense of self or to our collective mythology of teaching?

Finally, what we remember, as teachers, about school may also be influenced by the fact that we have chosen to teach. There may be a certain type of 'self-interest' at stake, so that we have a vested interest in remembering school a certain way.

Memories of Playing School

Many people remember playing school, which makes the phenomenon an excellent point of entry for self-study. We offer the following prompt around playing school (box 1.2) as 'a way in' to early memories of school. We have used this prompt in a variety of ways in our work with teachers. In some cases, teachers have written their responses individually and then explored them in small groups with other teachers. In other cases, teachers have simply used the protocol as a way to bring the memories to the surface during small group discussion. In either case, the idea that we can learn from other people's memories as well as our own is central. The prompt can also serve to structure discussions about 'not remembering'. For some teachers, there is nothing to remember; they didn't play school! Is there any significance in not playing school? What kind of play activities took place instead of playing school? Are there differences in how 'players of school' and 'non-players' relate to what actually went on at school? If themes of authority, control, helping and know-ing can be found in playing school episodes, are there other kinds of play where similar themes can be found? These are questions that ensure that rememberers and non-rememberers encounter each other's experiences.

When we initially pose the question, 'Did you ever play school?' in our workshops and courses, some teachers are surprised. What could possibly

Box 1.2

Playing School Prompt

Describe an early memory of playing school. Your description could include:

- a detailed account of where you played and how often, how old you were;
- who and what you played school with;
- how the play was organized;
- what you and other children did;
- how you felt about playing school;
- how the game usually started;
- how the game usually came to an end.

Is this the first time you have thought back to these experiences since becoming a teacher?

What meaning do you think that has now in relation to your work as a teacher?

---

be significant about such innocuous childhood play? It is just what they played, like hide-and-seek or hopscotch. Some people may think they have nothing worth remembering because it is not dramatic enough. Others forthrightly declare that they have no such memories (of playing school or any other early memories of school), noting that they have managed — successfully — to block out all early memories of schooling because it was so painful. These reactions are important because they remind us that recollections that deal with childhood can depict unhappy lives. Some memories really might be too painful to recall in the public circumstances of a workshop or class. As one of the interviewees in Sutherland's (1997) study responded, 'My childhood was so awful I don't even want to think about it. Even your asking the question has upset me' (p. 8).

Some teachers have 'confessed' to playing school, as though there might be something embarrassing about admitting to engaging in such a 'school-oriented' activity. Others have quite pleasurably 'come out' in their memories of playing school, going into great detail in describing ritualistic events — who got to be the teacher, who the students were, the positioning of certain objects such as chalkboards and desks, the role of recess and so on. Their recollections include memories of teaching younger brothers and sisters, other children in

15

the neighborhood, teddy bears, dolls, cats and dogs. In many cases they talk about the pride of actually teaching something to somebody.

Martha's Story of Playing School

Consider this account of playing school written by Martha, a teacher of more than 30 years and a grade 2 teacher — by choice:

> *My memories of early days are of isolated instances with no sense of how old I was when they happened. I think environment and possession of articles influenced how and what one played. Disregarding imagination that is.*
>
> *When I was 5, I received a doll for Christmas. With her came a box of handmade clothes — everything from bunting suit to winter coat, rubber boots, dresses, slips, sweaters, etc. That of course, influenced my play because I had something to dress and redress Daisy in as opposed to having one doll with one outfit that is not easily removed. My one vivid memory of that play is of having a clothes line the length of the kitchen laden with her wardrobe and Dad or my brother trying to walk underneath it.*
>
> *One girl who lived next door came to play with me when I was young. A memory there — she wanted to play nurse and various dolls had to be bandaged or cured or whatever. I never put in such a miserable afternoon! Nursing wasn't for me.*
>
> *When I should have been too old for dolls, I was given one plus a package of patterns — so I could learn to sew. I cannot figure out how old I was — maybe 12 more or less. I did not make clothes — Mom made them. Nancy was a Christmas present and I think I played with her for over a year. The age would be interesting to know because if I were 12, I would be in grade 8. Anyway, this doll and Daisy received a remarkable education. I remember hurrying home from school, setting up a little table, propping the dolls beside it and getting them to work. They each had their own workbooks, doll-size — I remember math and grammar. I would hold their hands and they would print in their answers. I doubt they ever got past grade 2. So as to keep the answers short!! Nancy's arms disintegrated later in life due to the excessive handling of them.*
>
> *I have a memory of Mom telling me I was old enough to put the dolls away. Whether that was before I got Nancy I have no idea but I think I can remember justifying my playing school as more permissible — more grown-up — than just playing with dolls. Spending all day in school and getting right to the classroom when I got home was a perfectly wonderful way to spend the winter.*
>
> *When I finally put the dolls away — which I don't remember doing — I taught kittens — the kinds of things that kittens should know — how to get in a house, out of a house, litter box, etc. Mike learned to eat from a fork and to come when we rang a bell.*
>
> *It's strange. I don't remember playing school with dolls before Nancy or what I played when I got the dolls dressed in one of their many outfits. The teaching flashback is more vivid than any others.*

   In Martha's story, we get a sense of the pleasure of the play, 'hurrying home after school', getting the dolls to work, teaching them useful things. We are introduced in her account to a number of very specific objects: Daisy and her vast wardrobe, Nancy and the sewing objects, the clothes line in the middle of the room. Martha makes the point that she played school because of the availability of certain objects, but some objects (those associated with teaching) are more attractive to her than others (associated with nursing), and certain actions had greater value over others — at least in memory. It is interesting that at such an early age playing nurse was distasteful to Martha. The attraction of specific play occupations varies. Some non-teachers (and teachers too) could never imagine anyone ever willingly engaging in playing school. The idea that Martha's play was in some way respectable because it was school-related seems important to her.

   The sheer detail of the story is interesting. How and why do we piece certain facts together and not others? For example, is there some significance to Martha's saying 'I doubt they [the dolls] ever got past grade 2'. Does it relate to the fact that she has almost exclusively taught the first or second grade throughout her career and often says, 'I'm just a grade 2 teacher', a phrase we still hear female teachers of young children say somewhat apologetically in relation to their work?

Objects and Retrieving Memories

The kind of detail around artefacts of play that we find in Martha's story is characteristic of many of the stories that we have heard, from both male and female teachers. These references to objects are important for several reasons. For one thing, using objects as prompts to remember is itself a strategy which can enhance memory work around childhood. For example, looking at photographs or yearbooks and — in the case of playing school — looking at particular artefacts such as a playroom chalk board can be important to the retrieval process. But the objects themselves are often imbued with meanings that are particular to the rememberer:

   The classroom was in my parent's half-finished rec room downstairs. Dad had installed a huge chalkboard down there on one of the walls and there was a 'real' eraser (just like the teachers used) and lots of white chalk — even colored chalk for making drawings of flowers or decorations on the board just like the teachers did. The chalkboard came from an old school room so that's what initially inspired us . . . We didn't have a 'chamois' though and I can't remember improvising one either. We didn't have real desks but we put together tables and chairs for makeshift ones and arranged them just like it was in the classroom at school. We took turns being teacher and student. Usually three or four of us at a time. We agreed to meet at a particular time after school. One of us would stand in the door as the teacher, with the rest of us all lined up until the 'teacher' rang a bell of some sort to let us in. The teacher had already made lines on the board and wrote on and made drawings and decorations on the board in preparation.

Other teachers recalled playing school by themselves — with imaginary students, but real school objects:

I remember assuming the role of teacher as early as 5 years old. My classroom was situated in the dampness of the basement. I had a desk, a chair, a makeshift blackboard and all the accessories associated with the teacher: masking tape, ruler, different chalk, etc. My mother was an elementary school teacher at the time and I was constantly browsing through the teachers' guide books to elementary math. I can remember teaching my imaginary class spelling, printing and basic mathematical operations. I never 'envisioned' discipline problems and the role I always assumed was that of teacher. I can't remember integrating my imaginary class into my lesson planning (i.e., I never pretended Susan was misbehaving or that Johnnie wanted me to answer a specific question.) I just recognized the presence of the class and taught the entire group as one uninterrupted.

The subject matter that play teachers teach may depend on the availability of certain concrete objects. For example, Joyce writes that her school play consisted of imitating the history teacher:

History was one of my favorite subjects and I remember learning about Montezuma, Cortez, and Pizarus. Our teacher had a funny way of pronouncing some words and so when I played school I would deliberately pronounce words wrong too. I remember that in my classroom where I was teacher I had a globe, a yardstick that I used as a pointer and a jewelry catalogue that had a world map on the cover as my text. I would ask my students to locate faraway places or to tell me customs of a particular country.

For Claudia, playing school at home was about the teaching of English, largely due, she recalls, to the availability of particular school texts related to English:

My brothers and I 'inherited' many school texts from our cousins who were a good 10 years or more older than we were and who had gone to school when parents were required to provide the textbooks. While there must have been science, math and history books, I only remember the literature texts such as Lorna Doone *(of which we had two or three copies from several of the cousins) and the play* The Admirable Crichton. *I don't ever remember reading these works right through, although I would sometimes read aloud bits to my imaginary students — and I did love the idea of having a play from which to read all the different parts. I also remember working out extensive tests although I am not sure how I arrived at appropriate questions based on my rather limited knowledge of the content!*

Another teacher, Nadine, goes on to describe a playing school episode involving Barbie:

> *Up to the age of 11, I remember, we played with 'Barbie' dolls a lot and often we tried to create the houses, churches, stores, that our dolls lived or worked in. We had a room (made of a cardboard box decorated with doll furniture, if we had them, leftover fabrics, scraps from catalogues and the hardware stores samples, or anything else we could scrounge up) for each 'setting' we play-acted our dolls in. I remember that one of these cardboard rooms was a school room. I had a Skipper as well as a Barbie, as did my younger sister, who was my major playmate. The Skippers were the students and usually my Barbie was the teacher. My sister's Barbie was usually the mother to whom the Skippers would return 'home' when my Barbie dismissed class. What I remember most is making sure my Barbie was dressed well — always neatly but nothing for a party. The Skippers wore nice dresses but not their 'Sunday best'. The Skippers would 'draw' pictures and ask questions, in turn. They had to be on time for school — the bell would be rung promptly (I can't remember what we used for a bell) and they had to line up and enter the class properly. The teacher walked around the front of the class talking until an assignment was given, then she would sit down at her desk and watch over the students who worked. The classroom had a makeshift chalkboard, bulletin boards — both of which had drawings and assignments or displays on it — we even drew little stars or 'good' work. Some assignments were put up to replace the old ones periodically. The drawings on the board would change periodically. Sometimes one of the Skippers could be the class monitor and help 'clean' the chalkboard and the chamois and erasers as well as put up assignments well done. We tried to put makeshift desks together — one for the teacher up in the front of the room and two in a row in the 'back' for the Skippers. Teacher's desk always had a big desk blotter and a can or something to hold pencils and 'chalk'. When my Barbie signaled the class was over, with our pretend bell, the Skippers could be excused to go home for lunch, come back after lunch, line up and wait for the bell again — have class and be dismissed, all over again. Funny, we never played principal . . . I can't remember us having a recess.*

Commodification of Playing School

These references to Barbie might also be read in the context of how school has become associated with commodification, a phenomenon best illustrated, perhaps, by parents eagerly purchasing such toys as magnet letter boards, Fisher-Price school house, and so on. Teacher Barbie, for example, comes in a boxed set complete with glasses, pointer, chalkboard, and her own doll students. However, while Teacher Barbie appeared in the 1990s, in the following account, Dale, who has been teaching for more than 30 years, shows that commercial 'playing school' toys have been around for some time. As she notes:

> *One of my earliest memories of playing school is associated with a small school set made up of a brown plastic teacher's desk with a drawer that really opened, a yellow plastic swivel chair for the teacher and two pupil desks, also made of brown plastic and which were of the type that were meant to be in row with the seat of one on the front of the other. The seats were hinged so that they could go up and down. I have no idea where I got this set and since I haven't seen it for years I am wondering about the accuracy of my memory. It seems like such an odd thing for me to have had for I don't remember having a lot of toys outside of dolls and doll paraphernalia. Because it was around 1955 I am thinking this must have been the early days of such plastic. I remember using a sneaker box to construct a classroom. I cut out windows and glued pictures on the walls. As far as teachers or pupils are concerned, I am not sure what I used other than a very small baby doll who must have 'stood in' as the teacher. What stands out in my memory, though, is the particularity of the furniture for playing school. The furniture symbolized for me the fact that school was clearly a special place.*

Accounts like Dale's raise questions about the relationship between these commercial 'playing school' objects and school itself. What is the significance of the 'commodification' of playing school? How are such toys marketed in terms of age or sex? Why are there so many play artefacts related to school? Asking such questions can deepen our understanding of school (and learning) in relation to society in more general ways, something that researchers of popular culture have brought to our attention. See for example, Ellen Seiter's essay, 'Buying happiness, buying success: Toy advertising to parents' (1993). We might look at how the television series *Sesame Street*, and all of its spin-off learning products (toys?) came about in relation to the perceived need for interventionist strategies for disadvantaged children in the United States. Such questions can also be posed, however, in relation to studying ourselves. *'Studying ourselves through our toys?' 'Toys ℜ Us?'*. Indeed, while a consideration of the social and political significance of *Sesame Street* may seem like a 'stretch of the imagination' from Martha's story at the beginning of this section, we return to her point about the sanctioning of doll play when it was linked to playing school '. . . *I think I can remember justifying my playing of school as more permissible — more grown-up — than just playing with dolls.*'

Authority and Control

Another feature that characterized Martha's account was the play teacher's sense of authority and control, of being in charge. While in her case, this control was not contested since she was teaching dolls and cats, we heard from others who had to negotiate the position of teacher.

> *I always wanted to be the teacher and never remember playing the student. I often gave my students (friends and/or younger sister) tests. I wrote on the*

chalkboard often. Once my girlfriend and I had an argument over who was going to be the teacher and who was going to be the pupil. She said she would be the teacher because her writing was better . . . School was fun but only if you were the teacher. The teacher was able to boss people around and tell the students what to do. I really liked writing on the board and yelling 'Silence!'

In many cases, the status of teacher seems to have been assumed by the person who was the oldest and who had access to the most knowledge of content and of how schools are supposed to run — hence the preponderance of younger siblings and inanimate objects as pupils. As one beginning teacher observes:

When I was about 9 or 10 years old, my two younger sisters were 8 and 6 and I would pretend to be their teacher while they acted like students. I would sit them down on the floor (carpeted) with three or four of their friends, hold the book up so they could see the pictures, and then read to them. Then I would ask them questions about the story. Occasionally, I gave them very simple math problems to work out, or we would colour and draw pictures (mainly of houses and flowers). Sometimes, when we played in our yard, I would pretend to be taking them on a field trip (like to a neighborhood variety store). I usually controlled the game, since I would force my sisters and their friends to play school. More times than not we had more recess time (skipping rope, playing hopscotch), than actual learning time. These sessions usually ended when my sisters had had enough and wanted to play another game.

Many teachers recall that their playing school activities were really about power and control rather than teaching actual content. For example, Gail writes about teaching her brother and his friends as students: *'I have vague memories (which I am sure are totally valid) of being the domineering one — i.e., the teacher. I'm sure those experiences are at the root of my brother's dislike of school! A great deal of importance was put on having the "right" answer; in fact I don't think any real teaching went on.'* Similarly Nadine writes:

I don't think we actually spent time on 'content' — actually teaching or learning anything so much as just play acting for the fun of it. We even had fire drills and made students who chewed gum in class throw it out and get 'disciplined'.

For another teacher, Carol, the management issues were more a type of 'leading from behind' rather than necessarily explicit control. As she writes:

There was a neighbour family where there were three children that were 3, 5, and 7 years younger than I was. I would go to their basement where there was a huge playroom full of toys all over the place. I would play with them.

> *Do some wooden puzzles to make sure no piece was missing before they could do it. Help them make some houses with cushions and blankets. Organize some puppet show for them and with them. Read them some books and help them in all kinds of pretend games. One thing I remember the best is the tidy up part at the end. I had the three of them clean up the whole room — trying to sort out the different toys. Pretend that we were making a great surprise for their mother. I was probably 8 or 10 at the time. As you can see I was not trying to show them how to read, but how to behave every day — not fighting over the same toy and being able to play together. I remember the mother telling me that I was a great mother's helper.*

We have other examples of teachers organizing themselves in non-hierarchical ways. Claudia, for example, recalls the experience of playing 'school staff' with her best friend. In particular she recalls how each had her own classroom 'mapped out' of snow. The classrooms were side-by-side and much of their play, as she remembers it now, was organized around discussions about preparing classes and dealing with recalcitrant students.

While we are not concerned with veracity in the memory accounts in this chapter, it is worth noting that they nonetheless 'ring true' when we read them in the context of research such as Weber's (1992) descriptions of children actually playing school (as opposed to adults remembering it). In the following case, she describes several English-speaking children playing school in a French immersion kindergarten:

> Alice, a lively redhead, approached another girl and asked her to play school. Together, they set off in search of additional 'students'. Soon thereafter, Alice had two girls and one boy sitting quietly and attentively at her feet near a bulletin board display that had been used by their teacher during a French 'circle time' vocabulary lesson that morning . . . (p. 53)

Weber then goes on to describe the ways in which Alice assumes authority and control over the others:

> Alice was obviously the play teacher and her very first actions were to get a little footstool to stand on and a long pointer 'to teach with' (her words). The other children at first accepted Alice as the teacher, as if the person who initiates the play is acknowledged as having the right to be the teacher first. (ibid)

As might be expected, there were power confrontations between Alice and other children who wanted to be teacher:

> Whereas dolls, teddy bears, or even imaginary playmates can be recruited as pupils, only real children can be the teacher and there is usually only one teacher at a time. Almost everyone wants a turn to be that powerful person — teacher — as illustrated in the following excerpt:

Child 1:   I want to be the teacher.
Child 2:   No, I am the teacher.
Child 3:   No, it's my turn; you were the teacher first last time. (ibid, p. 54)

Important to the work here is Weber's observation that 'playing school reflects an awareness of both the power that being an adult confers and that conferred by knowledge' (ibid). She also points out the significance to the children's play of both the teacher and the students being knowers. In one instance, for example, Alice asks the other children to pretend not to know the answer so that when she asks and gets them to repeat the correct answer, she is able to reward them 'very good'. 'Everyone was beaming and exchanging glances. There was cooperation and a shared secret between the play teacher and her students. It's a good joke, pretending not to know, and thus suggesting, that really, we do know!' (ibid).

Beyond what we have already said about being in charge and being in the know as important characteristics of much of playing school, the idea of 'authoritarianism' itself may be an important one in studying ourselves. Many of the accounts raise questions about a type of tyranny: making students learn, assigning questions which the play teacher herself cannot answer, taking charge of the smaller, the inanimate, the imaginary. As teachers we may catch ourselves using terms such as 'I'm going to *get* the class to do such and such . . .' or 'I'll *make* them work in groups first and then . . .' We may not actually mean that we are going to use force, but these phrases nonetheless suggest a particular positioning of ourselves in relation to our students.

But we are also thinking of how children in school often insist on the *correctness* of whatever it is that 'teacher says . . .' over whatever it is that parents might know. This is something that Jane Miller (1996) also refers to in her own accounts of playing school:

> Teachers had a lot more going for them than parents. They knew, for a start, how to handle children, and since that included children much older than I was, like the ones in Miss Cocker's top class, that meant you had earned the respect of the gods themselves. Parents — in my experience, at least — were often at their wits' end. Indeed, I realized that teachers could put your parents right about all sorts of things, and parents might very well not answer back when they did. (p. 67)

As teachers, we might interrogate some of these early experiences of authoritarianism. How do they carry over into what counts, for example, as official knowledge — both in terms of the expectations of the learners ('tell us what we are *supposed* to know') and the discourse of the school ('this is what you are *supposed* to know')? Questions such as the following might also be helpful in considering the roots of 'being in authority' and being a knower:

- What does it mean to have our authority 'challenged'?
- When do we assert authority?

- To what extent is being a knower linked to having authority or asserting authority?
- How do these constructs translate into our work beyond our classrooms, say, into our work with other professionals, school committees, professional development, and authority structures within our institutions?

Gender, Memory and Studying Ourselves

In this section we draw attention to some of the ways that males and females recalled playing school. We regard the similarities and differences in their recollections as significant for what they tell us about play (and playing school), and also for how they highlight the memory process itself.

Play and work

We start with Nadine's statement from the previous section, '*I can't remember us having a recess*'. For many of the women, playing school involved taking charge, being in control, and sometimes feeling the satisfaction of having a younger sibling actually learn something. But even when the memories were less about teaching and more about management, there were often associations with being helpful and doing something worthwhile. They almost always spoke to the idea of doing 'real work', not play.

Playing school seemed to occupy a more prominent space in women's memories. Many of the female teachers recalled that playing school was something which began on the day after the last day of school in June, or after the real school day was over. They remembered the game lasting until they were called for dinner, a friend left, they themselves had to go home — or the end of the lunch period came. Claudia, who was one of the 'van students' (students who were bussed to school) and who stayed at school for lunch while most of the town students went home, recalls spending every winter 'indoor lunchhour', of which there are many in the Canadian mid-West, playing school until real school resumed at 1:30.

In contrast to the women's recollections of teaching, the men we've interviewed were more likely to recall playing school as acting up in class, or fooling around at recess. As Nick writes:

> Although I can't specifically remember 'playing school' — sorry — just got a memory flash — I can remember when I was 8 or 9 and my sister 7, we had a makeshift classroom in our shed. There were two desks, a chalkboard (Fisher-Price type) and many school supplies (paper, pens, pencils, markers, etc.). I can't really remember what it was that we were trying to learn but I do recall setting time periods — recess time, lunch time.

Mark describes his playing school as 'playing the teacher's nightmare':

I know that I have played school but I forget where. I know that I played it with girls but I'm not sure when. Oh wait now — we were visiting a friend of my parents who had kids and they were girls. Here's some more data: It seems to me that I enjoyed playing the teacher's nightmare. I wasn't enjoying the company of girls and so it was profitable to ruin the classroom and its creative atmosphere.

The women also noted that mixed-sex groupings often led to the boys breaking up the game or 'not playing right' in contrast to the situations where they played in single-sex groupings until they were called in for supper.

I can remember we would all sit in rows on the lawn with Brenda as the teacher. Then things would quickly deteriorate. Arguments would erupt. The boys would sulk. The girls would yell at the boys. Then the game would break up. We would break into smaller groups and passionately discuss who started it and all would go home for supper. How did I feel? I was usually disgusted with the boys.

Even when the boys were remembered as taking the teaching seriously, as was the case in the memories of several of the women who recalled episodes where a brother or a male neighbour played the part of teacher, their play often had a disruptive quality. In other cases, the boys just did not 'play right'. Jan, for example, recalls an older neighbour boy taking it upon himself to teach her mathematics and not 'letting up' until she called her mother for help! While, on the surface, this can simply be read as an overzealous play teacher acting out a strongly authoritarian teaching style, the fact that the pupil has to call for help suggests that it is more than that.

The girls' recollections of playing school as 'real work' bears remarkable similarity to research about other types of childhood role play. For example, Susan Willis (1991) has examined the 'commodification' of women's work in children's toys through Easy Bake ovens, Little Sweepers and other play artefacts marketed for young girls. In asking adult males and females to recall their holidays during childhood, June Crawford and her associates (1992) found that men and women had quite different memories, particularly in relation to having fun and a sense of being carefree (male) versus feeling responsible (female). As they observe:

In our memories, as girls and as adult women, we noticed and described the work done by women, by our mothers and aunts and later by ourselves as adults. Holidays were a lot of work. The everyday tasks of cooking and cleaning and making beds, of children, of organizing outings, were not always, but mostly, done by women. These tasks were constantly referred to — in our childhood memories we were already engaged in helping perform them . . . There is no such preoccupation in the boys' memories. None of the boys' memories mentions any work; certainly they do not appear to have done any, or to be expected to do any. Nor do they refer, or appear to be aware of the work performed by their mother. Each refers to the other people and the place as part of the given of the holiday — the backdrop against which their own private drama was played. In essence this drama revolved around their own private excitement and pleasure at play. The memories were predominantly carefree and pleasurable: 'every day was fun and new', 'a sack of toys was at the end of the bed', . . . (p. 143)

The difference between the women's recollections of *playing work* and the men's recollections of *playing disruption* is important. Several women compared these play scenes from the past with the 'real thing' where they are still dealing with, in their terms, 'boys who won't play right'. The idea of 'not playing right' suggests that there may be competing agendas as to what the 'game' really is. Whose script is it?

However, it is important to acknowledge that 'hell raising' memories were not the only recollections that men had. Several male teachers also referred to the pleasure of work. In Andrew's case, the pleasure was in teaching himself something. Describing how he taught himself anatomy in the seventh grade using a playing school format he writes:

> *My sister had a blackboard securely attached to her bedroom wall and I can remember very distinctly teaching myself the 'notes' we were to be tested on the next day. I first studied them and then 'taught' the entire section to myself on the board. I can remember getting a perfect mark on the test.*

Part of the girls' pleasure might be attributed to the kind of 'taking charge' of playing teacher. As Crawford and her associates (1992) note in relation to the pleasure of self-reliance:

> As girls, in our striving to be responsible and competent, we tried to behave like adults, and to be taken seriously by them. Sometimes we succeeded, and were praised for being brave or patient or clever; for being a 'good girl'. Pleasure in competence was seen in some of our play memories and in many of our happiness memories where we developed new skills, a new independence. With competence came a greater freedom to be ourselves. This was a strong theme in both boys' and girls' memories, though the type of mastery differed. For the boys it entailed a control over the material world, for girls a control of self, of the body. (p. 186)

Similarly Jane Miller (1996) refers to an account of playing school that is written by Simone de Beauvoir, who taught for a short period of time at a lycée in the south of France. De Beauvoir is describing a playing school episode with her younger sister that highlights playing school as 'real work', not imitation work, as work that enhances the play teacher's feelings of competency:

Teaching my sister to read, write, and count gave me, from the age of 6 onwards, a sense of pride in my own efficiency. I liked scrawling phrases or pictures over sheets of paper: but in doing so I was only creating imitation objects. When I started to change ignorance into knowledge, when I started to impress truths upon a virgin mind, I felt I was at last creating something real. I was not just imitating grown-ups: I was on their level, and my success had nothing to do with their good pleasure. It satisfied in me an aspiration that was more than mere vanity. (cited in ibid, pp. 69–70)

Gender and the memory process

While the accounts above are significant for their content, we are also interested in what these stories reveal about remembering itself, and the differing relationships that male and female teachers might have to the past:

- *Mediated Memory:* What we remember as adults about our childhood is often mediated by what we are told about ourselves as children: Here we are thinking of how children ask parents over and over again 'Tell me again about the time . . .'. Kotre (1995) has observed that males are more likely to hear family stories about themselves as children that tell them that they are special — 'even sacred' (p. 227). They also hear that they were 'hell raisers' (ibid). Females are more apt to hear family stories that tell them they were well-behaved, docile and good — so good in fact, (ibid) that there are stories of them being left behind or forgotten 'in all the confusion', say on a family outing. As Kotre notes, putting aside biology, '. . . there is a huge difference between being told that you were special and being told that you were forgotten' (ibid, p. 228). What we remember may also be mediated by intervening factors such as how women teachers are depicted in popular culture. As Jane Miller (1996) writes:

  > They [these memories] will be overlaid by now, confused, distorted, reduced by time and age and the learning of many kinds of disdain for unmarried women who have worked all their lives with children and were probably quite poorly qualified. (p. 66)

  We may not have experienced our female teachers as 'bitter and twisted old maids' but in the intervening years may have been acculturated into the idea (through television, literature, lore) that all female school teachers are some version of the stereotypical 'old maid'.

- *Forgetting:* As male and female teachers look back on memories of childhood, they might also look at whether in addition to remembering differently, there are also differences in the amount that is remembered. In discussing the work of anthropologist Ruth Benedict, Ann Oakley (1994) observes that women tend to have more recollections of their childhood before the age of 6 than do men. As Oakley goes on to explain, this phenomenon of the 'forgetting of childhood is more common where there are radical discontinuities between childhood and adulthood. In Western culture, these discontinuities are more marked for men than women who . . . remain childlike in their sharing with children of the status of a minority group' (p. 29).

In relation to self-study, mixed groups of male and female teachers might want to explore these observations on childhood and forgetting.

- Can memories of such episodes of play as 'playing school' be related to differing expectations for adult males and females? Some of the women who gave accounts of playing school, for example, were initially somewhat embarrassed about talking of having engaged in such play. Yet once they got started, it was clear that this play to them was something that was very serious. We see this as a type of 'covering over' phenomenon (Gilligan, Rogers and Tolman, 1991) typical of women's recollections of their girlhood experiences. It is as though the memories are too trivial to be taken seriously, so that when they are brought out for scrutiny, it is necessary to apologize. But is this phenomenon exclusive to or even predominantly found amongst females? Some of the offhand and sometimes humorous comments of the men in the workshops, for example, could also be interpreted as somewhat revealing of a type of embarrassment — maybe even 'covering over' as well.

Both male and female teachers might talk about how they feel about retrieving these memories and whether or not there is a difference in how men and women relate to childhood experiences. This kind of insight could prove invaluable in 'reading' our present lives as teachers in the context of childhood play.

Playing Out Pain

Whereas the majority of the accounts from both male and female teachers had something of a pleasure theme — after all, people were recalling play — the following episode, written by Terri, a beginning teacher, stands out as an example of how playing school can have therapeutic value.

The Day I Played School

As a child I often played house or hide n' seek but the only time I ever played school was when I had an awful encounter with my grade 2 English teacher. Boy do I ever remember that fateful afternoon in Ms. M.'s class.

It was the day after the class's big spelling test and Ms. M. had them all corrected. As she began to call out the names, my heart began to beat rapidly, for I wasn't sure I had passed it. 'Terri' she called out. The moment of truth arrived. As I reached for my test, my worst nightmare became a reality. I failed! While my heart began to sink to the bottom of my stomach, I quietly mumbled my disappointment so no one could hear (or I thought no one heard — but someone did — my worse enemy in the class, Louise).

   After all the tests were given out, we lined up for recess but as I reached for my coat someone forcefully reached for my neck and pushed me against the lockers. When I overcame my initial shock, I was confronted with Ms. M.'s screeching voice. She was accusing me of using foul language when I received my test. Quivering, I swore to her that I didn't. I told her that the only thing I had said was 'fudge'. She didn't believe me! She said she was told otherwise. As her grip became firmer, Ms. M. forced me right up to the front of the class to admit to something I had never said. Out of fear and embarrassment I did.

   As the dismissal bell echoed in the distance, I remember feeling extremely angered towards Ms. M. and the way she had accused me of swearing at her. At that moment I hated her more than I hated Louise the tattle-tale.

   That day after school, instead of playing with our dolls, my best friend suggested that we play school. I agreed but only if I were the teacher and she the student. During the time we were playing I found myself re-enacting the situation that I had just experienced with Ms. M. but there was an important change. When I found out that a student might have used foul language, I asked both the student and the 'squealer' to meet after school to discuss the matter.

   It was, in a strange way, this experience which influenced me to become a teacher. To this day I promised myself that I'll be a fair and patient teacher, rather than one who is mean and aggressive like Ms. M. was!

Terri's playing school account evokes a type of questioning around *post hoc* constructions of childhood angst, showing how both play itself and thinking back on it can be constructive in dealing with pain. Terri is able to link this play experience to exploring the kind of teacher she wants to become. The episode also introduces pain as a motivation to teach, something that we pursue in the next section.

Painful Memories of Learning

In the introduction to this book, we spoke about Alison, a teacher in her late forties who is only now re-playing some painful memories of her third grade teacher in an attempt to try to re-shape the present and the future. As we mentioned, while her memory account led some beginning teachers to describe their own tales of horror, for others, there was a sense that people should just 'get over it'. We asked these same teachers, all beginning secondary teachers specializing in one subject or another, to recall a time when they themselves had experienced difficulty in learning something (box 1.3). We thought it would help them think back to themselves as learners, and that recalling struggles to learn a specific concept would have particular significance for them. As new teachers just starting out, what would they bring from their past? Could an account, say, of the struggles a future mathematics teacher had with learning history inform the practice of an aspiring History teacher?

Box 1.3

Difficulty Learning

Think of a memory of something that was difficult for you to learn in school.

Describe the memory in as much detail as possible, paying particular attention to smells, sounds, images and feelings.

Certain 'prompts' do not always evoke what we think they are going to. When we used the prompt above, we expected to hear detailed accounts of difficulty in learning to read, or do math and so on. While some of the accounts were indeed of specific subject areas, there were a surprising number of references to the role that teachers played in contributing to students' pain. It seems difficult to separate the teacher from the subject taught. We heard many stories of unfair teachers, humiliating experiences as a result of the abuses of teachers' power, and tyrannical and terrifying teaching practices. Where the playing school memories could be read as early memories of authority, control and so on, this set of memories might be read as early memories of humiliation and embarrassment associated with school.

What was also of interest was the time period when this pain was experienced. Most of the teachers in the group, who were in their early to mid-twenties, recalled experiences from high school or university, rather than from childhood. This does not necessarily suggest that the worst learning experiences happen after elementary school. As Salaman (1970) points out, the age of the rememberer may be influencing what is recalled. In her research, Salaman distinguishes between the remembering of people in their twenties and those who are in the forties, fifties or older. She observes that as the meaning of childhood memories becomes clearer in maturity, the pain of memories from childhood may be psychologically resolved. Thus, many memories which earlier had not been retrievable become available for recollection. When someone is just starting out in teaching, recent experiences in high school or university classrooms may be the ones that are the more significant in terms of 'illuminating' the present. For those who are in their forties and fifties, pre-school or primary school classroom experience may be more significant.

The memories of the beginning teachers had several other commonalities: They focused on what memory scholars call 'autobiographical memory', memory that is self-referential, and filled with imagery and interpretations of events from the past. Also common to these scenarios was the sense of pain vividly remembered. Although these stories are written by teachers who are functioning well within their respective classrooms and programs, it is clear that they are not necessarily 'over it'; the pain is still fresh and palpable. As Patricia Hampl (1996) writes:

> We only store in memory images of value. The value may be lost over the passage of time . . . but that's the implacable judgement of feeling: this we say somewhere deep within us, is something I am hanging on to. And of course, often we cleave to things because they possess heavy negative charges. Pain likes to be vivid. (p. 270)

The two cases which follow are examples of painful experiences that beginning teachers associate with their former teachers.

Case 1: Sam's Memory

Sam bounced off to school that fine spring day. It was the day that his social studies project was due. Sam loved social studies. Sam loved learning about other cultures and how people in other countries lived and worked. He took this project on with vigour and keen interest, spending hours upon hours making a poster and writing up a knowledgeable report. He neglected other classes and even friends to work on the project. After all, the Babylonians were a fascinating study for this grade 5 student. In his eyes, the project was more than just something to hand in. It was his creation. It was something tangible that represented his knowledge, interest and desire to learn.

The big day arrived. The project was due. Everyone told him that it was wonderful — even his nasty older brothers. Sam gave the project to his teacher and he was beaming with pride for a job well done. Now he had time to hang out with his friends. Everything was great until the end of the week.

Friday afternoon was a gym class and Sam was responsible for collecting the soccer ball and returning it to the rack by his home room. After doing this, Mrs. Baxter asked Sam if she could have a word with him. 'Of course', he thought. She probably wanted to tell him what a great project he had done. Instead, she said quietly 'you failed your project'. Turning back into the empty classroom, she took care of what teachers take care of on a Friday afternoon. Sam stood rigid in the hall outside of his class. He was frozen. At first it was disbelief. Complete and utter worthlessness took over him. After an eternity and a half he finally took a breath. He managed to carry his worthless carcass home. 'How could I have failed? I worked so hard.' repeatedly ran through his mind. 'Why did I fail?' 'Was his family crazy for thinking it was such a good project?' Sam was confused beyond belief. It was the longest weekend of his life. He did not want to return to school and even more, he never wanted to see Mrs. B.

Unfortunately, Monday morning painfully arrived for Sam. Sitting in his chair with his head lifelessly flopped on his desk, the return to class was made even worse by the fact that the teacher was going to present each

post-project to the WHOLE class and tell everyone what she thought of them!
Sam's project was the first to come out. Fear, terror, pain and asphyxiation
took on new meaning. He now hated Mrs. B but was equally terrified of her.

   'And now class, this is what an A+ project looks like' she said
quietly. She looked at Sam and let out an innocent chuckle as she showed his
project. Sam was even more confused and dumbfounded than before. 'What
was she doing?' 'How can she do this?' Of course he accepted the A+ but
that was all. She had taught him a tremendous lesson that day. Don't trust
teachers.

'Don't trust teachers!' The sense of betrayal and the awareness of
the sadistic use of power are still vivid in Sam's memory. What does it mean
for beginning teachers to enter a profession in which they do not trust the very
professional role they are taking on? When Claudia read Sam's account aloud
to another group of beginning teachers, she became aware as she read it that
the audience was anticipating some sort of 'happy ending'. Sam's straightforward narrative somehow captures the 'now' of a grade 6 boy: 'the big day
arrived', 'fear, terror, pain and asphyxiation' . . . and so on. We *feel* the lived
experience of a child who somehow seems to deserve a happy ending. As
Claudia observes:

What a downer to have read Sam's story at the end of class. As I was reading
it I could feel a type of tension in the room — or perhaps it was just a tension
in me. I knew what the outcome of the story was. Right in the middle of
reading it, I was thinking of how much I wanted to change the ending of it.
I wanted the class to hear this upbeat memory of how Mrs. B. had come
through in the end. That there would be more to it than this. 'Is that all there
is?' I am thinking the teachers are thinking. (Journal entry)

As with Sam's memory, Lana's story below also focuses on the
abusive actions of a particular teacher. In her case it is a high school biology
teacher, and while the account itself has all of the vividness and pain of Sam's
there is an additional factor of forgetting that is important.

Case 2: Lana's Memory

The faint smell of formaldehyde that clung to the air in the biology lab went
unnoticed by the students in his OAC biology. Mr. A. was reluctant to open
the window to air out the room because of the cold weather. Lana and three
other members of her study group divided their time between working on
their unit package and gossiping, with a heavy emphasis on the latter. Beth,
Rachel and Laura were laughing at Ben's latest obtuse remark when Mr. D.,
Lana's former calculus teacher, walked in to chat with Mr. A.

   As soon as he walked in a feeling of dread developed in her
stomach. Lana hated Mr. D. She didn't hate him because he was a hard

marker or because he gave too much homework; she hated him because she thought he was a bad teacher. He taught to those who already knew and understood, giving little time or attention to those who didn't. Lana had had few problems with math in the past; therefore her feelings about her teacher had little to do with how she felt about the subject. She just didn't like him.

Mr. D. couldn't help but notice the group of talkers because they were seated closest to the front door. He pointed to Lana and asked Mr. A. 'You have this one in your class?' Lana's dreadful pit grew larger. Mr. D. picked up a piece of chalk and drew something on the board — Sigma. Then he asked, 'Lana, what's this?'

'Sigma' she answered. Even though she had 22 per cent at mid-term when she dropped the course, she still remembered some of the basics, despite his teaching methods. He drew it again. This time he rotated 90 degrees to the left. 'What's this?' he asked again. 'Sigma'. He did this twice more. Lana's anxiety and confusion increased. Why was he bothering to ask her this now, in front of her biology class, no less? It didn't matter any more if she knew sigma from a doughnut. He drew another symbol. Then he asked her what her name was and wrote that on the board too. Finally he connected the points together. Lana was embarrassed and humiliated to discover that he had just drawn the figure of a pig labeled with her name.

There is another story that Lana's friends tell her that she cannot remember. When she was still a member of Mr. D.'s class, he was explaining a proof or something to that effect. Lana put her hand up saying she didn't understand and would he please explain it again. He did. She said, 'But Sir, I still don't understand how you got that. How did you get from step 3 to the end?' He walked over to her desk, placed his hand beside her cheek, pulled his hand back (as someone might do if they were going to slap somebody) and did nothing.

Lana's humiliation at being made fun of in class in such a cruel way is not unlike Sam's experience. While her forgetfulness of the second incident is entirely understandable, Lana's friends' recollections add another dimension to school memories, something that Jane Tompkins (1996) describes in the following excerpt:

I have an [other] image of the boy in third grade — his name was Steven Kirschner — a pretty blond child with sky-blue eyes and a soft-as-doeskin nature. He is standing at attention next to his seat, being dressed down by the teacher for some slight. I don't remember what it was, but I knew he didn't deserve such treatment. He stands there, stiffly, hands at his sides, in brown corduroy pants. His china-blue eyes brim with the tears he's trying to hold back. He is the very picture of innocence abused, yet the lash, metaphorically, fell on him just the same. And it fell on me, too, for strange as it may seem, I did not distinguish between myself and the unhappy scapegoat for the teacher's wrath. And so when Mrs. Garrity, the worst one of all, with her brown suit and red face made red by perennial anger, was heard screaming horribly and interminably in the hall at some unlucky person, it seemed to me entirely an accident that that person had not yet been me . . . (p. 5)

Similarly, Claudia remembers the day that her best friend's marbles fell from her desk during class — and were promptly confiscated by the teacher. First one fell and was taken away, and then one by one the whole collection fell. She remembers that it was her friend's birthday — something that is always 'special' when it falls on a school day, and that the whole confiscation seemed so much worse because of that. When Claudia mentions this to her friend years later, however, the friend has no recollection of it. Why is the memory more significant for Claudia than for her friend? Does Claudia record and read the memory as some sort of cautionary tale? Our own pain may be more accessible in other people's memories than in our own.

Pain likes to be vivid! As with the case of Alison, many of these teachers clearly had a great deal to 'get over' from their pasts. Consider for example Patricia Hampl's observations about the potential value of such remembering:

> Our capacity to move forward as developing beings rests on a healthy relation to the past . . . We carry our wounds and perhaps even worse, our capacity to wound, forward with us. (Hampl, 1996, p. 209)

Clearly, those who teach are in a position to re-enact, perhaps in unconscious ways, the very scenes that they themselves have experienced. At the same time, however, if we were to interpret such memories in the context of the power relations in the classroom and the broader social milieu, we would regard the accounts as ones that are less about wounding and pain at an individual level (Mr. D. versus Lana, for example) and more about the social conditions and structure of schooling: for example, many of the stories teachers remembered could be read in terms of sexual harassment in the classroom, the underachievement of girls in mathematics, the authoritarian or even tyrannical culture of teaching, and so on. Box 1.4 offers several types of questions which might take the discussion of Lana's and Sam's experience further in terms of how such stories might be used in our professional development. How might these different frameworks for asking questions contribute to interpreting the memories of others in ways that make us see our own experience differently?

Remembering Teachers

'No one forgets a good teacher.' (From an advertisement of the Teacher Training Agency campaign for recruiting teachers, *Times Educational Supplement*, (January 30 1998)

'The lady was a schoolteacher, I believe', says the undertaker . . .
'Yes', says my mother: 'she taught for over forty years'.
'Then she left some good behind', says the undertaker. 'A noble profession, teaching.' (From J.M. Coetzee's *Boyhood: Scenes from a Provincial Life*, 1997, pp. 165–6.)

Box 1.4

Reading Memories of Pain

Social

- How would you read power and control in the actions of teachers such as Sam's and Lana's?
- Are there fundamental differences between Sam's experience and Lana's?
- What are some of the possible 'lessons learned' for the other students who 'remember' for Lana?
- How might we read memories of these teaching–learning episodes (our own or Sam's, Lana's or Alison's) in the context of class, race, gender?

Individual

- Does the pain diminish when people are further on in their teaching career and if so, how does the act of teaching itself — being able to do something constructive — contribute to that diminishing of pain?
- Is the vividness of the pain about former teachers unique to teachers as compared with those who do not become teachers?
- Are there other professions that attract people who have something to be 'gotten over'? For example, do schools of dentistry attract candidates with a fear of dentists?

Social and individual

- What is the value to the rememberer of telling these stories?
- How would these stories be read by teachers who have been accused of inflicting pain? Is there any kind of confessional mode that is appropriate for teachers who discover that they occupy such a dark spot in someone's memory?

How can our early memories of teachers be used in systematic ways to explore our own teaching? We have been drawn to Kathleen O'Reilly Scanlon's book *Tales out of School* (1992), a collection of short accounts (some only four or five lines long) of people's memories of teachers. Their brevity and their poignancy make them ideal memory prompts. O'Reilly Scanlon's book offers vignettes on 'my most memorable teacher', 'a teacher I hated', 'a teacher I would like to be like', 'a teacher who changed my life', 'a teacher who ruined my life' and so on. As the author remarks in the introduction:

> What *do* people remember about teachers? It was this question that motivated me to write to more than 100 editors of daily newspapers across Canada and to ask readers to send in anecdotes about the teachers in their pasts. I knew that I remembered things about my teachers, but what about other people? What did they remember? (p. 7)

We asked beginning teachers to choose several memory accounts from the 100 or more letters and vignettes in the book to which they would respond in writing. The imperative 'Remember a teacher' is a very powerful springboard to recalling school generally. The prompt often led teachers into a grade-by-grade account of experience: 'In grade 1 we had Mrs. So-and so . . .', 'In grade 2 it was Miss Y . . .' and so on . . . Janine sums up the experience of reading these letters and vignettes:

> *All these memory accounts were really interesting to read. I find it amazing how much one teacher could change a person's life. Who would have ever thought that a teacher could be a hero and someone to admire. I never realized how much I appreciated my teachers until this semester. I really hope to make a difference in my students' lives, I would feel a sense of accomplishment.*

When she goes on to respond to the prompt 'The teacher who changed my life' (box 1.5), we see that there is an overlap between her life and the life of the one remembering.

Box 1.5

The Teacher Who Changed my Life

I was raised on welfare by a single mum with seven kids. My Dad left when I was almost 3 years old. My mother remarried a man who sexually abused me on several occasions. When he began to abuse my younger brother, I contacted the authorities and we were removed from the home. Five of us went to live with an aunt who favoured her two boys over my brothers and me.

My aunt received welfare money to care for us. Although one of my brothers and I needed glasses and another one required dental care, my aunt neglected to get these things taken care of. If we pressed her on these matters, she'd just get angry. I wasn't a destructive or bad child, but I was withdrawn and shy when I entered the eighth grade and met the teacher who changed my life.

Lydia Narancic was my homeroom teacher. She was almost 60 years old and had short white hair. She smiled a lot and as soon as I met her, I liked her. One day she called me to her desk to tell me she would like to talk to me. Mrs. Narancic told me she cared about me and she didn't like to see me so sad all the time. I hadn't realized I looked this way, but she said one of the other teachers had noticed my despondency too . . .

Audrey Hill,
Victoria, British Columbia
(O' Reilly Scanlon, 1992, p. 26)

As Janine writes:

My father is an alcoholic and has been for the past 20 years. When I was really young I didn't notice except that he had a really bad temper some days. As I got older, about grade 3, I noticed that my father was an alcoholic. I was always scared of him and he would mentally abuse me calling me stupid, no good for nothing, I should never have been born, etc. My mother couldn't really do much because he would just yell at her. I was really disturbed in school and my grade 5 teacher, Mrs. O. knew that something was bothering me. One day, after class, she asked me to stay behind so she could speak to me. I was scared because I didn't know what I did wrong. She told me that I could speak to her about anything and that it would stay confidential with her always. I broke down and told her about my father. She understood and told me if I ever needed to talk just to say so. I stayed after school with her very often and it felt good that someone actually listened and cared about me. After grade 5, Mrs. O. got transferred to British Columbia. I never saw her again but for two years we wrote to each other. I really think that she was a terrific teacher and I will always remember what she did for me.

Another teacher, Ann, chooses this same prompt to describe a teacher she remembers who made her feel like she was 'somebody'.

When I was in grade 4 my mother went back to work and I felt that we were so distant from each other. I missed her being home when I returned from school. I had no one to tell about my day. When my mom would get home she would be too tired to listen to what I would have to say. I felt alone and unimportant in my house; my father and I were never close. I needed my mother to be there and encourage me when I did things. I really lost my self-esteem that year until my teacher, Mrs. T. came into my life. She always pushed me to go further and to do better. She gave me a lot of attention which made me feel like I was important. When my grades would drop she would speak to me and tell me that she knew I could do better and that it wasn't like me to have these kinds of grades. At first I thought that she was picking on me but I liked the attention. I realized later that she did like me and she was trying to help me, she knew me and I felt special. My self-esteem was much better but it was hard when I would get home. I learned a lot from Mrs. T. and I wish I could thank her.

These stories are important because they remind us that we can investigate our own teaching through memories of exemplars and role models.

- What are the particular traits that we want to emulate?
- What is it about this teacher that is the most important thing that stays in our memories?
- What can we take away from the realization that not everyone's memories of a particular teacher are the same?

There were also numerous horror stories in O'Reilly Scanlon's (1992) book which evoked painful memories of teachers who were not unlike Alison's third grade teacher from the introduction, or the two teachers described by Sam and Lana. Consider the responses of Andrea and Catherine to 'She Would Bang My Head Against The Board' (box 1.6):

Box 1.6

She Would Bang My Head Against the Board

I'm 42 years old, but I still remember going up to do work on the blackboard in grade 3. When I didn't know the answer, my teacher would bang my head against the board, saying what a stupid girl I was and that she'd knock some sense into me.

One day in music class, the teacher caught me giggling as we sat cross-legged on the floor around the piano. As a punishment she made me sit scrunched up under her piano bench for the rest of the music lesson. I felt like an animal.

Jan Henkel,
Victoria, British Columbia
(O'Reilly Scanlon, 1992, pp. 78–9)

Upon reading the above letter Catherine writes:

She Would Bang My Head Against the Blackboard *is the humiliating story of Jan Henkel who remembers her grade 3 teacher calling her stupid and degrading her in front of the class. It is unfortunate that my grade 3 teacher also took her disciplining a step too far. I remember an instance where she broke a metre stick across the back of a student and many times where she scared some girls so much with her threats and insults that I would cry for them.*

In a similar vein Andrea writes:

How horrifying. I remember in my elementary school there was one teacher famous for his slapping. I hated him. All the kids feared him and avoided him. I'm never going to forget one incident where he slapped one of the students because he wouldn't stop talking. I remember telling myself 'I will fire this man one day when I grow older!'

In addition to memories of greatly admired teachers and teachers who were horrific, another 'genre' of memories of teachers deals with regret. In these accounts we see former students who wish now that they had been nicer, more humane to their teachers. Consider, for example, Gail's response to 'Mr. Ross' (box 1.7):

Box. 1.7

> ### Mr. Ross
>
> It has been over 45 years, but I still remember Mr. Angus Ross, our English and music teacher at Barrie Collegiate. Mr. Ross had to wear heavy braces on his legs, which made walking a chore for him. This handicap never took away his spirit, his energy to teach or his encouragement of students. I have always regretted that I never told him how sorry I was for not being on my best behaviour in his classes or what a special teacher he was to me.
>
> Eileen Nattrass,
> Victoria, British Columbia
> (O'Reilly Scanlon, 1992, p. 165)

Gail writes:

I find that people really do regret later on in life, the way that they misbehaved with their teachers. Many times I look back and realize how immature I was and didn't think how my teacher would feel about the students misbehaving. I remember one of my grade 2 teachers, Mrs. G. my music teacher, had only three fingers on one hand. All the students were either scared of her or made fun of her calling her 'retard, cripple' in her back. I admit that I did feel strange around her because it was the first time I'd ever seen someone missing fingers. She was a great teacher and after a little while I forgot about her missing fingers. I really feel ashamed though with the way I acted, but I'm sure Mrs. G. knew that children can be cruel and don't realize it. She never had any trouble with writing and playing music. I found her to be a very strong woman. I wish I could see her today but I have no clue where she is.

Gail's point about the regret we might now feel in response to past actions is an important one. How are we able to use such episodes to 'refigure' our lives as teachers? For example, do we handle difference in our classrooms more sensitively as a result of looking back? Do we understand more fully the actions of our present students, and if so, how can we apply such knowledge to our own lived experience of difference? Here we are thinking of the ways that as teachers we inevitably appear like Mrs. G. to our students by virtue of size, age, or position. We *are* different, and because we are in the minority (one teacher to thirty students) it is our difference that is apparent. In a group of 8-year-olds we 'stick out'. We are old. We are almost never *we* but rather mostly *they*. This is the kind of image that popular children's author Roald Dahl manages to capture in relation to the outsider role that adults (especially teachers and principals) occupy in the lives of children. Images such as those in his book *Mathilda* (1989) poke fun at the authority structures laid down by adults, and are also 'telling' in that they contribute to a sense of the culture of childhood as distinct from adulthood, learner as distinct from teacher. Even when we manage to transgress the boundaries, or to eliminate some of them, the more generic structures of difference remain. Our point here is that we are not simply remembering teachers and adopting, 'as needed', the characteristics we wish to emulate, or avoiding the ones that we despise. Rather, studying memories of our teachers is, in a sense, a way to construct a different 'gaze' on ourselves and our actions.

What Do These Memories Mean Now?

'It feels really good to go back and trace my memories; I feel like a child again.'
(Excerpt from the playing school narrative of a beginning teacher)

Does it matter whether we come to understand the past in relation to the present differently? Does it matter if we can remember back to what it felt like to be a child-learner? The fact remains, as it also does with parenting, that we are never separate from the generation which came before us (our own parents and teachers), and the generation that follows us (our children and students). A good illustration of this is the observation of Pascal, a beginning teacher, standing at the front of his empty classroom on his first day of student teaching. When Claudia, his university supervisor, comes in and finds him in this position, Pascal explains: *'I just want to get a feel for this space. I am thinking back to myself as a student. There are so many memories here . . .'* For Pascal, the value of these memories is that he can try to put himself in the place of the students. How do they want to be treated? How are they looking at this beginning teacher who, in this case, is replacing their regular teacher? There is also the example of a chance comment made by one of our students, Katherine, a beginning teacher in her early twenties who is 'remembering out loud' to her peers in a professional seminar. As she tells a story about one of her high school English teachers who was very disorganized, she suddenly stops, and as if jolted by a shock of reality (or imagination), she cries out, *'Oh no, what will our students be saying about us in 10 years?'* It is a sobering thought for the group. We remember our own teachers even as we are entering the memory space of our students!

Although many school memories are hardly earth-shattering, an analysis of them can reveal surprising things. For many teachers, the idea of retrieving memories, comparing and contrasting them with other teachers' memories, and so on, can be an empowering and liberating experience. Indeed, simply 'letting loose' on the cumulative experiences of school — in the environment of studying teaching — is itself illuminating. Many teachers are surprised about how much they have to say about a period of time that they often think is over and done with, and we are reminded of how much we are all survivors of a system over whose events and actions we have little or no control. Some, like Janine and Andrea whom we quoted in a previous section, are surprised at the intensity of the relationship between the past and the present:

Janine: *'Who would have ever thought that a teacher could be a hero and someone to admire? I never realised how much I appreciated my teachers until this semester. I really hope to make a difference in my students lives . . .'*

Andrea: *'I remember telling myself "I will fire this man one day when I grow older!"'*

How could we think that living such an extended period of our lives as students would not have any significance to our work as teachers? Indeed, as Sutherland (1997) points out, school, along with family and friends, is one of the three central elements in adult memories of childhood ('The Big Three').

Memory accounts and teachers' reflections on them are significant in a number of ways. At one level, they contribute to an understanding of *school-in-memory* or the space that school occupies in adult memories. At another level, they reveal a great deal about memory in relation to how people come to be teachers.

School-in-Memory

In an essay on memories of childhood, Neil Sutherland (ibid) points out that the 'life review' process is about how we go about piecing together the various chunks of our pasts, many of them from early childhood. We coined the term *school-in-memory* to describe the organizing function that school serves in our own narrative process. As John Kotre (1995) observes, children's experiences (and the resulting memories) may be shaped by the narrative style espoused by their culture. Kotre writes:

Their experiences are grafted onto the meanings and markers of that culture. As they learn to read and write, they discover new mechanisms and new models of memory. They learn a calendar of events, historical and mythical on which they pin their memories. (p. 136)

He uses the example of the logic of a first grader who wants to know 'What's April?' in order to point out how school operates as an organizing feature of memory. The child's mother corrects him:

'You mean, *when's* April?' 'No', he insisted, *'what's* April?' September, he explained, was starting school, October was Halloween, November was Thanksgiving, December was Christmas, January was going back to school, February was Valentine's Day, March was St. Patrick's Day. So what was April? Must be Easter, said his mother. (pp. 136–7)

The idea of school-in-memory complements what F.C. Bartlett (1932) describes in his classic study of culture and memory. Bartlett asked different cultural groups who were told the same story to recall the events of the story months later. The story included a reference to someone dying. In cultural groups who believe that death is most likely to be associated with 'just before dawn', they recalled that moment as being the time of the death; in those groups who associate death with dusk and the fading of the light, the death was recalled as taking place at dusk.

How does the process of school-in-memory work? School is significant as a feature of the memory process itself because of when it occurs in our life-histories, and because so much of school is about 'firsts' — first day of school, first time to be away from family, first self-selected friends, and so on. While the vividness of school memories that some people have may be proof of the potency of school experiences, this vividness may simply reflect the fact that adults tend not to remember that much before the age of 3 or 4, or before school 'age' and that, people tend to remember 'firsts' because of their novelty — which early days at school are full of. We live so much of school in terms of a new grade and a new teacher and first day of class. *'In grade 1, we had Mrs. Brimacombe . . . In grade 2, Miss Lane . . . In grade 3, Miss Montgomery . . .'* and so on, or *'My best year was grade 6 . . . My worst year grade 8 . . .'* As Sutherland (1997) notes from his study of the childhood memories of those born in Canada between the 1920s and 1950s:

> Although some people have few memories of the early years of their schooling, few have forgotten the excitement of the very first day: 'I could smell how clean my clothes were that day.' (p. 187)

The 'firsts' attached to memories of school — and of play associated with school — also include first memories that are related to the organization of schools and classrooms, especially around competency. *I wrote my name! I can read! We get to use ballpoint pens.*

We can also see the significance of school-in-memory in relation to the familiar question 'Do you remember . . . ?' which figures so prominently in our daily lives: 'Do you remember: what were you doing when John F. Kennedy was shot?; the day social studies teacher Christa MacAuliffe died in the Challenger space shuttle?' Years later, people will often associate an event with what they might have been doing at school at the time of that particular event (*'I remember we were right in the middle of a history exam when a neighbour came to the door to tell me about the death of my father'*). A birth or death in the family is remembered as being in June, because June exams were being written at the time. Indeed, we might be able to pinpoint the exact moment of an event because of its association with the teacher, subject or period of the day. For those who go on to become teachers, the academic year continues to be one that serves to frame the memory of particular events. Memory can be organized around the beginning of the school year, school holidays, exam periods and the like. As teachers, we teach through different historical events, ranging from wartime events, as represented in Alphonse Daudet's short story *The Last Class*, to such extreme weather conditions as flash floods, ice storms, intense cold or heat (*The Winter of '92*) and so on. It is this sense of teaching through history which provides the narrative structure of the movie *Mr. Holland's Opus*, which takes us through the chronology of American history in a type of time travel.

Confronting Destiny Narratives: 'How Did I Get Here?'

In her book *School for Women* (1996), Jane Miller talks about how a favorite children's story, *Ameliaranne Keeps School,* first 'caught her ambitions' to become a teacher. As she goes on to write:

> 'Keeping school' was definitely what I was after: the opportunity to explain what was what to children younger than myself, to adjudicate sagely and to ordain how time should be spent and space occupied. It was clear to me from a pretty early age that 'keeping school' had everything: power, glamour, rooms and rooms which belonged to you, the right to speak at all times and to demand a hushed silence as you did so, a fleet of children to run your errands, presents brought from home, and unstinting admiration. You were also in a position to bestow or withhold favour as you saw fit. (p. 67)

At a later point, Miller gets to realize a 'teacherly purpose' by teaching her younger sister who is ill with whooping cough: 'For a few happy months she became my bewildered pupil as I taught her all I knew and a good deal that I quickly invented in order to keep her there . . .' (ibid, p. 69). Such accounts are important in that they can help us probe how and why we become teachers, or the ways that our memories of playing school, for example, can contribute to our sense of being destined to become a teacher.

We often build mental schemas or structures for ourselves which contribute to an overall coherence or unity in our lives. One such structure that is significant to self-study is the destiny narrative, *'I wasn't meant to teach'*. People who enter faculties of education for example, are often asked in an interview or application essay to describe their reasons for wanting to be a teacher. Buried within the question there seems to be some sort of expectation to remember ourselves as having always wanted to be teachers. The question is an invitation to answer with a destiny narrative, something along the lines of *'I always wanted to be a teacher'*. So explicit is the expectation, that Claudia, a teacher educator, recalls an interview assessment rating scale used for a series of interviews with applicants to a Faculty of Education where the question of career aspirations *'Have you always wanted to be a teacher?'* occupied a central position.

If we appear to belabour the point around childhood memories and becoming a teacher (i.e., *'I always wanted to be a teacher'*), it is because we see it as a good example of the kind of memory narrative that infuses teaching generally, and which, when jogged, probed, and otherwise interrogated, offers the possibility of telling new stories. Destiny narratives can override what we know but wish to forget. Consider the ways in which circumstances, as much as anything, can account for our becoming teachers. Who actually becomes a teacher may be far more a matter of social conditions and mores than the professional literature on teaching would suggest or that teachers themselves remember or admit. Kathleen Weiler (1992) found, for example, in a study of retired school teachers who began their teaching careers during the Depression, that the rememberers sometimes attributed a type of 'free choice' ('I really wanted to teach') to a time and situation where there were actually few choices for young women. Girls (and not boys) were often asked the question *'What do you want to be when you grow up — a teacher or a nurse?'*

The converse to 'I was meant to teach' is 'I never wanted to be a teacher'. Eugenia, for example, has been teaching for over 20 years and has always carried around the belief that she never wanted to be a teacher. Upon revisiting her childhood memories, however, she realizes that it wasn't that she didn't want to be a teacher so much as the fact that she didn't want to be the kind of dictator-teacher that she had found her own teachers to be. She recalls actively resisting certain actions of her teachers. She also thinks of a comment of her mother's: *'You were always so headstrong and pig-headed'*. By interrogating these memories, she begins to tell new stories about herself. Thus, she moves from thinking of herself as one of those people who enter education 'kicking and screaming', to thinking of herself as someone who realizes in a more conscious way the significance of advocacy in teaching — of teaching 'against the grain'. In telling new stories about herself, she also finds herself gravitating towards a professional milieu where advocacy and change are at the centre. She begins to notice that there are teacher organizations that aren't just about maintaining the status quo. She meets teachers who write 'Teacher–Activist' on their business cards. She reinvents herself as an agent of change as opposed to someone who doesn't want to belong!

Beyond Retrieval

This chapter has laid out some ways to begin working with the past. If we want to reinvent ourselves in our work as teachers — to engage in living out and telling new stories — we need to start with the stories that are already there. Erica Rand (1995), however, cautions us that memory narratives, particularly around self, may be a mixture of history and myth. She observes that the frequency with which such memories *unravel* under scrutiny suggests that we should attempt to investigate how they unravel as part of memory work. She refers to the tendency of her respondents, adult women remembering their Barbie play, to see a direct progression from childhood to adulthood as itself an adult construction. In the course of engaging in memory work around

Barbie, some women became 'cultural activists'. Rand suggests that it is this process of engaging in the unraveling that is, in effect, 'the point'.

In this chapter we have offered strategies for reading memories that might otherwise be taken at face value. But we need to go further — to engage in a process for unravelling or working *back* through memories, a process that can allow us to explore what we have forgotten, why we have remembered particular details and, most importantly, what we want to take forward from the past to the present. Like the episode of Janet Frame and the broken beer bottle that we referred to at the beginning of this chapter, memory accounts can only have significance if the rememberer is actively seeking meaning. Strategies for unravelling are part of the process of reinvention. Re-playing school necessarily includes 'working back through' the memories. It is this notion of 'unravelling' and 'working back through' memories as a feature of reinvention that we explore in the chapter which follows.

Chapter 2

Working Back Through Memory

Memory (the deliberate act of remembering) is a form of willed creation. It is not an effort to find out the way it really was . . . The point is to dwell on the way it appeared and why it appeared that particular way. (Morrison, 1996, p. 213)

This statement by Toni Morrison, the Nobel-award winning novelist, alludes to the ways that certain literary texts both use and investigate memory, something she explores quite explicitly through the theme of 're-memory-ing' in both *Tar Baby* and her later novel, *Beloved*. In this chapter, we apply Morrison's conception of memory as a deliberate act by offering specific approaches to assembling, examining and 'working back' through memory. Annette Kuhn (1995) compares memory work to trying to solve a mystery novel 'except that in a novel there is always an ending, and usually a resolution. Memory work, on the other hand, is potentially interminable: at every turn, as further questions are raised, there is always something else to look into' (p. 5).

Morrison's use of the term 'dwell on' might connote a type of obsessiveness: 'Don't dwell on things so . . .' we hear people admonish others when they appear to be going needlessly back to something over and over. Here, however, the term 'dwelling on' is akin to the working through of memory — a type of analytic approach to memory that distinguishes the impressionistic retrieval of memories from the more analytic or interpretive approaches that we explore in this chapter.

Romy and Michele's High School Reunion

The idea of memory 'work' however, does not preclude 'play'. Rather it implies a kind of play involving memory and imagination. Consider, for example, the Hollywood film *Romy and Michele's High School Reunion* which plays with memory as the two main characters, Romy and Michele, prepare to go back to school. Although a Hollywood movie billed as 'harmless fluff' and a light-hearted fantasy may seem like a rather unlikely template for teachers' self-study and reinvention, this one does model and operate at a level of self-study throughout.

Upon learning of their forthcoming high school reunion, long-time best friends, Romy and Michele, revisit their high school yearbook. Through a series of 'zooms' from the yearbook photographs back to scenes from their past, we get a sense of how memory is operating for them. Because the two women are 'down and out' in California (indeed one of them is unemployed), they decide to attend the reunion, not as who they really are, but as successful business executives (who claim to have invented 'Post-its'). For the reunion dance, then, they 'reinvent' themselves as inventors, and replace the funky and colourful attire they would normally have worn to such an occasion with elegant black dresses, the kind of conventionally chic clothes that they imagine executives would wear. At first, their former classmates are suitably impressed with what Michele and Romy seem to have achieved since leaving high school. Inevitably, of course, their covers are blown, unravelling everything and forcing them to remember and confront their high school social status as outsiders. Their memories of that status differ:

Romy: All I ever wanted was for people to think we were better than we were in high school and now we're just a stupid joke, just like we always were.

Michele: No Romy . . . Can I tell you the truth? I never knew we weren't that great in high school. I mean we always had so much fun together. I thought high school was a blast and until you told me our lives weren't good enough I thought everything since high school was a blast.

Michele's observations might be taken as an indication that memory-work may not always be a good thing — the unexamined but happy memories she was carrying around with her have been disrupted. However, this confrontation proves to be beneficial: the realization of who they were then — and who they still are — gives them both strength. They are able to use the past to imagine a new future, one that capitalizes on the very thing that set them apart from the others in high school — their avant-garde sense of fashion and creativity. By the end of the movie they are ready to venture forth as themselves — 'self-made' clothing designers (who they always had been) now 'reinvented' as entrepreneur/designers.

The 'looking back' feature of this movie is an example of making the past usable and is emblematic of what Liz Stanley (1992) describes as *post hoc* understandings:

> Memory is the key here, that slither of constructed *post hoc* understanding that apparently acts as a shaft of light reaching from now back into 'the past'. (p. 51)

The film operates with a level of self-consciousness about it. For example, the opening scene shows Romy and Michele watching *Pretty Woman* on video for the nth time and teasing each other about their deep emotional attachment and reaction to it. And as much as *Romy and Michele's High School*

Reunion is a playful fantasy, it also addresses serious issues about social status and marginality. Beyond this content though, we can also see the processes of memory — including reinvention — 'at work'. Understanding the past allows Romy and Michele to rewrite their future.

Dwelling on/Working Back Through Memory

The line separating 'writing memoir' from 'doing memory work' is not easily drawn, and some scholars use the terms interchangeably. But we do find the distinction between them useful for highlighting shifts in accent from the personal to the social. The remainder of this chapter is divided into two sections. In the first section, we attend to unravelling personal memories through writing memoir. In the second, we focus on memory work that is more clearly situated in the context of the social and collective.

Writing Memoir

Do teachers write memoirs or is that sort of activity reserved for elderly politicians, famous writers, serious travellers, and movie stars? Memoirist Patricia Hampl (1996) describes memoir writing as a type of travel writing — not tourist travel writing where there is a brief stop-over to take a few snapshots or video tape the scene and move on, but rather the writing of a

> traveller who goes on foot, living the journey, taking on mountains, enduring deserts, marveling at the lush green places. Moving through it all faithfully, not so much as a survivor with a harrowing tale to tell as a pilgrim, seeking, wondering. (p. 211)

Teachers — beginning or experienced — could be viewed as seasoned travellers. Their work is informed by travels through their own schooling as well as their teaching. As Nancy K. Miller (1997) points out in an essay on the burgeoning number of published memoirs by women, the memoir is often itself a type of curriculum vitae that goes beyond the usual type of entry such as '1979–1986: attended "x" elementary school' to include thick descriptions of school memories. Our contention is that writing memoir as a richly textured curriculum vitae can contribute to professional development.

Writing memoir — as we describe it here — refers specifically to a genre of writing where the focus is both on what is remembered and how it is remembered. This is done by remembering and then remembering again, or by telling a memory and then engaging in a re-telling where we attend to why we have remembered something a certain way and what this might mean in our work as teachers. Patricia Hampl (1996) states:

> Memoir is the intersection of narration and reflection, of storytelling and essay-writing. It can present its story *and* reflect and consider the meaning

of the story. It is a peculiarly open form, inviting broken and incomplete images, half-recollected fragments — all the mass (and mess) of detail. It offers to shape this confusion — and in shaping, of course it necessarily creates a work of art . . . (p. 209)

As she goes on to write:

If we learn not only to tell our stories but to listen to what our stories tell us — to write the first draft and then return for the second draft — we are doing the work of memoir. (ibid)

Hampl observes that even the first draft is not simply a matter of transcribing what is already there in memory; even at this stage of getting it down on paper, there are certain fragments that come to be associated as a matter of invention more than as fact. For Hampl, the first draft is often full of lies and half-truths — what one *seems* to remember. As she writes: 'I try to let pretty much anything happen in a first draft. A careful first draft is a failed first draft' (ibid, p. 206).

I don't know why I remembered this fragment about my first piano lesson. I don't, for instance, have a single recollection of my first arithmetic lesson, the first time I studied Latin, the first time my grandmother tried to teach me to knit. Yet these things occurred too, and must have their stories.

It is the piano lesson that has trudged forward, clearing the haze of forgetfulness, showing itself bright with detail more than 30 years after the event. I did not choose to remember the piano lesson. It was simply there, like a book that has always been on the shelf, whether I ever read it or not, the binding and title showing as I skim across the contents of my life. On the day I wrote this fragment I happened to take that memory, not some other, from the shelf and paged through it. I found more detail, more event, perhaps a little more entertainment than I had expected, but the memory itself was there from the start. Waiting for me. Or was it? (ibid, pp. 203–4)

The significance of the first draft is mostly to 'give shape' to the confusion of images in memory:

Personal history, logged in memory, is a sort of slide projector flashing images on the wall of the mind. And there's precious little order to the slides in the rotating carousel. Beyond that confusion, who knows who is running the projector? A memoirist steps into this darkened room of flashing, unorganized images and stands blinking for a while. Maybe for a long while. But eventually, as with any attempt to tell a story, it is necessary to put something first, then something else. And so on, to the end. That's a first draft. Not necessarily the truth, not even *a* truth sometimes, but the first attempt to create a shape. (ibid, pp. 209–10)

As she goes on to describe the second draft, we see that she regards it as a type of re-visioning, 'a new seeing of the materials of the first draft. Nothing merely cosmetic will do — no rouge buffing the opening sentence, no glossy adjective to lift a sagging line, nothing to attempt covering a patch of gray writing' (ibid, p. 210). In a memory account of her first piano lesson, Hampl begins to work backward to unpack what's true and what's not on her first draft and demonstrates how 'what's not' true is significant. In this unpacking of her memories, she devotes a great deal of detail to her first piano book: the red *John Thompson* book.

> When I reread what I had written just after I finished it, I realized that I had told a number of lies . . . I didn't have the Thompson book as my piano text. I'm sure of that because I remember envying children who did have this wonderful book with its pictures and children and animals printed on the pages of music. (ibid, p. 204)

In the second draft the memoirist goes over the memory, challenging certain points, questioning certain interpretations and the ways in which the details and images — the specifics — are often contained within the language of symbol. As she writes:

> Now I can look at that music book and see it not only as 'a detail' but for what it is, how it *acts.* See it as the small red door leading straight into the dark room of my childhood longing and disappointment. That red book *becomes* the palpable evidence of that longing. In other words, it becomes a symbol. (ibid, p. 208)

In talking about the significance of particular details she notes:

> Their work is the creation of symbol. But it's more accurate to call it the *recognition* of symbol. For meaning is not 'attached' to the detail by the memoirist; meaning is revealed, that's why a first draft is important. Just as the first meeting (good or bad) with someone who later becomes the beloved is important and is often reviewed for signals, meanings, omens and indications. (ibid, pp. 207–8)

For Hampl this kind of re-visioning serves a personal function in that the memoirist engages in a new relationship with the self of the past. This idea of a new relationship with the self of the past is also touched upon in the work of Naomi Norquay (1993) who describes it as doing *homework* on ourselves. Her use of the term *homework* is an interesting one to us — not only for its obvious association with school, *but for the idea that we ought to do our homework as teachers* — at home — *and not use the classroom as the place to 'work out' our pasts!*

Norquay (ibid) provides an example of homework that led her to see her work in anti-racism in a different light. She began with a memory of herself as an activist in the sixth grade, one in which she initially cast herself as hero. We reproduce Norquay's complete account in order to give an indication of the length and detail that is helpful in writing first drafts.

A Memory

Mr. J. explains the Rhodesian situation — Toronto, 1968

It was grade six. We had just finished 'Current Events' and Mr. J. was trying to explain to us why Rhodesia was at war. I do not recall feeling any tension at the beginning. But after a while I began to notice that my best friend C, the only black kid in the class, was beginning to look uncomfortable. Mr. J. just kept on talking. I began to notice that as he continued, the other kids were making furtive glances at C.

'The problem is', I remember Mr. J. saying, 'is that a quarter of a million whites have to keep the lid on four million natives running around. It's almost impossible . . .'

What he said after that is gone from my memory. All I remember is watching C get more and more tense and the other kids getting more and more nervous watching C's rising discomfort. As Mr. J. talked and the class watched, I became acutely aware of C's blackness; she was no longer simply my friend who had moved to Toronto from Bristol. Her 'Englishness' that had attracted me to her in the first place was no longer apparent.

Suddenly she burst from her seat and ran out of the classroom. As if on a reflex, I too erupted from my seat and ran after her. We cried in the girls' washroom for awhile and then I said we should go and tell the Principal. Anger surged in me. We went to the office and I remember demanding to see Miss M. immediately. We were called into her office and I told her what had happened and what Mr. J. had said. C was still crying.

Miss M. told me to go back to the classroom and tell Mr. J. that she wanted to speak to him. When I reached my room, Mr. J. ordered me to wait out in the hall. When he came out I started to shake so I leaned against the wall.

'Stand up straight!' he demanded.

I don't remember what happened after that other than a bunch of us sneaking by the office windows after school and seeing him sitting in Miss M.'s office. I remember that my emotions were very mixed at the time. I was angry at Mr. J. but also terrified because I had challenged his authority in a most unorthodox way. I also realized for the first time that C was both my friend from England and my black friend and as the latter she was vulnerable to prejudices that had up until then gone unnoticed. I somehow felt responsible for her. In that one incident, I became her advocate in a white world. (ibid, pp. 241–2)

Norquay goes on to describe the homework that she engaged in years later, working in a deliberate way to reconstruct the memory.

Mr. J. was racist (but after all, it was the sixties), C was black (and no longer just any friend from England), and I was the heroine (a socially responsible 11-year-old willing to challenge authority). Until now, I have been quite comfortable with this reconstruction. I had taken a risk and had challenged authority from the righteous position of a child from an upper-middle class 'educated' family who knew prejudiced remarks were wrong. This reconstruction seemed to support my belief that I had grown up in a family with

> *a 'strong sense of social justice'. Furthermore, it has long confirmed a com-*
> *fortable version of my current self: someone committed to anti-racist work.*
> (ibid, p. 242)

When she goes back over this memory, she 'reinterrogates' her construction of it — and in so doing begins to see herself a new way:

> *I am no longer the empathetic, understanding friend. Rather, I am the one*
> *who took control and orchestrated the events to quell my own anger and*
> *indignation. Looking closely at my memory of the event, I was the one who*
> *did all the talking. I was the one who demanded to see the Principal. I was*
> *the one who expressed the outrage. Looking back now, I cannot remember C*
> *saying anything at all. My memory is that she just followed along and cried.*
> And I do not know why she was crying! *Was she embarrassed? Angry?*
> *Humiliated? Or did she want me to stop crusading on her behalf? My actions*
> *were clearly not based on C's feelings, but on my assumptions about her*
> *feelings.* (ibid, p. 247)

In her reinterrogation, Norquay is not so much contesting what happened as her initial interpretations of what happened. She begins to understand her 'here and now' differently by probing her 'there and then', realizing that her self-image as an activist may be masking some painful truths. This leads her to question more deeply the challenges people may face in speaking out from a position of privilege.

In the two examples of writing memoir that we have presented, the writers have a number of commonalities:

- they use their childhood memories to probe the 'now';
- they each tell a memory in a first draft form and then go back over it critically in a second draft;
- in their second drafts, they look for inconsistencies, 'lies' (silences?), and symbols;
- they include references to the remembering process;
- they use school-related childhood memories to probe the 'now' rather than specific school prompts such as those we provided in the previous chapter. Norquay's use of the title 'A Memory' suggests a rather broad, unspecified and very idiosyncratic approach here: what is important to the rememberer?

In the case of Norquay's memoir, we have some indication that this remembering is of practical significance to her in her work as an anti-racist activist. For one thing she questions her privileged mainstream position. This does not mean that she will cease to be an activist, but rather that she needs to understand and articulate how her position of privilege operates in order to relocate herself.

In doing our own homework, we followed Norquay's idea of using a first and second draft, sometimes with an unusual twist. In the example that follows, Claudia's 'first draft' was actually written as a lead into an essay on the subject of 'making do' that she wrote some ten years ago for a professional journal.

Making Do: Claudia's First Draft of Writing Memoir

When did I first learn about making do? 'The backs of the calendar pages will do' my mother said, 'for drawings or stories or grocery lists. No need to waste a fresh piece of writing paper.' Outgrown clothes were never thrown out. 'This will do for a floor cloth, rags for the garage or tractor. Old Rosie on the reservation could probably use them for braiding mats.' Mostly, my mother was right about the mats, although one day, uptown and right in front of the post office, I chanced to see before me my old play coat (it had made do for outside and just being around) being worn by one of the Indian children from the reservation. Unmistakable the coat was, with patches on the cuffs and elbows made from the heel of my father's grey-beige work socks. Someone had managed to make do even beyond our own making do. (Mitchell, 1988, p. 16)

Claudia notes that she applies this 'making do' philosophy to process writing. Conditions never seem exactly 'just right': 'If only we only had a week . . .', 'If my mother had only given me some regular writing paper instead of the backs of those sheets from the Harriet's Magic Mirror calendar . . .' (ibid, p. 18). She concludes, 'I revel in the essence of making do and the magic and will of the human spirit that not one of us is saying "if only I had something to say"' (ibid, p. 18).

At the time that she wrote this, Claudia was not consciously engaging in memory work. Now, however, inspired by the interrogations of racism in Norquay's memoir, Claudia revisits her memory account in the second draft which follows.

Making Do: Claudia's Second Draft of Writing Memoir

As Claudia goes back over this first draft of childhood memory, she slips into a second draft mode — looking for gaps, new associations, symbols. Although her point about process writing — and just getting on with things — may have been a relevant one when the essay was written, it is the 'lead in' memory that commands her attention this time. As she writes:

This memory offers concrete evidence — in writing — of an arrogance, a glibness, a 'covering over' — particularly of the details of Old Rosie and the jacket being worn by one of the Indian children. Why was the shape of the sock-patch so important? I remember now that it was a boy who was wearing the jacket. Why was I so general then as to say 'Indian child' when there was no sparing of the detail of the heel of the sock as a patch on the elbow? Where was I when I saw him? Was it a face to face contact with the wearer of the coat? Did we make eye contact? Did I even regard this other child as a child like myself? In rural Manitoba in the 1950s, native children either attended schools on the reservation or they went to residential schools, not the regular schools I attended.

I remember my father had parked our car — a new Oldsmobile — in front of the post office — on an angle to the sidewalk — as parking was (and still is) in many wide-streeted small towns. If you were sitting in the car, you thus had a full view of pedestrians — like a spectator and in fact that is something that people would often 'just do' — particularly on Saturday night when the stores stayed open late. I probably saw the jacket go by from the vantage point of the front seat of the car. I am a spectator. In a consciousness now around racism and multiculturalism, I wonder not only about the initial event (seeing the jacket on someone else — that someone being one of the children from the reservation) and what I have felt or thought (or not) some 40 years ago — but also what I could have been thinking about even 10 years ago when I wrote the essay.

The idea of interrogating a *written* account from 10 years ago may seem like 'stretching the limits' of memory work, particularly since this one was crafted for publication and was not specifically written as a first draft account. Nonetheless, like so many texts, logs and letters that we write over the years, it contains gaps and silences that take on new significance when interrogated from the perspective of who the rememberer has become. In this respect, Claudia's second draft highlights the importance of confronting rather than dismissing past writings which may often seem, years later in our careers, as though they were from 'another life'.

The significance of silences is also a feature of the memory work/ memoir writing of Chelsea Bailey (1997), a former pre-school teacher. For Bailey, the silences tend to be the everyday events of our teaching that are so ordinary that they seem to be mere passing moments.

For her, the point is not so much to tell a true story or even an important one so much as to reconstruct those moments which have left her with uncertainty and doubt (ibid, p. 143). As we see in the following vignette, these reconstructions serve as disruptions, they break the silence of the ordinary.

Power

A 4-year-old child sits with two other children and two adults at a snack table. I make a request of him, to pass the crackers, to pick up his napkin, to stay seated while he is eating, each request referring to how I think snack should proceed. He stares deeply into my eyes and crushes his cracker in his hand and lets the pieces fall on the floor. I feel my chest fill. My heart beats more quickly. I have just been blatantly defied and challenged, and it makes me angry. I begin to think, 'this is the first day I have ever met this child and he has just declared war against me. What the hell am I going to do?' . . . I am hurt. My authority has been threatened, threatened by the will and glance of this child. This feeling of being threatened is not altogether different from fear. (ibid, p. 149)

For Bailey, this reconstruction isn't so much about resolution or what would have been the right thing to do here so much as a memory of the tension — and the ways that the retelling/reconstruction of what seems to be just a 'passing moment' can serve to deepen her understanding of what her dilemmas are in her teaching. As she writes:

> I am confronted with and unable [to] resolve the tension between the ways in which the knowledge available to me about teaching and children produce certain locations of power and prohibit others and my efforts to perform as 'teacher'. (ibid, pp. 150–1)

Writing Memoir From 'Lived Experience'

The use of the specifics — visceral, thick descriptions — can also be found in phenomenological approaches to memory which focus on *lived experience* as phenomena. As John Kotre (1995) writes:

> Phenomenologists who study memory speak of the body as a 'memorial container'. You must touch old objects, they say, smell old aromas, hear old sounds, stoop down to the level of a little person to recapture the experience of childhood. And you will experience your memories more deeply if they are embodied in gesture and movement. (p. 17)

As we noted in the previous chapter, many events lend themselves well to rich, thick descriptions: first days of school (as a teacher), standing in empty classrooms, returning to the school (or a school) after a prolonged absence and so on. A good description of a 'lived experience' can be found in Jane Tompkins' *A Life in School: What the Teacher Learned* (1996). Her memoir begins with a dream — one that she speculates is shared by 'thousands of teachers':

> I'm in front of the class on the first day of school, and for some reason, I'm totally unprepared. (How did this happen?) Throat tight, I fake a smile, grab for words, tell an anecdote, anything to hold their attention. But the strangers in rows in front of me aren't having any. They start to shuffle and murmur; they turn their heads away. Then chairs scrape back, and I realize it's actually happening. The students are walking out on me. I have finally gotten what I deserve. (p. 1)

Tompkins describes this as a private agony but also as a 'collective anxiety' about authority. In her book, devoted to excavating the 'why' of this dream, she revisits her need to be a high achiever throughout her 'curriculum vitae' and what this has meant to her various teaching projects. Of particular interest is a chapter that she calls 'Reverie' where she uses the phenomenon of rows as a catalyst to engage in memory work around order, control and the authority of institutions. As she writes:

> *In my mind's eye I keep seeing rows. Rows of desks, running horizontal across a room, light yellow wooden tops, pale beige metal legs, a shallow depression for pencils at the far edge, and chairs of the same material, separate from the desks, movable. The windows — tall and running the length of the classroom — are on the left. Light streams through.*
>
> *The rows are empty.*
>
> *Now the desks darken and curve. They're made of older grainier wood; they're the kind with a surface that come out from the back of the seat on your right and wraps around in front. The desk top is attached to the seat where you sit, which is clamped to the seats on either side or to those in front and in back. The desks metamorphose in my mind. Now they are hinged, tops brown and scarred; they open to reveal notebooks, textbooks covered in the shiny green and white book covers of Glen Rock Junior High; there's a bottle of mucilage and a pink eraser. On top, there's a hole for an inkwell, black and empty. The seat, when you stand, folds up behind.*
>
> *Sometimes the desks are movable; more often they're clamped down. Always they're in rows. And empty. The teacher's place is empty, too, another desk, or table-like thing. Sometimes it's a podium on a platform. The blackboard behind.*
>
> *The scenes are all mixed together — grade school with graduate school — but always the windows along one side of the room, and always the desks in rows.*
>
> *After babyhood we spend a lot of time learning to sit in rows. Going from unruly to ruled. Learning to write on pages that are lined. Learning to obey. There is no other way apparently. Even if the desks were arranged in a circle or were not desks at all but chairs or ottomans, still they would have to form some pattern. We would have to learn to sit still and listen.*
>
> *The first part of life goes on for a long time. The habit of learning to sit in rows doesn't leave off when the rows themselves are gone. Having learned to learn the rules, you look for them everywhere you go, to avoid humiliation. You learn to find your seat in the invisible rows.* (ibid, pp. 153–4)

What is significant about this reverie on rows is how Tompkins subsequently relates it to her dream at the beginning of the book wherein she questions both her own authority to be there and her on-going ambivalence around order and control. It is something that she still struggles with and does not neatly resolve in her teaching. Thus, while her memory work is not a cure for Tompkins' ambivalence, it does provide a deeper understanding of how the unresolved tensions in her teaching — course after course, semester after semester — are in fact part of her pedagogy.

Tompkins' notion of 'rows' is one example of the many images, sights, sounds or events that can evoke 'lived experiences' of schools — and which can serve as 'prompts' for excavating memory (see box 2.1). Consider the significance of the cane as it figures in the memory work of South African novelist J.M. Coetzee (1997) who revisits his childhood:

> *Every teacher at his school, man or woman, has a cane and is at liberty to use it. Each of these canes has a personality, a character, which is known to the*

boys and talked about endlessly. In a spirit of knowing connoisseurship the boys weigh up the characters of the canes and the quality of pain they give, compare the arm and wrist techniques of the teachers who wield them . . .

Among the canes it is not Miss Oosthuizen's that leaves the deepest impression on him. The most fearsome cane is that of Mr. Lategan the wood-work teacher. Mr. Lategan's cane is not long and springy in the style most of the teachers prefer. Instead it is short and thick and stubby, more a stick or baton than a switch. It is rumoured that Mr. Lategan uses it only on the older boys, that it will be too much for a younger boy. It is rumoured that with his cane Mr. Lategan has made even Matric boys blubber and plead for mercy and urinate in their pants and disgrace themselves . . .

When his father and his father's brothers get together on the farm at Christmas, talk always turns to their schooldays. They reminisce about their schoolmasters and their schoolmasters' canes; they recall cold winter mornings when the cane would raise blue weals on their buttocks and the sting would linger for days in the memory of the flesh. In their words there is a note of nostalgia and pleasurable fear . . . (pp. 6–9)

Box 2.1

Uncovering Memory: Writing About Lived Experience

1 Focus on a particular example of or incident surrounding the object of experience: describe specific events, an adventure, a particular moment.

2 Describe the experience from the inside, as it were; almost like a state of mind: the feelings, the mood, the emotions, etc.

3 Describe the experience as you live(d) through it. Avoid causal explanations and generalizations. For example, this is not the place to state what caused your illness, why you like swimming so much, or why you feel that children tend to like to play outdoors more than indoors.

4 Try to focus on an example of an experience which stands out for its vividness, or because it was the first time.

5 Attend to how the body feels, how things smell(ed), how they sound(ed), etc.

6 Avoid trying to beautify your account with fancy phrases or flowery terminology.

(Van Manen, 1990, pp. 64–5)

We see how the lived experience of the passage of time is particularly significant to schools. In the introduction to this book we alluded to the cover which features a clock that can evoke the impatience often felt when waiting for the bell. The clock is emblematic of the kind of control that the institution of school holds over us. However, as the following account written by a teacher/teacher educator indicates, school bells do not necessarily evoke the memory of waiting to be released. Like most prompts, they can also be part of what Goodson and Anstead (1995) would describe as a 'dissident memory'.

The bell . . . the bell . . . the b-e-l

School bells — my first recollection is of being in grade 1 and out on the playground at recess. Was it a hand-rung bell or a buzzer? The bell would ring and as we ran to line-up to go back into the school we would chant to the rhythm, 'the bell, the bell, the b-e-l'.

Why do I write about school bells? What do they mean in my life? First of all they say something about other people being in control of my life. One of the most 'shattering' moments when I visit a school now is the sound of the bell, the reminder that human activity (including adult activity) is totally controlled by the bell. Unlike when I was a child when at least it was a human being who rang the bell (or even in my first teaching position when it was always one of the grade 8 or 9 girls who got to ring the buzzer — it was as though one of these students had more power than I did), the buzzer in most schools is on a timer — it rings no matter what — and even driving by a school when it is not in session one might hear the buzzer go off.

The link between bells and freedom is an important one. As a student being enslaved in school — waiting for the bell to ring. Being 'let out' for only short periods of time for recess before being 'brought back'. As a substitute teacher in a junior high, praying for the bell to ring so that the day would be over. As a classroom teacher, urging students to get 'x' or 'y' done before the bell — knowing that if they don't it will throw the whole plan off.

Then there are silent bells in the university where I teach. In the middle of a lengthy explanation or anecdote towards the end of class I suddenly notice students squirming or putting on their coats, while others stack their books to carry away. They mean to leave. The undergraduate students in my class will simply be gone. The graduate students will be more polite. A small group of them told me in confidence one night after class that while they really enjoyed the class it always seemed that I would launch into a 20-minute roll when there were just 10 minutes left in the period.

This element of control is important. But then, when I remember the 'bell — the bell, the b-e-l' it seems to me that there is another type of control operating as well. I remember the significance of being the first child to hear — or acknowledge — the bell calling us back inside. I was the one to start up the chant. Now it seems to me that there was something almost praise-worthy — teacher's pet-like, the displacer of other people's happiness — about being the first person to detect the sound of the bell. I could call it another type of control.

She goes on to speculate about a number of things regarding her teaching, asking herself: Is this another one of those 'I always wanted to teach' signs? And if so, what kind of teaching does this 'control' image point to? What about the position of being a teacher's pet? Do teacher's pets go on to become teachers? In the above account, to what extent is there a control factor operating whereby the teacher/teacher educator 'keeps' students in when they are trying to heed the 'silent bells' that the teacher ignores? Memory texts such as this one illustrate how private memories (for example, bell associated with feeling like teacher's pet) often conflict with more public texts (for example, bell associated with feeling confined).

Memory Work: From the Private to the Social

The previous section focused largely on how we can work back through personal memories of school to make the past usable in our teaching. In this section we attend to how memory work can be used in a social (collective) context. Here we draw, in particular, on the systematic and deliberate approaches to memory work advocated by June Crawford et al. (1992), Frigga Haug et al. (1987), Annette Kuhn (1995), and Janet Zandy (1995), all of whom attend to what might be described as a 'border pedagogy' one that uses elements of the past that link to issues of race, class, gender — or anything on the margins. Their work interrogates memorability in relation to difference.

In her edited volume *Liberating Memory: Our Work and Our Working-Class Consciousness*, Janet Zandy (1995) writes of the significance of memory work to the 'amnesia' that has surrounded working class experiences in North America:

> It [memory work] is a bridge between the subjective and intersubjective — the private and unprivileged circumstances of individual lives — and the objective — the collective history of class oppression. It is a way of moving from personal pain to public and cultural work. The 'stuff' of one's life can be transformed into fruitful practices. Even grief can be put to good use. (p. 4)

This idea of grief being put 'to good use' when uncovering memories from a type of amnesia is an interesting one. Retrieval of those memories can influence one's work both in the classroom and in professional life generally. An example of this is a memory that Zandy includes by Julie Olsen Edwards (1995), an early childhood instructor. In her description we see how some painful childhood memories infuse the present — both in her classroom and in the rest of her academic life:

> *Every semester on the first day of class I welcome the students.*
> *Special welcomes to those who are immigrants — my awe at the task they have taken on to learn a new culture, a new language — my hope they will teach us some of what they know from their original home, that they*

will gift us with a bigger understanding of our world. Special welcomes to the reentry students, and to the 'first in family' to come to college. I talk about pioneering — finding new paths to travel, new languages, new ways of thinking and doing — that it takes courage, effort . . . Why do I write this here? Why does this seem so closely allied to having a working-class/left identity?

Memory: sitting in the second grade. New child in class. Chinese. The teacher stumbles over her name, then says in loud and exaggerated clipped syllables 'That is not an American name. Your name in this school will be Wendy.' Not knowing why, I feel a sweep of embarrassment, discomfort, shame. It is somehow very important that I go up to her at recess and try to play. She only stays in class a few months and I never learn her real name.

Memory: Valentine's Day. It is my turn to pass out the cookies and milk for snack time. I have laboriously figured out the calendar and have been waiting for this day. The cookies will be heart shaped . . .

'Don't you ever wash? Someone else will have to hand out the snack.' She goes on talking, someone else is given the box of cookies. I remember looking at my hands as if they belonged to someone else. It had never occurred to me that there was an underside to nails, that one was supposed to do something to them.

Recent memories: I still carefully clean under my nails before any faculty meeting, interview, speech, conference. It is a source of great frustration to me that I cannot grow long nails. (pp. 345–6)

When teachers like Edwards use their own memories of being an outsider to teach students who might also be outsiders, they draw us into the question of voice and person in doing memory work. Who are we remembering when we use 'I', 'you', 'he or she', or 'we'? The pronoun referents in memory work are important. Here we are thinking of when women teach girls, men teach boys, teachers from working class backgrounds teach students from working class backgrounds and so on. 'I', for example, may seem to be an autobiographical referent. However, as Naomi Norquay (1993) observes in relation to her own memory work, the 'I' can also be situated somewhere out of herself:

I have also discovered that when I take up memories of my childhood, both the cherished ones and newly discovered ones, I detach myself from them. I have come to view them not so much as the private details of my own life, but as representative of the kinds of incidents that have taken place and continue to take place in the lives of many others. (p. 250)

In a case like Norquay's then, the 'I' is a type of speaking 'on behalf of', a speaking for and about, but also still speaking as herself. The uses of 'I', 'you' 'we' and 'he or she' speak to the boundaries set for those about whom and for whom we speak. As Antze and Lambek (1996) write:

If selves and communities are imagined, then the boundary between them is also likely to be mobile and permeable. Although westerners tend to think of their memories as being uniquely theirs, as specifying singularity, this may itself be the product of specific narrative conventions and systematic omissions. Even in the West memory talk is fraught with pronouns that extend beyond the I. (p. xx)

Here we are thinking of the ease with which formulations such as the following are used: 'you will remember . . .' or 'a person remembers . . .' or (as we find ourselves slipping into) 'we remember . . .'. When is the referent really 'you', 'a person' or 'we', and when is it really 'I'?

In her memoir *Patterns of Childhood*, Christa Wolf uses the third person pronoun to refer to herself as a child, and the second person 'you' to refer to her adult self — something that serves as a strategy for 'self-scrutiny' (Frieden, 1989, p. 175) both for the writer and the reader. As Frieden observes in her analysis of Wolf's use of second and third person pronouns:

Rejecting conventional rules of pronoun reference, Wolf recreates and refers to her childhood self in the third person, with a different name, and addresses her adult self as 'you'. The 'difficulty of saying 'I' thus becomes the driving force behind the work, as she attempts to reconcile the past and present self, to enable the writing adult to refer to the childhood self as 'I'. The use of second-person address for herself is a strategy also designed to draw readers into the text, since the conventional understanding of 'you' would be an address to the reader. Wolf's narrative strategies thus disrupt conventional readings of her life story in favor of an ongoing process of self-scrutiny: both content (her search for self) and form (the expression of that search) resist a comfortable or insulated familiarity. (ibid, p. 175)

As in other types of literary inventions, rememberers may 'invent' various voices for expressing memories in writing. Wolf's idea, for example, of having a different referent for her child self and her adult self is an invention which provides for a particular form of disruption. The reader is forced to pay close attention to who is speaking and why she has switched pronouns at a particular moment.

In the case of Eva Hoffman (1989) who moved in her teens with her family to North America from Poland in the late 1950s, her dilemma in relation to personal writing is first whether she will write in Polish or in English. She decides on English because, as she reflects, 'If I'm to write about the present, I have to write in the language of the present, even if it's not the language of the self' (p. 121). Indeed, she acknowledges that the language which is 'about me and not about me' also 'is beginning to invent another me' (ibid). However, what is also significant is the 'person' in which she chooses to write: As she observes:

It seems that when I write (or, for that matter, think) in English, I am unable to use the word 'I'. I do not go as far as the schizophrenic 'she' — but I am driven, as by a compulsion, to the double, the Siamese-twin 'you'. (ibid)

At times the writers themselves may see emerging what seems to be their own unconscious impulses to use an unconventional pronoun form.

While we were in the process of writing this chapter — moving back and forth in our pronoun referents — we accidentally used first person pronouns with third person verb formations: 'I sees . . .', 'I wonders . . .'. While we did end up 'correcting them', we also wondered if perhaps 'I sees . . .' provides a different 'reading' on the identity of the speaker worth noting.

Memory in the Third Person

A form of memory-work that makes use of the third person explicitly was developed by Frigga Haug and her colleagues, a collective of German feminist scholars. They first began to develop a set of systematic memory procedures advocating the use of the third person when they realized that research often privileged the personal and the individualistic over the social and collective. For them remembering is about taking collective action.

Following Haug's work, another collective, June Crawford and her colleagues in Australia, explored the significance of emotion and gender to memory work. In their work, groups of men and women come together to recall particular memories of saying sorry and being sorry, of happiness, fear, danger, and holidays. What is fundamental to the work of both Haug et al. (1987) and Crawford et al. (1992) is:

- expressing memory in the third person;
- writing the memories;
- group/collective memory work.

Expressing memory in the third person

In our own professional work, we have explored Crawford et al.'s suggestion that writing in the third person 'encourages description and discourages interpretation' (1992, p. 48). In the various memory-work projects in which we have engaged, we have found that once people start referring to themselves by name or as 'he' or 'she', they observe how easy it is to work with this formulation. The accounts from chapter 1 involving beginning teachers recalling a memory of some difficulty in learning were collected as third person writings. When we first spoke of memory in the third person to one group of teachers and librarians, we were taken with the comment of Joanne, a language arts teacher with 10 years' experience working with young children: 'Oh, third person! That sounds like exactly what happens when I give one of the children in my classes a puppet through which to speak!' Like writing in the third person, a puppet on the hand may relieve the speaker of a 'self-focus', making it possible to 'step outside' one's self.

Writing the memories

Crawford and her colleagues list the advantages of *writing* within a collective or group — a list which we adapt here:

- Writing gives us permission to bypass the 'normal' or proper conventions of spoken narrative, we are not influenced as the story unfolds by audience reactions/expectations.
- Having to organize thoughts and ideas in order to set them down in writing lends a certain structure and discipline to the memory-work group that a discussion group may lack.
- Writing is less likely to involve justification and interpretation.
- Writing provides a fixed and permanent record.
- Written text gives the everyday experience of our lives, the 'unimportant and uninteresting', a status, a significance that is worth exploring. (ibid, pp. 47–8)

Group/collective memory work

Haug et al. and Crawford et al. demonstrate the value of working as a group/collective to take memory work out of the personal and autobiographical and more into an exploration of the social (see box 2.2). Key advantages to this approach are:

- A group has a wider base of theories, judgments and opinions that may be pertinent to any one theme than an individual has (i.e., individuals can share the workload of acquiring appropriate knowledge).
- There is a level of analysis inherent to group work that is not available to the individual (for example, providing for a type of 'compare and contrast' in terms of experiences).
- 'Writing against the interpretation of others' (Haug et al.) encourages self-examination for clarity and precision since the rememberer has to make herself comprehensible to the others in the group.
- Sharing stories within a group brings out the social rootedness of personal experience. (adapted from Haug et al., 1987, *Female Sexualization*)

As with memoir writing, it is important in group memory work to write more than one draft. It is important that each rememberer has an opportunity to run through his or her entire first draft without interruption, and that each person in turn read his or her memory. Only when all the memories have been heard does the group begin to engage in a close reading, asking such questions as:

- Are there ambiguities?
- What cliches are used? why?
- What's missing from these memories?
- What are the commonalities? How does the group account for anomalies?
- How do these memories run 'against the grain' of the expected?
- What symbolic language is used? what does it seem to symbolize?
- What concrete links can be made to a teaching episode now?

Box 2.2

Collective Memory Work

Step One

The group decides on a particular theme (for example, School).

Each member is then instructed to:

- Think of an early memory related to the theme (literacy, going to school, etc.)
- Describe (in writing) the memory providing as much detail as possible. What was happening? Do you remember any particular tastes, sounds, or smells?
- Write in the third person.

While this writing can take place over a short period of time, say for the purposes of a workshop, ideally it will take place over a couple of days so that the participants have time to let the ideas percolate.

Step Two

- Small groups come together to exchange and analyse the texts. This is different from a conventional discussion group in that the focus is as much on our own interpretation of someone else's text as asking questions such as 'what did you mean by . . . ?'
- The group looks at each person's memory in turn. Each group member expresses opinions about the memory, looks for possible meanings; little heed should be paid to literary conventions or style.
- It could be useful to use such prompts as:
    what does this remind you of?
    what pictures come to mind?
- Group members might ask each other (and not necessarily just the author):
    what's missing?
    clarification of ambiguities
- After each memory has been read, the group members can look for similarities and differences, continuous elements; are there aspects of the memories that don't appear to fit?

Step Three

Participants rewrite their texts, paying attention to the questions raised during the analysis.

Adapted from Haug et al. (1987) and Crawford et al. (1992)

Prompts

In the previous chapter we used prompts around 'memories of playing school', 'memories of a difficulty in learning something' and 'memories of teachers' to explore the usable past.

Box 2.3

Prompts for Memory Work

The possibilities for retrieving memories which might serve an educative function in professional development seem endless and could include earliest memories of

situations:
- math class;
- music class;
- being a student;
- teaching someone;
- playground experiences

emotions:
- pride;
- accomplishment;
- failure;
- boredom;
- fear

objects/symbols:
- school bell;
- desks;
- smell of chalk dust, of new exercise book;
- intercom;
- globes

While these kinds of generic school memories are ideal for group work, there are also localized and idiosyncratic prompts, which, while often school-related, are not universal. Some prompts have localized 'currency' and are more related to childhood in a certain geographic region than specifically to school.

Not all prompts end up being equally rich in evoking insight or in producing the expected. Crawford et al. for example cite a memory 'trigger' in their work on emotion of 'saying you are sorry' that was expected to lead to memories of guilt and shame. In actual fact this led more to memories of anger and injustice, and it was the memory trigger of 'secrets' that led to the richest material on guilt and shame. They also suggest avoiding traumatic memories as the starting-off point — bearing in mind, of course, that any prompt has the potential of leading the rememberer back to such memories.

Dale's Memory Work: Using Principles of Collective Memory Work for Individual Self-study

Whether doing memory work individually or collectively, the initial step is to follow the first and second draft approach, interrogating the first draft using questions along the lines suggested previously. Expressing the memory in writing is key in both individual and collective memory work. Ideally, in both cases, the written memory work it should also become a public document so that it is read, heard and critiqued. With some third person memory work, such as that of Annette Kuhn, the public document is more likely to be a 'published' document so that the model of 'living historically' (the term Haug and her colleagues use) becomes available for others to read and critique in terms of their own lives. In this respect, memory work accounts are self-study documents both for the rememberer and the readers.

To illustrate the process, we offer as a case study the memory work of Dale, a former teacher who is now a teacher educator. The initial memory is 'a school memory' but the prompt was actually a visit to Dale's home town which she left 30 years ago. On her return visit, she came in contact with both her grade 3 teacher and a school friend, Gwen. We present Dale's memory work through a series of memories rather than just one recollection. The conditions for the remembering differ from those in the work of Haug et al. and Crawford et al. in that the memory work was not produced as part of a group or collective. We explore the memories here — complete with the protocol for group analysis — with the expectation that the reader (or readers who constitute a group) will engage in a collective interpretation.

In the memory accounts below Dale uses the protocol outlined in box 2.4:

Memory 1: Black hands

Dale finds herself located in a rather strange time zone as she visits her mother who still lives in the small town that Dale grew up in. Her mother mentions that Dale's grade 3 teacher often asks about her, and that she would really like to see her when she comes home. Dale telephones her, and her teacher immediately launches into the most familiar of conversations, and yes she is dying to see Dale. They arrange for Dale to go the next day. Seeing Miss T. again, almost nothing had changed. She recalls that when Miss T. taught her in 1955, over 40 years ago, she was already in her late 40s, just about the age that Dale is now. Dale recalls thinking that her teacher was very old then! Now she is in her nineties and she looks exactly the same to Dale. Dale observes that she feels exactly the same as she did 40 years ago — not frightened necessarily but certainly deferential, aware that she is in the presence of the teacher who later became the Principal. Miss T. asks after

Box 2.4

Individual Memory Work Protocol

I First draft

    A   Prompt: Think of an early memory of school.

    B   Describe (in writing) the memory providing as much detail as possible. What was happening? Do you remember any particular tastes, sounds, or smells?

    C   Write in the third person.

    D   Give each memory a title as if it were a short chapter in a novel you are writing.

II Second draft

    A   Continue to write in the third person.

    B   Reflect on the details of the first draft: What meaning do these details have? How might they link to race, class, gender?

    C   What meaning does this memory have to your teaching?

---

various members of Dale's family. Dale says that she is aware that she is sitting there with some credibility — not because she has a PhD or a career in teacher education, but because her grandmother who has been dead for over 30 years but who used to live next door to Miss T. is somehow guiding her through this experience. Although they talk of many things and Miss T. is very interested in Dale's career and her work in literature and with beginning teachers, there is no question for Dale that she is still very much in grade 3. They speak of the many artefacts of Miss T.'s classroom — the doll house with the real electric light; the floral print curtains that were used to cover over the next day's work board; the cardboard hands (one black and one white) at the front of each row — a black hand would appear if even one person in that row had dirty finger nails. Dale finds herself looking down at her nails to check to see if they are clean.

    When Dale reads over her memory account, she realizes that her focus has been very much on positioning herself in relation to this teacher. Dale writes:

    The teacher, Miss T., is still the teacher, and she, Dale, is still the little girl. Little girl, though, or is it some other form of outsider status? And why is the exotica of the classroom so important — still? The doll house with the electric light, the floral curtains on the blackboard? Is it enchantment or a type of foreignness of the classroom — quite outside anything that anybody in Dale's personal world would know? School is about the exotic, about someone else's knowledge, not one's own. Why does she go back to the cardboard hands? Dirty fingernails. Health. The food groups. They hearken to the days when you had to describe the perfect healthy breakfast: bacon and eggs and toast and cereal and a glass of milk and a large glass of orange juice and half a grapefruit. Dale never knew anyone who ate all that for breakfast but whenever called upon in class to describe what she had had that day she always listed everything from the chart — just in case. Breakfast itself was memory work. School was a foreign affair. Dale thinks about the degree to which she tries to ensure that her students never feel foreign, that everything seems to be as 'okay' and everyday as possible. Things that happen can be outlandish and outrageous and extraordinary, but they must seem to be ordinary.

Memory 2: Penguin pins

Dale spends an evening in the local hotel coffee shop with Gwen, the person who was her best friend throughout elementary school. Without really discussing it, they gravitate towards the back of the coffee shop — out of reach of the juke box and the main traffic. There is a lot to say, and they both realize that they don't necessarily want an audience. Dale feels that it is as though they are back in the cloakroom of their old school (cloak and dagger room, she now thinks), or in the washrooms — illicitly, of course, since everyone is supposed to be outside for recess. Gwen still lives in the town. While news of their respective lives, children, partners have to be caught up on, most of the conversation is interwoven with accounts of teachers. Some of this discussion emanates from a consideration of class photos. The conversation, recalls Dale, is mostly about themselves in relation to teachers and to school, and less about other classmates. They refer to a particular photo from the eighth grade where they are wearing skirts of the same pattern. Because they are sitting side-by-side in the photo they almost blend together. They laugh about this; the skirts they are wearing are the square-dance skirts that had been made up for a school competition. However, as Gwen points out, clearly these skirts had been chosen freely for the photo since if it had been a 'square dance day', every girl in the picture would have been wearing them. Practical deductions.

When they get talking about their elementary school teachers, Gwen speaks of their sixth grade teacher whom some others had feared but whom they had both liked. Gwen points out that she thought this teacher had particularly liked her and recalls the memory of a set of penguin pins that she had received as a special award at the end of the year.

Dale has forgotten about the penguin pins, but as the memory begins to come back, she experiences an odd sense of envy that she had not been the one to receive the penguin pins.

The penguin pins! So long ago and such an important thing to Gwen — after all these years. Dale, though, wonders about her own sense of envy so many years later too, and feels a sense of guilt for still harbouring such thoughts — particularly when she realizes how awful school must have been for Gwen. Gwen had even mentioned in her letter 'you were always so smart'. Thoughts of these words cause Dale to feel an additional sense of guilt for coveting what meant so much to Gwen. She thinks about how important it is for individual students in her classes to feel special. They must all see themselves as getting the penguin pins.

These two episodes, 'black hands' and 'penguin pins', are rooted in a history that spans a period of 40 years. They rely on and invoke particular memories of relationships to teachers and schools. However, they are not about nostalgia or about trying to recapture those good old days. Dale has chosen to 'come back to school', literally, as a way to begin an investigation of her work now as a teacher educator — by re-visiting the town she grew up in, her grade 3 teacher from 40 years ago, and her best friend from the same time period.

The coffee shop conversation between Dale and Gwen came about as a result of a series of letters they had written to each other around a particular class photograph — one from eighth grade in which Dale and Gwen are wearing square dance skirts of the same fabric. As part of her own memory project, Dale had written to Gwen, asking her about the grade 8 class photo and her memories of school. Gwen wrote back in detail about her memories of schooling — and added her own 'take' on the picture. Thus, when Dale and Gwen met a month later, they were both consciously involved in trying to retrieve and articulate certain scenes of schooling. They were each engaged in some version of 'what meaning does this have?'.

In Dale's accounts there are a number of important features:

- Each memory episode includes *two parts:* a first draft account and then another one of looking back again. Dale remembers and then looks back at how particular details guide her consideration of what this has to do with her teaching now.
- The two drafts are written in such a way that the text reads like the *story of someone else's life.* It is a 'life out there'. The accounts are written in the third person (Dale/she) rather than the first person.
- The *naming of the memory* piece is an approach to giving the work a life of its own — separate, in a sense, from the memoirist — regardless of whether it is a very simple descriptive title, as in 'Penguin Pins' or a title that operates more on a 'meta' level as in the case of '(Post)colonial Memory' (to follow in Memory 4).
- Details from the first draft of the 'life out there' take on *symbolic value* when they are re-appraised or re-examined in the second draft. For example, the details of the 'black hands' and the floral curtains covering over the math assignment are examined as symbols.
- Ultimately, the second draft moves into a consideration of *what does this mean — now?* In the case of these school-related memory accounts, the point is, what do these memories have to do with becoming and being a teacher? Thus we see Dale coming to more of an understanding of what she does and why: Why is it so important to her that the classroom be a welcoming, non-exotic place — regardless of the content — for her students? She thinks of how she consciously works at ensuring that students feel special — all winning penguin pins. She is also conscious, however, of what might be termed a shadow, a dark side, the envy she feels about Gwen's penguin pins and how much the world of teaching and academia has a competitive side to it.

In these next two accounts, a localized or regional prompt of the mail order catalogue is central to Dale's memory:

Memory 3: Mail order memory

As a child, Dale recalls spending many hours going through mail order catalogues finding clothing and toys and furniture to order — filling in all of the categories including colours which were always referred to by number. She remembers playing with the order forms that were inserted into the back of the catalogue — sometimes they would be separate, sometimes they would be integrated with a perforated line. These forms entertained her long after an actual mail order office was opened in the town she grew up in. Her family never actually used the catalogue forms, which happened to be similar to the ones that she used to watch the clerks in the order office filling in.

She recalls feeling hot in her heavy winter coat as she stood in line with her mother, and later her best friend on a Saturday afternoon when these orders would be placed. She remembers being very proud of using cursive form and making very 'adult-like' signatures at the end of the form. Another thing Dale recalls is that almost at the same time as she was playing 'mail order', she was being taught the conventions of the business letter at school — probably grade 4 or 5. Frequently they would have to write sample letters to order sporting goods such as a basketball or a baseball bat. In the letter, they had to demonstrate correct business letter form and include the quantity, price, size and other details of the order. Dale recalls feeling that it was really quite silly learning to do a business letter to order goods such as basketballs. Everyone knew that you ordered on a form, not in an open letter!

When Dale goes back over her memory, she writes in response to the question 'what meaning does this have?'.

Dale feels that some of her earliest memories of the split between school work and the real world are encapsulated in this anecdote. The things one did in school were always just to please the teacher, never useful in and of themselves. It never occurred to her, for example, that anything she ever did in nature study had anything to do with her, even though she grew up in nature, on a farm, surrounded by trees, birds and wild flowers. Now she thinks about it in terms of class; didn't the teacher realize that people don't have to write order-letters, or that farmers didn't necessarily have time to stop and identify species of birds or flowers — that they were just 'birds'?

She is also curious now about the role of the five sets of encyclo-pedias in her home and their disjuncture with home literacy. Not only did farmers not have time to stop and name species of birds, they also did not have time to read the twenty-volume Book of Knowledge *series or* Grolier Encyclopedia, *or* Lands and Peoples *or* Nature and Science *or* Popular Science. *Consequently, she has no memory of ever seeing anyone else actually using these books. While Dale recalls looking through these, and eventually discovering for herself the kind of knowledge contained within these sets, she also feels that there was something significant about these early lessons on auto-didacticism and how she came to eschew teachers' knowledge, particu-larly as evident in fixed reading lists, prescribed texts and so on. So strong is Dale's revulsion to this isolated scientific knowledge that picking up a copy of the nature study book at a country school restoration some 40 years later, she finds herself 'transported back in time', recalling the ugly black and white photographs of schoolgirls in starched gingham checkered dresses and boys in short pants and white shirts — something no one at that time would ever be caught dead wearing.*

The point is that valid knowledge, for Dale, is knowledge obtained from outside school; school knowledge is not something anyone would really want to know. She now recognizes that this also has something to do with her revulsion of 'textbooks' — both for herself and her students. With her grade 8 class, she recalls, it was always more intriguing to find material from outside the sanctioned curriculum. She realizes how 'ready' she was to teach in a learner-centred multitext classroom, regardless of the subject, as opposed to teaching from the text. It had always been there.

In a second mail order catalogue account Dale writes about growing up in Canada at a time when it was still very much a colony, when the 'mother country' Britain was still very central. For this reason she refers to it as her (post)colonial memory:

Memory 4: (Post)colonial memory: the catalogue family

Dale remembers that when she was about 8 or 9 — and in the third grade — she had created a whole mythical family of cut-outs taken from the Eaton's catalogue — made up of a mother, father, and about eight or nine children (with several sets of twins). This family was cut out of sections of the catalogue and used to create many play narratives. For example, the family was often getting ready to travel or to go away on family picnics. They also had all sorts of baby paraphernalia from the catalogue such as brightly coloured strollers, playpens, and highchairs. There were several important features of this family: first, Dale recalls talking about this family a great deal at school, telling everyone about them and how they lived in her backyard on the farm. In her mind they lived in a small granary that was always hauled up to the backyard in the summer to store bicycles and the lawn mower — and which in the fall was dragged back out into the field to use for grain storage. The granary was a relatively new construction, still retaining the scent of new plywood — hence its somewhat exotic flavour relative to the rest of Dale's surroundings. Dale would often share with other girls at school her experiences of babysitting the young children in this 'catalogue' family. In her account the family was always made up of preschool children so of course none of them could be found on the school grounds. They seemed to come mostly in twin versions — which was quite easy to do from the catalogue because there were so many duplicates of each model wearing different outfits. A second feature of this family was its origin — which was British. Dale doesn't recall all the names of the children now — except for the little boys who had names like Nigel and Nyall, seemingly drawn from British school stories. These boys were always dressed in little short pants or sailor outfits.

Looking back, Dale observes that this catalogue memory seems to be significant for a variety of reasons. The British references are particularly important now in relation to received truth and privileged knowledge. Everyone of any significance in the nearby town was from England or

Scotland — the medical doctors and the church ministers who came or went. The voice of authority had a British accent. Knowledge and literature — education — was related to Britain. Nothing of any significance seemed to happen where she lived, and she recalls entertaining her parents one Sunday afternoon with one of her first compositions when she was about 8 — a biography of Charles Dickens in which she stressed his British heritage. The references to the perfect family made up of lovely cherubic toddlers are also important. As the youngest in the family, she seldom had the opportunity to interact with younger children, unlike many of her friends in school whom she envied because they had younger brothers and sisters. Was this an early sign that she really wanted to be a teacher?

The details in accounts such as Dale's take on symbolic value upon re-appraisal or re-examination. For example, the doll house and the floral curtains covering the board work in her third grade classroom symbolize for Dale the exotic nature of learning. The cardboard hands — one white and one black — at the front of each row symbolize for Dale the judgment placed on one's private life, in terms of cleanliness and diet — from the outside. Dale recalls that her mother and father often commented about other facets of privacy — noting the boldness of people who asked probing questions about the history of the farm or personal details of one's life and so on. This theme of 'outsider' also pervades her two mail order memories: the gap between personal knowledge and school; and the gap between local culture and real culture. Even the penguin pins that provoked a sense of envy convey the kind of insider/outsider meaning, with the teacher being the one who confers worth and value 'from the outside' on the student.

Dale recasts the significance of these early experiences of schooling to her own teaching in a number of ways. For one thing, she locates these memories in her on-going quest to make things relevant in the classroom. For example, she recalls how her very first teaching assignment in the early 1970s coincided with the heyday of A.S. Neill's *Summerhill* and his belief that everything you need to learn in school could be acquired in six years (as opposed to twelve), and how ready she was for moving towards integrating school knowledge with 'real' knowledge.

Further, she regards it as very important that her students, be it those in junior high school or in university, feel 'at home' in their learning in her classroom. She wonders whether it is mere coincidence or of some more personal significance that she became so passionate about Canadian literature, the 'home literature', when she was in university — the idea that there were novels written by Canadians and about Canadian experiences. When she started teaching literature to 13 and 14-year-olds in 1970 she sought out examples of Canadian short stories, poems and plays that would speak to them — the kind of literature she would have wanted to read. Since this was a time of Canadian fervour — beginning with Expo '67, the emergence of Canadian nationalism and so on, perhaps the attitudes stemming from her own personal colonial experiences were part of a larger social movement. As she observes, it is difficult to know, since right around the time that she began teaching, the educational movements of the time were very centered on humanism, free expression, being in touch with one's self and so on. While such an approach has now become firmly entrenched within a learner-centred pedagogy, she also sees it not just as a movement about personal growth but also about social change. The idea that the teacher, 'the institution' is the ultimate authority was something to be critiqued and overthrown.

When we ask participants who have engaged in working with this third person memory formulation to reflect on the experience, their comments reflect a great deal of interest and engagement, as well as a growing awareness of the value of memory writing to themselves and to others. As Dale notes of working back through memory using the third person accounts:

> *It was amazing. The more I wrote about Dale and not 'I' the more I could attend to the details which I otherwise would have thought irrelevant or banal. As ordinary as these details are/were, they didn't seem quite so ordinary — they seemed more worthy of being remembered — explored 'as though' I weren't writing about myself. The details took on a life of their own.*

Dale's reference to the details taking on a 'life of their own' suggests someone else's life, someone else's classroom. What is important about this is that it becomes a classroom that we can not only visit and travel through (Hampl, 1996), but if we follow Toni Morrison's (1996) notion of 'willed creation' — one that we can all study through dwelling in and on!

Living Historically

Haug et al. (1987) observe that:

> living historically [through memory work] should be taken to mean a refusal to accept ourselves as 'pieces of nature', given and unquestioned, and a determination to see ourselves as subjects who have *become* what they are, and who are therefore subject to change. (pp. 50–1)

Probably no point is more important to the practice of self-study than this. Writing memoir and engaging in memory-work is undertaken in the service of understanding our classroom life better. Providing protocols for assembling and analysing these memories does not necessarily guarantee 'sudden breakthroughs'. Working back through memory is not some sort of quick fix, and the immediate benefits of writing memoir or engaging in third person memory work are not easily discernible — or describable. Nor do they give us the whole picture. In the next chapter, we turn our attention to school photographs as a way to enlarge the picture — both figuratively and literally, to look at how some aspects of school memory are constructed through photography, and to question the ways that school photographs can themselves contribute to 'deconstructing' our work as teachers and learners.

Chapter 3

Picture This: Using School Photographs to Study Ourselves

The act of photography anticipates the future by ripping the appearance of a moment out of its time, creating a tangible image for the future of what will be the past. (Walker and Moulton, 1989, p. 157)

Every photograph is a record of a moment forever lost — snapped up by the camera and mythically presented as evermore. The family album is always torn by the sorrows of loss: lost childhoods, lost friends, lost relatives, lost memories, lost objects, lost newness. (Barthes, 1981, cited in Mavor, 1997, p. 119)

Photographs are something we just take for granted; they get taken, we look at them, we hide them away, or we display them. How often, however, do we look *into* them, or really consider them as either 'tangible images' of the past or as records of lost moments. Yet, photographs can play a very important role in framing our sense of the past and shaping the course of our future. Consider, for example, the following inscription which appeared on the back of a school photograph:

To my two bestest teachers Mr. and Mrs. M. From me — 20 years from now you may forget my name so — Cathy Banks

Almost three decades ago, an eighth grade student named Cathy gave a photo of herself to Mr. and Mrs. M., who were then in their first year of teaching. Mrs. M. has been in possession of this photo for over 25 years, even longer than the 20-year span specified by her student who did not want to be forgotten. Not only has Mrs. M. not forgotten Cathy, she has kept up a regular correspondence and friendship with her throughout the 25 years. It was nevertheless a surprise to Mrs. M. when she happened upon this snapshot recently while going through a box of old photos. The inscription seems almost eerie now because it has been discovered so far into young Cathy's future — the projection of a 13-year-old girl into '20-years-from-now', anticipating someone looking back, insightfully acknowledging the degree to which a photo remains a tangible reminder of the past.

In this chapter, we investigate the use of school photographs in studying ourselves as teachers. School photographs include individual portraits such as Cathy's as well as group shots showing the entire class with the teacher. As artefacts, these photographs can evoke school rituals, idealized

74

notions of 'schoolgirl' and 'schoolboy', and much more. They invite us to remember, speculate, and fantasize, an invitation that we will take up in quite literal ways. School photographs contribute to some of our most lasting impressions of school and of our lives as school children, reminding us of what we once were, and what we are no longer. But like the school memories examined in chapters 1 and 2, school photographs also provide perspectives on who we have become. In this regard, they extend the work of memory and reinvention into a more visual form, inviting us not only to look back on ourselves as former students, but also forward to ourselves in the classroom now.

School Photos as Phenomenon

Photo-theorist Max Kozloff (1994, p. 76) writes, 'Still portraiture is one cultural index of how people are *schooled* to regard themselves.' (italics added). Kozloff's use of the term 'schooled' is interesting, since one of the most regularized and routinized practices in portraiture in many Western countries is the taking of the school photograph on 'picture day'. The actual event usually involves an employee of some national photography company arriving at the school already armed with appropriate backdrops for the pose. In many Western schools, these settings consist of scenes of a sky, forest or library, or some other unobtrusive background image. Other conventions include a snappy repartee with the subjects who are directed to say 'cheese', 'sex' or 'my father has smelly socks' — anything to get them to smile. Posing for the class photo is susceptible to all the dynamics that operate within any social grouping: having to stand beside someone who is detested, being 'exposed' in the front row, being hidden in the back row and so on. When posing for their individual photos, students are often treated to the running commentary of onlooking classmates, all awaiting their turn in front of the camera.

Figure 3.1   School photo, Dorian reading

Consider the following excerpt from a 'photo memory' discussion with a group of 10- and 11-year-old girls — Abby, Norah, Dorian, and Gretchen. During an interview with the girls, it became clear that they had already informally begun to engage in what we would call memory-work around their school photographs. (Six years of schooling yield six picture days! Indeed, they were aware of 'being schooled' to look a certain way in these photographs, of actively colluding with the photographer to construct certain images. We were also struck by the ease with which they were able to speculate on why the photographer had them pose a certain way (see Figure 3.1).

Abby:	*Oh grade 2 — they made us sit at the desks with the open book — a geography book! (shrieks and screams)*
Norah:	*Oh no — mine was a dictionary.*
Interviewer:	*A dictionary?*
Gretchen:	*Mine was an encyclopedia!*
Norah:	*Mine was a Larousse dictionary.*
Gretchen:	*That year I had forgotten it was picture day and I remember I was wearing a mickey dress.*
Interviewer:	*What's that?*
Everyone:	*A mickey dress — it has Mickey at the front and Minnie at the back.*
Gretchen:	*It was so awful, plus I had to sit at this desk . . . uh . . . in front of this book that I would* never *read. I looked a bit stupid reading this book.*
Norah:	*I remember my hair was going all over and I had these little strings attached . . .*
Dorian:	*I guess they wanted to make us feel like we looked so smart.*
Interviewer:	*Do you think that's why they put you in front of a book which you probably couldn't even read. Hmm — was it a difficult book? Was it a French book?*
Gretchen:	*Uh yes some of them.*
Norah:	*Some of them were English.*
Abby:	*I remember my book was English plus they made me do this (demonstrates how she had to look down at the book and point).*
Interviewer:	*Oh you're kidding. You mean they actually made you point your finger like they do in kindergarten?*
Abby:	*(offers another demonstration).*
Interviewer:	*And is that what you were doing in the photograph?*
Abby:	*(nods head)*
Norah:	*You wouldn't believe what I was reading — because to make me look like I was reading they made me read it. I was reading the definition in French and the word was 'alphabet' (laughter all round) . . . and the next word was . . . uh acqua . . . and it was all these weird definitions.*
Interviewer:	*Imagine reading the definition of the word 'alphabet' while you get your picture taken in front of a book so you look like you can read.*
Norah:	*I remember they used these books for the kindergarten kids too and they couldn't even read!*
Interviewer:	*Oh you're kidding. Did they make them look at the page with their finger?*
Norah:	*(nods).*

Gretchen: *Well, they didn't do that for me; they just made me look at a weird book . . . Then they made me hold the book like this (holds out her hands in the book reading position) and then I had to go like this (demonstrates the way in which her eyes had to land on the page).*

Interviewer: *Why do you think they made you do that?*

Gretchen: *I think they were trying something out that year.*

Dorian: *Maybe it's because it was supposed to look like a school . . . I feel like it was kind of like to make the parents think we are really smart or something.*

Abby went on to note that part of the posing is '*to look good*', but much of this is determined not only by the photographer, who insists '*on making you smile with your mouth open, even though you've practiced a more serious look*', or makes you point to words on a page, but also '*by your classmates, who are all standing there waiting for their turn and wondering why you're taking so long, because everybody knows you aren't going to look that great anyway*'. The four girls also agreed that teachers can '*ruin your pictures*' and described a teacher who wore what they considered to be inappropriate outfits, more fitting for a party or a night club than a classroom.

The posing explored by the four girls gives us a sense of what Kozloff (1994) refers to as 'routine deception'. As he observes of still portraiture:

> Portrait photographs are invested with a routine deception. Normally, one thinks of them as the result of a moment that has been taken out of time to exhibit the fact. In such images, all psychological slack has been pulled taut to assert the prepared, immobile display of the person or persons. The characterizing process should look stable, with details consistently presented throughout the frame. A subject may appear self-absorbed or unconcerned about a later audience, but this is only a device that masks the fact that he or she is primed and ready for inspection. (p. 3)

The resulting 'vernacular portraits', as they might be called, more closely resemble poses taken at Sears or Walmart than Karsh or Cartier-Bresson portraits. They are unlikely to end up on a gallery wall or in a coffee table art book, but they *are* likely to end up just about everywhere else: in offices on employees' desks, in living rooms on top of the television set or mantelpiece, in the wallets of parents, grandparents, boyfriends or girlfriends, best friends — sometimes even former best friends. Photo albums may be full of the products of these annual picture-day events. Often to the embarrassment of a former school child, they may be displayed in a relative's living room long after schooldays have ended. In the case of a class photograph of 25 or more students, the images aren't just owned by one subject; all of the class members continue to have access to the image. Similarly photographs in school yearbooks have this public quality about them, since even if we don't own the picture, or have managed to lose it or hide it away, many others still have it in

Harry Weber
Romania, 1910

Figure 3.2   *Grandfather's school photo*

their possession. In a sense, the photographs take on a life of their own, a life that we can no longer control. Every once in a while, someone must be coming upon such photos and saying 'I wonder whatever happened to so and so?' or 'Is that what he looked like then?'.

Imagine, for example, the surprise and deep emotions Sandra felt when she stumbled upon a school portrait of her deceased grandfather taken in Romania in 1910, a photo she never suspected even existed (see Figure 3.2). Her beloved grandfather — whom she had never seen read or write — had gone to school! And look at the professional pose and background — strikingly similar to the portrait of Claudia's daughter Dorian taken in the 1990's (Figure 3.1). This old photograph illustrates that the phenomenon of picture day as we know it now (posing to look the serious student, using props such as books and professionally staged backdrops, etc.) is neither a recent nor a strictly North American ritual.

A point that is made in much of the literature on family photographs is that, in many respects, everyone's family photos look the same. There is a social and public dimension common to all of these representations, and only in the personal and private stories can differences be found (Holland and Spence, 1991). As Holland (1991) writes in her introduction to *Family Snaps: The Meaning of Domestic Photography,*

[. . .] our 'own' family pictures, however ordinary, remain endlessly fascinating as we scrutinize them for exclusive information about ourselves. The images of relatives we never knew but whose influence is felt, reminders of the optimistic youth of our parents and their parents, these things seem to throw light on our present condition. (p. 2)

It is important to point out, as Carol Mavor (1997) does in an essay called 'Collecting loss', that part of this generic look is related to what families can agree on as a 'cover' or 'myth'. In her essay, Mavor cites author Marianne Hirsch, who explores the generic look of family albums:

Happy Holiday, Happy Vacation, Happy Graduation, Happy Birthday, Happy First Bicycle, Happy New Home, Happy New Baby, Happy Wedding. Though, as family members, we can read other stories between the lines, there are solid similarities between family pictures (the pose, the occasion, the smiles, sometimes the clothes), a general covering over that perpetuate[s] dominant familial myths and ideologies. (Hirsch, 1994, p. 122, cited in Mavor, 1997, p. 126)

Although we are all familiar with the saying 'a picture is worth a thousand words', it is probably more accurate to say that a picture evokes a thousand words (or more). In *Snapshot Versions of my Life* (1987), Robert Chalfen points out the significance of the verbal interpretation that often accompanies photographic images. Some of this verbal interpretation comes in the form of captions or inscriptions written on the backs of photographs or beside them in an album, which might take the form of cryptic messages

('Taken from our balcony'), dedications ('To my darling Ann'), or identifiers ('Sandra in the Dead Sea, 1993'). Further interpretation is provided by the stories told while photographs are shown or viewed. Consider, for example, the following comments made by Rae, a pre-school teacher:

> *For some time, I was quite involved in tracing my genealogy. It was fascinating for me to go back through the microfilms of the original farm censuses in Sweden to find the list of yet another large family that I was related to. But more fascinating for me still is having a chance to pore over my grandmother's photo albums, asking her once again which long-ago relative that was, or to please tell me again the story that goes with this picture.*

Chalfen goes on to describe how verbal accounts structure the viewing of images:

> Comments, in the form of storytelling and various recountings, serve to expand and complement minimal identifications common to other kinds of written captions. Complete silence during a home mode exhibition event is socially inappropriate behaviour — viewers and exhibitors are expected and conditioned to say something. These accompanying remarks appear to be as conventionalized as the imagery itself. (p. 129)

School photographs, too, carry with them their own myths. What reality are they covering over? They become symbols in and of themselves, but of what? Perhaps of ordinariness, in the sense that they could be anybody's history. Or is it that they point to a universal truth about schoolgirls and schoolboys? The group photographs might be regarded as 'tableaux': tall people — mostly just heads — in the back row, and shorter people with shoes, socks, legs and hands in full view. Who stands next to whom? What can only the insider know about these arrangements? We scan the image to see if there is anything in the photograph to suggest the extraordinary — that this child would go on to become a great statesperson, a Nobel prizewinner, a victim, a mass murderer, our future spouse or partner? School photographs — both group and individual poses — are highly evocative, and are used in ads, opening scenes of movies, newspapers and newscasts. For example, it was a class photo of grade 1 pupils and their teacher who were shot and killed in Dunblane in 1996 that was broadcast around the world. The images of missing children on milk cartons are generally school photographs. In Joel Sternberg's photograph 'Highway 101, Petaluma, California, October 1993', we see on the billboard a school photograph of Polly Klaas, a young girl who was abducted from her home during a slumber party on 1 October 1993 (see Figure 3.3). When a child disappears or dies unexpectedly, the school photograph is often the most recent tangible image of him or her.

In spite of, or perhaps because of, their ordinariness, school photographs have not received much attention in either the literature of photography or the literature on schooling and teacher education. Drawing on current

© *Joel Sternfeld. Courtesy PaceWildEnsteinMacgill, New York.*

Polly Klaas was abducted from her home in Petaluma during a slumber party on October 1, 1993. Within hours, a massive volunteer effort was organized to find the twelve-year-old girl. Millions of flyers bearing Polly's photograph and a police composite sketch of her abductor were distributed nationally. Large banners were affixed to billboards across Northern California.

Two months later, Richard Allen Davis, an ex-convict with a history of drug and alcohol abuse, led police to a wooded area fifty miles north of Petaluma where he had buried Polly Klaas's body.

Figure 3.3   Highway 101, Petaluma, California, October 1993

work which examines family photographs as tools of 'narrativisation' (Dewdney, 1991), we see school photographs as ideal sites in which to explore the past and present.

School Pictures as Method — Revisiting Picture Day

Annette Kuhn, in *Family Secrets: Acts of Memory and Imagination* (1995), writes about using photographs in memory work:

> Making do with what is at hand — its raw materials are almost universally available — is the hallmark of memory work's pragmatism and democracy. Anyone who has a family photograph that exerts an enigmatic fascination or

Figure 3.4 A Great Day in Harlem

arouses an inexplicable depth of emotion could find memory work reward-
ing. (p. 6)

The idea of deliberately using staged or arranged photographs as a
site of study and reflection first occurred to us when we viewed Jean Bach's
documentary film on jazz musicians: *A Great Day in Harlem.* The film is
organized around a single photograph (Figure 3.4) that was taken by photographer Jonathan Kane for *Esquire* magazine in 1959. A number of jazz musicians, including such 'jazz greats' as Dizzie Gillespie, had been invited to show
up at an address in Harlem to be part of a group photo. Drawing from raw
footage of the taking of the photo, the makers of *A Great Day in Harlem*
concentrate both on the picture-taking process and the resulting photograph,
so that, more than 35 years later, the subjects interviewed for the film are still
talking about 'that day'. Participants talk about what they remember: how they
felt about being in the photograph, where they stood, what the photo shoot
was like and so on.

As Claudia notes after viewing *A Great Day in Harlem*:

*It was like seeing the film version of that country and western song from the
sixties 'The Class of 57 had its dreams'. I couldn't wait for the film to end so
that I could race home and look at my grade 6 class photograph. I wondered
what it would be like to go back over that photograph again. Instead of*

showing up at a designated place in Harlem, we [my grade 6 class] had all lined up in the school gymnasium some time between morning recess and noon-hour. It wasn't so much that I needed to know what everybody was doing now. It was more a case of wondering what we were doing even then — and what that had to do with what we had become. I was dying to try out the film-makers' method. I immediately wrote to my best friend from the sixth grade. I wanted to know how she 'read' herself in that picture. What would she say about some of the other people? I imagined us looking closely at ourselves, at each other. I wanted us to look 'into' the picture. (Excerpt from Claudia's fieldnotes)

The Method

The questions proposed in box 3.1 can be used to guide either an individual or collective reflection on school photographs. We suggest that group members start by assembling as many of their school photographs as possible, choosing several to talk about in some detail. Even if someone cannot find any school photographs, he or she may still find the questions helpful.

School Photograph Workshop

We invited teachers to participate in 'picture day workshops' where they got together in small groups to look at and talk about their photographs (Figure 3.5). They were asked some weeks ahead of time to gather as many of their school photographs as possible. This is because the official trustees of school photos and family albums are often, we discovered, mothers and grandmothers, and the teachers often had to 'call home', make visits to their families, or make other arrangements to get the photographs.

Some of the teachers who participated in the sessions had not been able to locate their school photographs. In other cases, the families had never purchased them in the first place. However, an absence of photographs does not prevent the rememberer from engaging in memory work. People often retain vivid memories of actual photographs or the process of having photographs taken. Participants without photographs often remembered posing, or the highly anticipated day of getting the photographs back. In fact, it was not always the photograph that was brought to the session that was necessarily the most memorable, and for those who had no photographs, the memories and group discussions around the photographs were often very powerful. As Lorraine noted:

I still had plenty of memories about those photographs . . . It made me think that one day I will be the teacher within the group photographs and I want students to remember me as a good teacher. It also made me think about what the characteristics of a good teacher were.

Box 3.1

Revisiting School Photographs

1   What can you remember generally about picture day?

2   Pick one picture you have strong feelings about. Describe it. What grade were you in? Why do you think you have such strong feelings (positive or negative) about this one?

3   Which picture do you regard as your best school picture and why?

4   Which picture do you regard as your worst school picture and why?

5   What do you remember about being photographed in a group/class? (getting lined up, who you had to stand beside?)

6   What do you remember about being photographed in an individual pose?

7   Do any of your school pictures have pictures of teachers in them? Describe some of these photographs. What comes to mind when you think about these pictures now?

8   Do you remember making any special preparations for having your photo taken? (for example, was there a certain look or pose that you wanted to achieve? Why? Do you remember details regarding clothing?) What comments were made by other people (for example, by the photographer, teacher, your classmates, parents) before, while or after you were photographed?

9   What was done with the school pictures in your family (did you usually buy them, display them in the house, exchange them with friends, send them to relatives, give them to the teacher?)

10   Do you have any specific memories of the photographers themselves (what they said, how they acted, what the name of the company was?)

11   Thinking back, what kinds of images of yourself as a student/learner are 'captured' in your school photos? Do the images change? How?

12   Have you ever looked at school photos of your parents? What comes to mind?

13   Are there any inscriptions on the photographs?

14   What do these photographs mean to you now that you are a teacher?

Figure 3.5   Picture day workshop

A number of teachers spoke of the experience of assembling the pictures and thinking about their possible meanings even before the sessions. In some cases, they described revisiting the photographs with family members. For instance, Margaret, who has been teaching since the late seventies, sat down with three of her children who were also looking at their school pictures. As she writes:

What a rich experience it was last night sitting down with Ben, Christie and Jay to talk about school photos. My own school picture was a class photo. In fact, I don't think we ever had individual photos until high school, and those because of the yearbook. Since I don't have the picture in front of me, I must rely on memory. While I only have vague recollections of having the picture taken, it is still the picture that stands out most in my mind. Maybe because it has been in my history the longest — and all school memories begin with this picture. It was taken outside in front of the school, and since we are all wearing light jackets and the girls are in summer frocks I am thinking that it was very early in the school year. Not the first day of school though because I recall that Hans Bach's mother took a picture of me that day. Hans brought it into school to give to me weeks later. I carried it around with me for days so that by the time I gave it to my mother it was quite crumpled.

One significant factor, in retrospect, was that Glen, now my ex-husband and then a classmate, refused to pose for the picture and therefore isn't in it. In fact, because he isn't in that picture, I have little proof that he was ever there. Somehow the fact that he is not in the picture seems very

*significant. The camera doesn't lie! My one memory of him that year is that
he bit into a chocolate bar I had taken for recess. I had to go up to sharpen
my pencil or something at the beginning of recess, or maybe I was called up
by the teacher. When I came back, it had a bite out of it — right through the
paper! I found this so repulsive I threw it away. Such a silly idea — I could
have broken off one end — but somehow the idea of germs (of a boy) getting
through was too much.*

*Photo day for me was a little like vaccination day or eye-test day!
It was filled with anxiety and yet, a little excitement — something, anything
out of the ordinary, time out of class. We got to stand around, line up, have
a little time before a class would start up again — all in the service of novelty.*

*While the teachers are also in the class photos, they don't stand
out in my mind as having much significance. Most of my teachers 'in memory'
are old and cranky. They seemed to me then as mostly 'old ladies' who wore
old lady dresses, and were not in the least like ordinary people — they had
little calendars on their desks that advertised Investors Syndicate [which I
myself later bought shares in until I had to sell them!]. They were mostly
unmarried and were institutional — like sooner or later you would get them
— Miss G. in grade 2, Miss H. in grade 3, Miss I. in grade 4 and so on.
Occasionally, because there were always two classes of each grade 1, there
would be a new teacher who would be a 'wild card'.*

While Margaret's story might appear to be 'all over the map', moving from the photograph, to the ex-husband, to the chocolate bar, to getting
out of class, to the teachers themselves, it is a good example of *how we
remember schooling as a whole*, a tendency that child historian Neil Sutherland
(1997) has also identified in his work. As Sutherland notes: 'To my interviewees, learning to read was inextricably tangled together with such matters as the
sort of teacher they had, how they got along with other children, and how
their parents felt about schooling' (p. viii). What appears to be a generic
school photograph composed of the usual class line-ups is rich with personal
detail. In Margaret's case, there is the memory of the crumpled snapshot from
the first day of school, interspersed with the class photo where her ex-husband
is 'conspicuous by his absence', along with the memory of the missing chocolate bar piece. Mixed in with these images are memories of getting out of
(missing) schoolwork in order to have the photo taken, and the unmarried
teachers (*Miss* G., *Miss* H. and *Miss* I.) Why are these details important? Among
other things, Margaret's references are interesting examples of the presence of
absence. What or who is not there is as significant as what is. These images
foreshadow the presence of ghosts in photographs, which we discuss later on
in this chapter.

Many of the teachers in the workshops not only retrieved their
photographs, but also mounted them all in an album or special folder, while
others organized their photographs chronologically. Patricia, a beginning
teacher, had managed to hang on to all of her school photographs from elementary school and had assembled them chronologically. We cite below her

entire narrative on these photographs to give some sense of the recurring themes this exercise produced:

> *The following pages include some of my school photographs from elementary school. These are the only pictures I have — the pictures from high school are in the yearbook. We were not given a copy of our class picture, because we did not have a home room class. Getting our picture taken in elementary school was a big deal for everyone. I remember everyone being so excited to get their picture taken. The girls came to school with their prettiest outfits and some boys actually wore suits. If I remember correctly, our parents were sent a letter from the administration reminding them that we were to have our pictures taken.*
>
> *There is one thing I especially remember about having our class pictures taken. The photographer always made the short people sit on the bench and the rest were allowed to stand. I remember hating that. I wanted to stand too! I also remember that once we were given our many copies of our pictures, we all exchanged individual pictures with our classmates and had them signed by the person who gave them to us. The rest of the copies are just sitting in a box somewhere. My mother didn't give our relatives any of the pictures. My grandmother may have one or two, but that's about it.*
>
> *Grade 3 — my grade 3 teacher was Miss Boileau. She was probably the kindest teacher I had in elementary school. This picture is really strange because of the division of the sexes. It's such a typical picture — boys on one side and girls on the other. I'm the first one seated on the left hand side.*
>
> *Grade 4 — I remember grade 4. It was the worst year of my life. We all look like happy little kids, but the truth was that we were all miserable. Everyone was terrified of Miss Perry. She was very strict and naturally we all feared her. I'll never forget this picture. Everyone laughed about it for weeks. Everyone knew that Ronnie had a crush on Linda. But we actually got it on print. Notice the way Ronnie (the boy sitting on the far right) is looking at Linda!*
>
> *Grade 5 — this was my favourite class. I was in the same class with eight of my best friends. This is probably the picture I hated most. I had my hair cut short for the first time and everyone said that I looked like a boy. I can't believe I chose to wear such an ugly outfit. I'm the funny-looking one with the red and white striped knickers.*
>
> *Grade 6 — once again I'm sitting! The only reason I can think of is that I probably didn't grow enough to stand with the taller kids. This was also the year I wore braces on my teeth. I refused to smile when I had my individual picture taken, but the photographer managed to get a smile out of me. At least my braces matched my long silver earrings!*

Patricia comments on the taking of the picture and the importance of clothing, facial expression, position in relation to other school children and so on. These are important points to think about in self-study. How do we remember the posing? What were we trying to convey about ourselves? Why were (and are) we so concerned about how we ended (or end) up looking?

Figure 3.6   Teacher revisiting her yearbook

What can we see now in these photographs that could be useful to us as teachers?

Themes of Picture Day Narratives

The picture day memories written by workshop participants contained several recurring themes, of which the following are the most representative.

Special day

Following from the previous chapters, where we focused on school as an organizational feature of memory, it is important to note the 'memorability' of picture day — something outside the everyday routine of school life — however dreaded the event might be for some (even akin to a visit from the school nurse). What is not easy to convey on paper is the vividness of the recall and the 'definite' quality of the responses. As one respondent noted 'it just all came back to me when I looked at these pictures!' In a sense, picture day serves as a once-a-year 'memory-making event' amidst a vast number of school days that all blend together. For some, like Laura, picture day was particularly special:

> *When I was younger, school picture day was one of my favourite days of the year. My mother and I would pick out my best dress the night before, and I*

Figure 3.7   Class photo

would model it for her to make sure it was the perfect outfit for my big day. In the morning, I would wake up extra early to get dressed and make myself look very special. I could not wait to be organized in line with the rest of my class and hear the photographer say 'cheese'. I anticipated that moment from the first day of school . . . I never once missed a picture day at my school. One year I was really sick on picture day, but I made my mother dress me up, make me look healthy (with a little make-up) and take me to school especially for the picture.

For others, however, as we see in the themes which follow, picture day was more of a 'marked day' than a special day. Moreover, this once-a-year event had a type of 'taking stock' about it.

Class line-ups

Many of the participants spoke about where they were positioned in group photographs. As we have seen in some previous accounts, it makes a big difference whether one stood or sat. In Rebecca's case this had a great deal to do with size. She always minded having to sit in the front row because she was short. How exciting it was for her then, in fourth grade, when she almost made it to the second row! She recalls, however, that just as the photographer was about to snap the picture, he suddenly did some rearranging of the group and she was placed back in the front row. For other people, 'class line-ups' were about social status and who one was obliged to stand or sit next to:

> *I remember that fights would occur because some people didn't want to stand next to each other in the group picture. It all seems silly now, but at the time it had great importance. One of my friends reminded me of one particular year when a girl in our class was always teased because they said she smelled bad. So, a guy who stood next to her in the class picture is seen with his fingers crossed to protect himself from her 'germs' (kids can be so cruel!).*

Another teacher refers to the fact that she can recall standing at an extreme angle away from the boy who is next to her in the photograph. It was important that she position herself as far away as possible so that no one could possibly associate her with him.

Control and resistance

Like the playing school narratives we explored in chapter 1, many of the photo narratives raised issues of control. For example, several workshop participants noted that looking at their school photographs brought back memories of being 'controlled' and colonized. In some cases, as in this example offered by Anna, the control was that exerted by parents over their children — even in photographs:

> *I think the reason I hate my elementary school pictures is because parents have complete control over what you will wear and look like. A child has basically no say. I realize that if some children were to dress themselves, it could be a disaster, but why do parents do it on purpose to make you look funny?*

This comment is reminiscent of the interview with the four school-girls cited earlier in this chapter, in which they used phrases like *'they made us . . .'* and *'we had to . . .'*. However, although many participants complained about being controlled in their school photographs, there were also several accounts of resistance and 'sabotage' — not everyone complied with the pose! Zac, for example, adopted an oppositional stance towards school photographs, which he saw as an opportunity to rebel against being 'schooled' to look a certain way. One year, his mother insisted that he wear a particular v-neck sweater. Convinced that, in combination with his long hair, the sweater made him look like a girl, he decided to use the one thing his parents couldn't control — the expression on his face — to ruin the picture altogether, and thus succeeded in asserting his autonomy. Like many of the men's playing school narratives seen in chapter 1, Zac's account is an example of refusing to 'play right'.

Female teachers also had recollections of subversion. Consider Connie's narrative in relation to her grade 3 photo:

> *The morning of the picture I asked my Mom how come she did not have my good dress ready for the class picture. She told me that the pictures were being taken the next day and that she would let me wear my dress only then. I*

argued with her and begged her to let me wear the dress because I knew the pictures were that day. Still she insisted she was right and she had accordingly laid out a pair of pants and a plain sweater for me to wear that day because it was cold. So, I left that morning crying, and caught the bus wearing a pair of dark green corduroy pants with patches on the knees and hoping to God that mother was right. Well, guess what? She was wrong! How terrible. Everyone was dressed up in their best clothes for the picture and there I was in my corduroy pants with the patches. Somehow my mother was going to pay for what she had done. So I made the most sour of all faces any child has ever made in any picture — anywhere! Ironically, I could not find that grade 3 class photo. I think my mother hid it for fear I would destroy it.

It is interesting that the photo is now missing, and that Connie thinks her mother has hidden it for fear of its being destroyed. It does not occur to her that her mother might be hiding it because she doesn't want anyone to see it either!

Pictures of learning

Some teachers went on to look closely at their pictures to discover what they might reveal about their identity as learners. Anna, for example, writes:

I find that when I look at my school pictures, I can see that at an early age I really looked like I loved being at school. I looked like I wanted to learn. As I get older, that look diminishes, perhaps because school was no longer fun. It was too competitive and too serious.

Anna's observation is interesting in that it invites a 'compare and contrast' approach to looking at a series of pictures over time: are there particular 'looks' that might be taken as signs of being eager to learn, of losing interest, or of being acquiescent? How might these photographs be read in the context of looking at other 'school learning' artefacts such as report cards, or old notebooks and assignments which contain teachers' comments? Valerie Walkerdine (1990), for example, offers an interesting analysis of teachers' comments on her report cards, reading the phrases 'Valerie seems gifted' or 'Valerie is a steady, reliable worker' (p. 166) 'against' her knowledge of what they really meant ('steady reliable worker', for instance, equals 'boring, ordinary, lumpish, snail-like').

Intergenerational comparisons

At our suggestion, some teachers found and scrutinized the school photographs of their parents. For example, Rae, a teacher of 17 years, uses her parents' school photos to reflect on how her role as a teacher is different from that of the teachers belonging to her parents' generation:

It is interesting to me that neither shot, from different cities and different years, has a teacher in the photo. When we take school photos now, all the

> *teachers are in the photos! Maybe we see our role differently than teachers did
> in the 40s and 50s. Perhaps we are more buddies, or at least parents to the
> children, and they in turn see us more that way.*

Other teachers compared their own pictures to those of their parents at the
same age. Nadia, for example, writes: '*I've seen some of my mother's school
pictures and I do have to laugh. The styles were different then and everyone
was the same.*' Nadia's comment points to how each generation reads those
which have come before it. This perception of a previous generation's uni-
formity ('*everyone was the same*') contrasts with the commonly held impression that everyone in our own photographs is unique. However, previous
generations are not always perceived as uniform and distant from our current
reality. Jan, a beginning teacher, looks at photographs of her mother in a way
that suggests identification more strongly than detachment:

> *I compare myself especially with my mom's pictures. I try to see whether I
> looked older at a certain age than she did.*

Although not unique to teachers or school photo projects, this
comment has important implications for the professional development of teachers. In her work on mothers and daughters, Carol Mavor (1997) writes:

> For the birth of a girl can be an everlasting process of cutting and stitching be-
> tween mother and child, between stereoscopic images. (One of my students
> recognized this complex imagining and re-imagining in an old high school
> photograph of her mother, and wrote: 'Not only does it have a sense of aura
> because it is old, but because it is my mother/me . . .'). (p. 122)

In a related way, teachers might compare themselves with the
images of teachers in these photographs. Is there a particular teacher look? Do
we ourselves look like our former teachers (our teachers/ourselves)?

Gender and dressing up

Do women and men have similar memories of picture day? Yes and no. On the
one hand, some female teachers noted that they felt that school photographs
were much more of a 'big deal' for them than for the males. As Ann writes:

> *I found that girls were always worried more than boys about having their
> picture taken. Boys would come out of gym class, their hair a mess, and have
> their pictures taken. They never checked their hair or face like the girls did.*

Indeed, in Rob's account, this point is confirmed:

> *What do I remember about my picture days? Not very much, except that I
> would always leave the house in the morning looking like a little gentleman,
> but by the end of the first recess, I'd already be a wreck.*

Similarly, Craig writes:

*Pictures were always fun, and even now, when I look back on my grade 1
and 2 pictures, I can't ever believe that I was that small, and I have a hard
time remembering much of that time (mmm . . . come to think of it, I don't have
a good memory when it comes to my personal life — just useless 'jeopardy' facts).*

On the other hand, the following narrative written by Brian offers a
different male perspective on picture day:

*As a young child I was quiet and shy and sometimes got picked on. This self-
conscious feeling wasn't helped but was catalyzed by the fact that my dad
dressed me up in a brown suit — supposedly stylish in those days. So I went
to school all dressed up like a good boy and realized my fate when I was
dropped off for school. This was at its climax when I realized everyone else
was more or less in casual clothes. I was immediately greeted by the teacher
who told me I looked nice. My concentration was not on her but on all the
kids staring at me in my brown suit. Although I endured several jokes and
snickers, the teasing soon stopped and I believe some students became jealous
of the praise of the teacher and other adult helpers in the classroom. This
made me feel extremely proud. To this day, I thank my father for dressing me
up in that brown suit. At a very early age, he taught me to be proud of myself
and that appropriate dress is one way to show that pride.*

Similarly, Marcus recalls being all dressed up in a white shirt and
bow tie for his first grade picture while the other boys were wearing scruffy
t-shirts and jeans. Like Brian, he was proud to be dressed up for the photograph. Even Zac's account, cited earlier in this chapter, of making every effort
to sabotage the school photograph, is an indication that boys too are self-
conscious about the picture-taking process.

Inscriptions and captions

Like Cathy's note to her teachers cited at the beginning of this chapter, inscriptions provide an additional layer of meaning to photographs. Inscriptions can
take a variety of forms, including additions to the visual text such as those
described earlier by Karen (moustaches drawn on people's faces, the words
'nerd' or 'geek' accompanied by an arrow pointing to someone's face). Many of
the teachers in our workshops remembered scribbling over the faces of people
of the opposite sex. Rebecca, for example, has a photo of her kindergarten
class where she has combined sign and verbal text, including an inscription on
the back of the photo: '*I hate the boy how [sic] has blue on his face*'. Margaret
now wonders why she scribbled out the face of one of her classmates in her
first grade photograph:

*Why? She [Jean Sharp] was not a powerful person or a popular person. Why
did I scribble out the face of an unpopular person? Or is that the point? Did*

> *I do it under the tutelage of a more powerful person like Annette King whose father ran a local business? She once convinced me to put glue on the back of Jean Sharpe's desk in grade 1 so she would stick to it. Of course Jean didn't stick to it since the glue immediately dried, but what was it about the relationship? Why were we so mean? I think her family had less than many others in the class. Was this our own form of class discrimination operating?*

Her question is an important indication of how we can be moved to look back at ourselves critically. How do certain inscriptions serve as 'proof' now of how we were then? For instance, John Kotre (1995) writes about a 30-year-old gay man who revisits his high school yearbook as an 'archival dig', in search of clues on the genesis of his sexual identity. The inscriptions written by a teacher and by a friend in his yearbook are very revealing in this respect. As he writes:

> *I've got a high school journal downstairs. I just found it a few years ago. Some of the details I'd forgotten, though I did have a memory that I had written, 'I think I am a homosexual.' There was this very awkward language about how I had a date with Mary and it was time for me to at least put my arm around her and I would try very hard to do it, because you were supposed to. I was really madly in love with a friend called Robert. I spent all the time I could with him, and I described this in the journal.*
> *When I was home in the spring I hunted up my high school yearbook, and there were two things in it that really leapt out at me. One was from the teacher I was closest to. She wrote, 'I have been pleased at the value you place on three of your friendships. I think it indicates the kind of person you are.' That's ambiguous, but they all would have to have been male friendships. I thought she knew something she wasn't saying. The other comment was from Robert, who wrote a long thing that included something like, 'It's been so good being close to you and having all this time with you. I feel I know you like a book from cover to cover except that most pages are blank.'*
> (p. 166)

What is interesting about these inscriptions is the comparison between their short cryptic formulation — the 'surface structure' — and the deeper meaning. Consider, for example, the inscription written on the photo taken sometime early in the 1920s of Claudia's mother Elsie as a young girl (Figure 3.8). According to the family graphologists, this inscription was written by Elsie's father. Elsie, now looking at the snapshot and inscription some 74 years later, struggles to remember exactly which year it could have been, and where it was that she and her family were going. She thinks she was in the second grade and that it was 1922 or 1923. Because her father worked for the railway, they moved often and it was not at all uncommon for the family to have to be uprooted in the middle of a school year. Thus, the destination could have been one of several small prairie towns. Elsie looks again at the snapshot and thinks that the coat she is wearing was probably cut down from

This is a snap of Elsie taken by her teacher the morning she left Belmont

Figure 3.8   Elsie — photo and inscription

a larger coat, something that would have been a common occurrence, given the shortage of money, and the fact that she had two older sisters and several younger ones coming along. Aside from these 'bits', she has no memory of the photo being taken, the name of the teacher, or why her father wrote on it. She does recall that she was never a very good student, so that her recollections of her school days are rarely about the more academic aspects of school. In a conversation about the photograph, Claudia and Elsie speculate about a teacher — *the* teacher — (a) taking the time (and having the resources) to photograph one of her departing pupils; (b) mailing it to Elsie's family after it was developed; and (c) Elsie's father, a railway worker who normally paid relatively little heed to such domestic matters (according to his family) taking the time to inscribe the photo. The 15 words in the inscription say more than the 'thousand words' that the photograph itself is supposed to say. Issues of patriarchy, class, the actions of a caring teacher are all embedded in this short inscription and, like some significant memories, would have remained hidden beneath the surface structure, had they not been teased out, either by a prompt or by a deliberately self-reflexive activity.

Annette Kuhn (1995) has looked at inscriptions — or captions, as she calls them — as potential sites of contestation or 'power-plays'. For example, she refers to a photograph of herself at age 8 that both she and her mother have written on. The mother has identified the photograph as having been taken at one place and point in time, while the daughter locates it differently.

Claudia sees a similar contestation in a photograph of herself at around the age of 7 or 8 when she is sitting at the piano, posed in the 'playing position'. Her mother has written on the back 'Claudia practicing the piano'. Claudia wonders about the inscription. She hated practicing the piano and rarely did so. Was her mother being ironic, hopeful, declarative? For whom was the inscription written?

In the final analysis, the act of inscription does not have to be tangible at all (for example, scribbles, writing, etc.). Meaning is also symbolically inscribed onto school photographs. For instance, where and by whom are the photographs now kept? By whom are they valued? How are they kept (contained in a cardboard box, mounted in a special 'school days' album along with report cards and concert programmes)? Robert Chalfen (1991) draws our attention to the ways that culture and ethnicity may be inscribed onto school photographs. For example, examining the photograph collections of two Japanese-American families, he notes the prominence of school photographs in the albums of these immigrant families, in contrast with the relatively few school photographs to be found in the photo albums of Anglo-Americans.

Chalfen goes on to discuss the ways in which photographs of schooling might be connected to a feeling of belonging and a search for identity in the new country. School is an important part of learning to take on a new identity. Chalfen notes the consistency of school-related references in many other photography collections of Japanese-Americans, although he also discusses the ways in which school photographs are also a regular part of the documentation of life in Japan too. In contrast, Elsie's photos found in a cardboard box, while mostly from the same era as the ones referred to by Chalfen, are rarely in-school pictures, and are never pictures of teachers. Rather, they are snapshots of school sports days or of dressing up for concerts. The official 'business' of school (i.e., learning) is not something that is documented. The ways that these collections differ in focus gives rise to questions about how we value particular aspects of school, say, for example, sports, schoolwork or, in some cases, the teachers. How might these various forms of valorization contribute to future relationships to school and to being teachers ourselves?

What Does This Mean to You?

The 'picture day' project has a number of dimensions to it. In one sense, it could be read purely as an exercise in 'looking back', 'going down memory lane' and 'being nostalgic' — something for which there should be a place in teachers' lives. In some cases, this nostalgia might be seen as a tribute to the teachers who influenced the lives of other teachers. As Grace writes: '*It was interesting to note that the majority of my group brought in pictures of group photos as opposed to individual ones. The major reason for this was because they really liked their teacher*'. However, when we asked participants to think about how their readings on picture day might contribute to their work as teachers, they indicated that photography projects such as this can also take us beyond nostalgia and forward into the future.

Rae, for instance, looks back on the idealism that she sees in her school photographs, reading it against what she now feels:

As I look upon these [photos] now, I am thinking back to what I thought and the idealism, naivete, and dreams that I had. I can't really say that I don't still have some of this; maybe rather than looking wistfully at this time, I instead feel that I'm glad that I held onto a lot of that. But I can't help thinking, as I gaze upon myself — could you ever have imagined then what the world would be like now and what your place in it would be? I guess this exercise is causing me to reflect.

The further significance of these photographs is that they facilitate discussion about what it means to occupy a new position in the photograph. Former students re-vision themselves as teachers. Jean, a student teacher in her first year of education, calls this repositioning 'standing on the left side':

And can you imagine, in a couple of years, I will be standing on the left side of the photograph next to a group of 20 or more students? I can't wait.

Another student teacher, Mary Frances, observes:

I looked closely at my elementary teachers and said to myself 'Wow, who would've thought that many years later I'd be studying to be in their place or maybe following in their footsteps. I wondered if they'd always wanted to be teachers, or if, like me, it was more of a recent decision. I wondered if they liked their profession . . . I also noticed something I'd never given a second thought to back in those days: only one of my teachers (other than gym) was male. I wonder now how he got there and how he must've felt in an all-female environment.

Some teachers began to critique their own 'complicity' in the picture-taking event, questioning, for example, the pose that subjects are 'schooled' to take on, reminiscent of the comments of the four girls cited at the beginning of this chapter. As Grace observes:

[. . .] that smile was [. . .] practiced beforehand. Why did we care about the smile anyway? Why didn't we just smile as we always did? This is a question that perplexes me to this day.

In her comments below, Shelly situates the school photograph in a socially constructed text that includes family:

What's interesting to note is that as I look back and remember all the school pictures I had to have taken, my parents' image of me somehow follows. For some reason, as I look at myself in pictures from the age of 5 to 12, the pictures somehow resurrect my parents' pep talks, disappointments and proud moments of the past. I'm actually realizing how significant pictures are — memories and life and being photographed — and how they become someone's history.

Her remarks draw attention to the ways that photographs allow us to 'live historically'.

Stirring up Memories: Working With Photographs

Now that I look back, I realize that it is me in those pictures, whether I like them or not. I can't go back and change them, therefore I have to accept them as they are. (Excerpt from the workshop journal of Natalie)

Had the teacher who made the above observation walked past a small photograph shop in Montreal which featured an ad display for 'Family Photo *Restorations*' (italics added), she might not have seen photographs as being so final. She might likewise have come across a flyer for a company called Creative Memories which advertises workshops on photography: 'Make sure your memories will last . . . You get them developed in one hour and excitedly thumb through your latest package of photographs. Weeks later those same anxiously awaited photos are stuffed in a shoe box under the bed . . .' The flyer goes on to provide information on cropping, layout, mounting, and journaling: '*Use creative cropping*', it reads, '*to trim excess baggage and non-essential elements out of the picture*'. We thus don't have to accept our photographs just as they are. By trimming excess baggage and non-essential elements, we can get rid of images we don't want. We are not even limited to trimming techniques. Digital cameras and software such as Photoshop have made it remarkably easy to 'create' memories anew by entirely altering original images.

Theoretically, the idea of being able to modify our photographs is interesting. Some teachers in our workshops, as noted in previous sections, spoke of making literal alterations by scribbling out faces, attempting to lose certain photos, or actually cutting out the faces of offensive persons with scissors. Others might have wanted to make such alterations, since they spoke of hating their photographs, hating the whole experience really, and of remembering how painful picture day could be due to anxiety about facial expressions and features, having clothes that weren't as nice as the other children's, not being able to afford to buy the pictures, and so on. As a number of the memory accounts we have seen indicate, children can be very cruel — the 'snobby girl', or worse, a whole class of 'snobby' children, might go to great lengths to humiliate and intimidate others, who live in eternal dread of being the butt of jokes, or the one whose face is regularly scribbled out in class photos. In the following section, we examine how self-study can involve working in a 'restorative' way with photographs.

Working With a Single Photograph

A single photograph can serve as a basic tool, the 'raw material' of self-study. In box 3.2, we include some lead questions which touch on both the production and consumption of photographs. Such questions take us 'behind the

Box 3.2

Memory Work With Photographs

1 Consider the human subject(s) in the photograph. Start with a simple description, and then write an account in which you can take up the position of the subject. In this part of the exercise, it is helpful to use the third person ('she', rather than 'I', for instance). To bring out the feelings associated with the photograph, you may visualize yourself as the subject you were at the moment the picture was taken: this can be done in turn with all of the photograph's human subjects, if there is more than one, and even with the inanimate objects in the picture.

2 Consider the picture's context of production: where, when, how, by whom and why was the photograph taken?

3 Consider the context in which an image of this sort would have been made: what photographic technologies were used? What are the aesthetics of the image? Does it conform to certain photographic conventions?

4 Consider the photograph's currency in its context or contexts of reception. Who or what was the photograph made for? Who has it now, and where is it kept? Who saw it then, and who sees it now?

(Adapted from Kuhn, 1995, p. 7)

---

scenes': who owns/controls the camera? Who photographs what, under what circumstances and for what reasons? What is it that a family (any family) regards as worthy of being photographed? What does the choice of subject reveal about the person who took the photograph? What happens to these photographs? Are they displayed prominently and abundantly, or are they reserved for a 'gallery space'?

As an example of this kind of photo-writing, Annette Kuhn (1995) writes of a photograph of herself as a working class schoolgirl in Britain in the 1950s in her new school uniform. She was under a great deal of pressure to *pass* — both the 11-plus exams in Britain to win a place at a prestigious grammar school, and as someone who was *not* from a working-class background. The photograph becomes a symbol of the resulting alienation she felt and the bitter conflict she was caught up in at home:

Sadly, the photograph of me in my newly bought uniform is lost now, but I retain a clear sense, not just of what the picture looked like, but also of how it felt to be inside those clothes at that moment. I did not particularly like the photograph: to me, the girl in the too-big uniform looked fat, graceless and out of place. What was there to be proud of? Did the sleeves of my blazer cover my limply hanging hands, as my memory-image insists? Were its shoulder seams several inches past my sagging shoulders? Was the hem of the dress six inches below my knees? Did strands of badly cut hair stick out from underneath an awkwardly placed beret? These clothes, in every sense, decidedly did not fit.

And yet this uniform was proof for all to see that, as an 11-year-old bound for a good school, I was different, cleverer, a cut above the rest: it singled me out from the rest of my contemporaries. The fact that the photograph was made at all is proof that, for a brief time at least, I was once again special, the credit to my mother I had stopped being several years earlier: the photograph was her own idea, and she went to some trouble to arrange it. (p. 91)

Kuhn goes on to talk about how the uniform (and the lost picture of it) symbolized a class agenda and de-sexing of the schoolgirl, and was ultimately symbolic of a type of amnesia, a loss of certain memories:

The price they [working class children who went to grammar schools] were asked to pay for their education was amnesia, a sense of being uprooted — and above all, perhaps, a loss of authenticity, an inability to draw on the wisdom, strengths and resources of their roots to forge their own paths to adulthood. (ibid, p. 98)

Inspired by this account, Claudia examines a photograph from her childhood to work back through images of herself as a reader. While the photograph was not one taken in school, it nonetheless relates to her identity as a learner and to the type of literacy work she is involved in now.

Claudia regards a photograph of herself taken on Christmas Day some time in the late 1950s. It is a black and white photograph. She is around 8 or 9 years old, and she is sitting by herself on a couch at her aunt and uncle's place, reading an Annie Oakley novel, Danger at Diablo, *a book that she received that day from her grandmother. In the picture, she seems engrossed in the book and it is unlikely that she knew the picture was being taken. Who took it? Her father or her aunt. Unusual for her father to take it, unless bidden by her mother, and then he would almost always cut off someone's head.*

She can only vaguely remember reading the book that day, although she remembers reading it over and over again later. She is interested in its gender-appropriateness. Annie Oakley for a girl. She would never have been given something that wasn't exactly for a girl, and clearly distinguished from what 'the boys', her two older brothers, would receive. What did they receive? Was that the year they received Jules Verne's Twenty Thousand Leagues Under the Sea *and Mark Twain's* Huckleberry Finn? *The books were all part of the same series: shiny, plasticized contemporary-for-then covers, neatly laid-out table of contents, newsprint-like pages, but with red edging. The endplates always had some sort of content-related design. What interests her now is that she was allowed to engage in such a solitary activity as reading on a social occasion like Christmas. Where were the boys? Is she excluded from being with them (again) or does she want to be reading? It is a very small house that she was visiting; why was there no one else in the room at the time? Family photographs are almost always an occasion for a group photograph: 'Come on — let's get everybody together.' Someone had to say 'let's get out the camera', picture-taking being a regular feature of family events such as Christmas. The 'someone' who gets the ball rolling may be more important than the photographer here. Who would have thought that a solitary subject — Claudia reading — was worthy? Somehow to take a picture of just one person was wasteful, indulgent. Why devote a whole photograph to just one person unless it was the person's birthday? As for taking an unposed picture — no one ever took candid shots. Again, they could be wasted. Get everyone lined up and posed — one shot fits all!*

Is this where the construction of herself as 'always reading' was conceived and formulated? To her knowledge, this is the only known photograph of herself reading until adulthood. The snapshot always lived in the photo box, a large Eaton's coat box. It was not the kind of photograph that was displayed; snapshots never were unless enlarged (and even then only if there was no possibility of a studio photograph — for instance, if someone had died and this was the last picture). The only photos put up on display were formal shots of weddings or a studio portrait of some child, customarily at age 1. Surviving to the age of 1 is the last major occasion until high school graduation. But being stuck in the coatbox did not mean that these less formal photos were never looked at. Going through the pictures was a regular family pastime for the women, especially when her aunts would come over. Claudia probably saw this same photograph two or three times a year and probably also heard as frequently 'Oh there's Claudia reading!' It is not just Claudia who carries around the solitary image of herself reading. It is also their image; it fits in with life's events. Claudia continued reading, eventually studied reading, and now teaches reading while continuing to read. When she goes home now to visit her mother and picks up a book (as opposed to say a magazine or newspaper) her mother still says 'oh there you are with a book'. Lasting impressions.

Now, as an adult, Claudia owns the picture and it is only she and her daughters who see this picture. Her mother, who has always been the repository of all family photographs, has started passing on these photographs to those whom she regards as being the rightful owners — the subjects. It is not uncommon to receive a letter from her mother with old snapshots enclosed. Is her mother now finished with these memories, or does she simply want to make sure that the 'owners' have them while there is still time?

The value of the single photograph lies in its potential to help uncover layers of meaning. As is the case with most memoir and memory writing, Claudia's 'essay' serves as a forum for going deeper. Is it just speculation, or does it also have a fantasy quality to it? What started out as a treasured photograph portraying a childhood pastime of 'just reading' becomes an opportunity for the rememberer to work out the unique characteristics of the photograph. In this essay, close attention is paid to the modes of both production and consumption, as well as the ways in which the photograph has a bearing on the past and present. We also see how contextual features such as where and by whom the photograph was kept can have meaning. For example, since it is primarily Claudia's daughters who have access to the photograph now (and not her aunts or mother) she no longer hears the Claudia-the-reader story, as her daughters have never heard it. When does a story end? How powerful are the images that are set up outside our 'jurisdiction' in the classroom? Does a photograph make a reader? Or how do such photographs contribute to our own ongoing constructions of ourselves as learners?

Working Chronologically: Laying out Photographs

> *These photographs from the past never agreed to get lost. Odd, because she had tried hard enough, over the years, to lose them, or thought she had. She had treated them carelessly, shoved them away in seldom-opened suitcases or in dresser drawers filled with discarded underwear, scorning to put them into anything as neat as an album . . .*
>
> *I've kept them, of course, because something in me doesn't want to lose them, or perhaps doesn't dare. Perhaps they're my totems, or contain a portion of my spirit. Yeh, and perhaps they are exactly what they seem to be — a jumbled mess of old snapshots which I'll still be lugging along with me when I'm an old lady, clutching them as I enter or am shoved into the Salvation Army Old People's home or wherever it is that I'll find my death.*
>
> *Morag put the pictures into chronological order. As though there were really any chronological order, or any order at all, if it came to that. She was not certain whether the people in the snapshots were legends she had once dreamed only, or were as real as anyone she now knew.*
>
> *I keep the snapshots not for what they show but for what is hidden in them.* (Laurence, 1974, pp. 13–14)

Margaret Laurence's character Morag, in *The Diviners*, attempts to put her parents' photographs into some sort of order. Morag's 'technique' of laying out photographs in chronological order is one used by a number of photo-workers and memory advocates. For instance, bell hooks (1994) writes in an essay entitled 'In our glory: Photography and black life' about how she and a friend explored the significance of photographs and racial identity: 'Drawing from the past, from those walls of images I grew up with, I gather snapshots and lay them out, to see what narratives the images tell, what they say without words' (p. 52). Hooks observes that when a male friend of hers, who is also black, 'lays out' his photographs of himself, his particular goal is to find out when he began to 'lose his openness'. She remarks: 'Through these images, he hopes to find a way back to the self he once was' (p. 53). In a similar vein, a colleague of ours, Judith, describes a project of taking pictures of girls who are around the age of 11 or 12. Her interest is in how girls take on a different look as they move into adolescence. In laying out photographs, she is interested in examining 'the look' that characterizes the changeover from girlhood to adolescence. Is it the positioning of the mouth, the fixing of the eyes in a certain way, the positioning of the head? Or is it an image of something lost, hidden, gained?

In her essay 'Reworking the family album', Jo Spence (1995) offers a straightforward method which she calls 'some practical work for you, the reader to do' in order to construct a 'self-history' using a chronological approach. The chart outlined in Box 3.3 is adapted from Spence's essay and can be used to examine general childhood photographs as well as official school photographs.

Teachers in our picture workshops sometimes followed this idea of 'laying out' school photographs in quite spontaneous ways. In some cases, people used this format to comment on teachers: 'In grade 1, we had Miss X . . .'; 'here I am in grade 2, when we had . . .', and so on. Lynn 'reads' her entire curriculum vitae from grades 1 to 11 through depictions of her hair and her smile.

> *All I can remember from being photographed is that I hated it. I was always so self-conscious. I was worried about my hair, my clothes and especially my smile. How was I to smile? I remember the famous talks we used to have about which smile was the best, or how we should place our hair. This was of course during or approaching adolescence. When I was young, I would never think of it, or I don't think I did. Everyone thought that they were ugly. I could name so many things I hated about myself. Looking at these photographs and remembering how I felt makes me laugh. I know I'm still like that, but I am not as 'complexed' by it.*

The idea of a teacher now doing an entire curriculum vitae according to hair may seem like a rather shallow way to look back at the self and recall school. We are drawn, though, to Lynn's references to hating being photographed, and the number of things she hated about herself; her language is anything but vague. These memories from not that long ago (since she is in her early twenties) indicate that the experiences of the body are also part of schoolwork — a topic we take up further in the next chapter. Lynn is also not alone. This same kind of fixation with hair can be seen in the work of Haug's (1987) collective, where members engaged in memory work around hair, legs and mouth.

Similarly, Valerie Walkerdine (1990), in *Schoolgirl Fictions*, describes a photo project that includes looking at slides of herself, some of them 'school-girl-type' photos drawn from family snapshots which again draw attention to body. For her, the project is focused on the mouth (voice) and body:

Box 3.3

Laying Out Photographs

- Get together all the pictures of yourself which you can find. Also look through other people's collections in the family.

- Lay them all out on the floor, and sort them into piles with a separate one for each year. Now sort out one single picture for each year of your life, and lay them out on the floor, starting with the earliest year.

- Lay the chosen pictures out onto a long piece of white paper and write down the approximate date of each photograph.

- Try to remember key emotional events in your own life which link up to the years you are dealing with, and write them down.

- At a later session, concentrate on key events for each year organized around social or economic factors.

- Add a layer of comments to each photograph: who took the photograph? what is their relationship to you? If there is space, tack the whole thing to a wall so you can work with it in an easily accessible, highly visual way.

- Take one or two photographs from your 'self-history' and find a quiet space to do more detailed work on them.

- Either talk into a tape recorder (giving date and time) or write in a scrapbook or 'creative journal' everything you can think of about the photograph and the events surrounding it.

- If you have a close friend to work with, ask him/her to interview you. This person should be there as a prompter, not as someone who comments . . .

- Once you have done enough work at this stage, go back to your original 'self-history' and start to think about what's missing.

- Make notes about pictures that might have been taken but never were.

- Start to think about how you might photograph a day in your own life. Notice what your patterns are, what gets repeated day after day, what seems trivial, what seems important. When you are ready, put a new roll of film in the camera and record the day as you go along.

> Do you want to do it from your own vantage point, or do you want to be included?
>
> • Make a close-up photographic self-portrait of somebody in your family, a friend or a partner. Concentrate on making yourself or them as idealized as possible. Then restage it to show them at work, or doing something active. Think about the differences between the pictures and what they do and don't show.
>
> • Consider keeping a photo-diary.
>
> (Adapted from Spence, 1995, pp. 192–4)

On the first image of myself as a smiling and pretty little girl, I first wrote the caption 'as pretty as a picture'. But I knew that was not all there was to say. I drew a second. I crossed out the mouth and stuck a piece of tape over, obliterating the mouth altogether. As a caption I wrote 'all mouth'. This was a profoundly shocking piece of self-mutilation to the image, since the one thing I worked hard at not being was a talkative and cheeky child who could possibly be described in the negative connotations of 'shouting her mouth off'. I think what I achieved was a kind of censorious silencing of myself, without ever necessarily having an adult to tell me to keep quiet. I mean that I have no recollection of being told to keep quiet or even of being told off. I suspect, then, that what I was doing was censoring myself so that I could not possibly be in the position where I would have to be told off. (p. 149)

She goes on to talk about a photograph taken when she was about 11, in which she crosses out her mouth and her abdomen, observing: 'I could hardly bear to work on the image, so hateful did I find it' (ibid, pp. 149–50). Claudia's description of reading Annie Oakley and the photo descriptions from Walkerdine and Haug et al. suggest that the lines between a school identity and just 'being in the world' are not easily drawn: Who we are 'in school' is not separate from who we are outside school. In Claudia's case, the reading pose 'captured' on film on Christmas Day is linked with the image she holds of herself as a dedicated student at school. Similarly, many of the hair accounts in Haug et al.'s work are not just about the styling of the hair, but how it is 'read' in the context of school and being controlled. Walkerdine's references to 'self-censorship' — what lies behind the painted smile — address the issue of a social construction of silence. Moreover, the lines between who we were as children/learners and who we are as adults/teachers are blurred. What is the relationship between the photo of the studious child as learner and becoming an academic (Claudia)? Similarly, what are the connections between self-censoring a photograph from childhood and becoming someone who now writes about those silences (Walkerdine)?

Men and Women Looking at Photographs

How do men and women use photographs? Do they interpret them differently? Almost all of the examples that we have been able to find in the published literature have been in relation to women's lives, and many of the references have been to clothing and body. We know, however, from our work with generic school photos, that some males were concerned with these issues, making references to being physically smaller than others in the class, or to memories of having to wear different types of clothing to that worn by the other boys. At the same time, feminist literature informs us that constructions and deconstructions of body already bring a gendered 'reading' with them. It should thus not be surprising that narratives through photography also reflect differing preoccupations.

Thinking back to Alison's memories of her second grade teacher in the introduction, and the responses of those (often, although not only, males) who said 'get over it', it seems significant that so many of the women we spoke with identified connections between what they looked like and how they learned, while conversely, the men had a relatively 'casual' attitude towards looks and learning. We are eager to find methods and openings for men and women teachers to work together, particularly since they often work in mixed sex schools together. Andrew Dewdney's (1991) work on the use of photographs in multicultural settings might be applicable to gender work. In Dewdney's projects with immigrant families in Australia, people brought in their family snapshots and through a 'compare and contrast' session, worked together to reorder them:

> We then took the next step of trying to locate our families in a broader social and political history to see if we could find points of connection between them . . . As people struggled with this broadening of their family album, other narratives began to emerge within those already established of colonialism, imperialism, migration and dispossession . . . The process of narrativising family photographs through the project was one which continually surprised people. However familiar individual photos were, ordering them according to a narrative concept continually brought with it unexpected elements. The familiar was made strange by its insertion into a socially shared context. The narrativisation of parental histories required the speaking of what was absent from or hidden behind photographs. (pp. 120–1)

A project in which men and women work together with photographs could involve them 'laying out' their photographs in whatever way seems appropriate: grade by grade (in the case of school photographs), or according to events such as holidays, birthdays, achievements and so on. The 'narrativisation', as Dewdney describes it, would emerge in the reorderings. For example, pictures could be reworked according to the kinds of questions we outline in box 3.4:

Box 3.4

Laying Out Gender Visually

1 In mixed sex groupings, lay out photographs (school or other) according to categories such as 'worst year', 'best year', 'most social year', 'worst academic year', 'most studious-looking' etc. What kinds of differences and commonalities do you notice?

2 Are there any photographs that might be associated with feeling a particular sense of pride, embarrassment, accomplishment, apprehension? Again, what differences and commonalities do you notice?

3 Pay close attention to pictures that might depict a time of being 'on the edge' (of early childhood vs. school-age, childhood vs. adolescence, or adolescence vs. adulthood). Are there any features peculiar to males 'on the edge' or females 'on the edge'?

4 Look at photographs that might include school friends. What do you notice that might be the same or different? How do people stand? How are they positioned? What do mixed-sex photographs look like?

5 Compare photographs of your students and yourselves at the same age as your students. Beyond obvious comparisons involving hair and dress, what commonalities do you see? Differences?

6 How does laying out the photographs this way link to your understanding of yourself as a teacher — now?

By sparking 'compare and contrast' discussions, these verbal–visual collages could make a space for men and women to begin to hear each other's school chronologies in new ways, and to tell new stories.

What Can a Teacher do with a Camera?

Our title for this section is adapted from Jo Spence and Joan Solomon's (1995) book, *What Can a Woman Do With a Camera?*. The authors contend that, historically, women have been largely the objects of other people's (men's) gazes, and propose that women take control by presenting images of themselves, so that 'the boundaries fall away giving fascinating leaps of the imagination' (p. 1). In her introduction to the book, Solomon expresses her hope that the ideas in the book will 'encourage women to use their cameras fearlessly as tools of exploration' (p. 14).

The idea of cameras being used fearlessly in schools is certainly not one that is new to teachers, although the question has more frequently been posed as 'what can a student do with a camera?'. This is something that Alex (Nick Nolte), the social studies teacher in the movie *Teachers*, does. Confused and disturbed by an impending lawsuit against the school, Alex asks his students to use whatever means they can to find out 'what's wrong with this school'. One student uses a camera (which he 'borrows' without asking from the audiovisual room) to capture, visually, the ways in which the school has failed its students. In one segment of the film, we see the school through the eyes of this student and his camera lens: the drugs, abuse of students, teachers asleep on the job and so on. He presents these images to the rest of the class through a slide presentation so that they too participate in exposing the school. The use of photography here is key, because it asks simple, yet central questions about the aim of education. One way of seeing it — the way that it is presented in the scene — is that the blame for a dysfunctional school rests squarely on the shoulders of the teachers and administrators.

In a real-life context, there are projects like Wendy Ewald's *Portraits and Dreams: Photographs and Stories by Children of the Appalachians* (1985). In this book, Ewald describes the significance of the photographs that her students take, and the ways in which she and they use these photographs to look at their lives differently. In a similar vein, Kamina Walton (1995) describes a photography project in which 8- to 11-year-old girls explored issues of physical and verbal harassment in their school. Working with cameras in a studio context, they created photographic images and print texts which gave expression to some of their anger and frustration. The outcome of the project was a series of posters which were produced for display in the school library. They carried messages like: 'We hate you punching us' and 'We hate you lifting up our skirts'. This photography project thus gave the students a means not only to tell their story visually to everyone, but also to engage in a type of activism.

Walton's work is characteristic of the type of photography projects done with students within a resistance framework in Britain in the 1970s and early '80s. A prominent example is the work of Jo Spence and Terry Dennett compiled in Spence (1995), the 'mainstay' of the Photography Workshop project carried out in London schools. Their mission was to use photography in a cultural studies framework as a way to work with student resistance. Commenting on this work, Dewdney and Lister (1986) note: 'Without conscious and active engagement with the content of young people's resistance, teaching is bound to reproduce more than it transforms' (p. 31). Student expression through photography is also taken up in the cultural studies work of Buckingham and Sefton-Green (1994) who document creative photography projects in which students 'inserted' themselves and their photographs into popular television and film narratives. The authors conclude that it is the 'dialogic play between the subjective self, and the social self' that is important . . . 'In educational terms, it is crucial that students learn both to reflect upon this dialogic process and to make explicit the tensions between the individual and the stereotypical' (p. 106).

This idea of a 'dialogic process' is equally significant for teachers — and so we repeat our initial question: 'what can a teacher do with camera?'. Much of our work with teachers using school photographs draws inspiration from a short essay written by British teacher Anne Krisman (1986) entitled, 'You shout at us one minute, you take photographs the next . . .'. This essay was one of the few formal references we could find *anywhere* to teachers taking school photographs, and yet many teachers in our workshops — especially elementary teachers — spoke of regularly taking class snapshots of special projects, field trips, first days of school, last days of school and so on. One man, who has been teaching for more than 20 years, has a photograph of every student he has ever taught. Another retired school teacher that we know not only has the group photos of every class she ever taught, but extensive scrapbooks of newspaper clippings on events related to her school and students. Kathleen, a teacher educator, spoke of asking one of her students to take candid photographs of her university classroom 'in process'.

Krisman's (1986) essay draws attention to the pedagogical significance of taking pictures in class:

> I have always taken photographs of the children I have taught. In the past, they have been 'special occasions' ones, at parties, school trips, the Annual Fete. I must have had problems with these children in lessons, but the photographs give none of this away. The children smile, pose as a united group, offering Miss as a Photographer a great deal more respect than they gave her in class. When I took photographs inside school, after the initial queries about my camera and the fears that Darin would drop it as he told me about his Dad's superior Canon AE1, I was often heard to say, 'Look, I'm not taking a photo of you until you look as if you're working.' I was amazed at how this threat worked, and the willingness of children to co-operate as we set up photographs that indicated either that they were swots (signified by top buttons done up, arms folded, head erect) or rough kids (signified by lunch on table, feet up, laid-back posture). The photographs were displayed on my wall, created a mass of interest and often minor stirs. (p. 122)

She goes on to describe some of the student 'interventions' that took place as part of the 'minor stirs':

> One girl ripped a photograph from my wall display as it had her on it (her face = her possession). Someone drew a moustache on the Head of Music and some children on the photos were pricked with compass points. (ibid)

At a first glance, these interventions might seem to be an innocuous (or deviant) playing with the photographs. However, for Krisman, the entire gamut of responses — from the students and her colleagues — represent a type of pedagogical project. As she writes:

When my photographs were developed, I showed them, in no real order, to people who weren't teachers at my own school. I found myself explaining the images, making sense of them . . . I was more aware of the children I was teaching. My eyesight had sharpened. I felt as if I knew them better, after coming to terms with them in their second form and in their developing, alive, vibrant state. Schools as institutions still rile me, but by restating it for myself in terms other than anger or bitterness, I feel better equipped to survive to fight again. (ibid, p. 124)

'Better equipped to survive to fight again'. Krisman's use of the photographs from her classroom sounds very much like her own form of professional development.

When we spoke about Krisman's article to some of the teachers we know, many of them noted that while they often took pictures of their classes, they had not necessarily thought of the particular images they were 'capturing'. It was just something they did, for a variety of reasons.

Two photography narratives, written in our workshops in response to Anne Krisman's (1986) essay, make some interesting points about the nature of photographs and picture-taking. Consider Deborah, an elementary school teacher of 20 years. For Deborah, picture-taking activities, both in and outside of school, have always had an ambiguous quality to them. As she writes:

I have always been fascinated by photography, black and white photography in particular. My beginnings in photography go back to the Brownie box camera days, the first camera I ever used. The first picture I took (at least from what I now remember) was of my grandparents' dog, Sparky. He was a farm dog, a black and white border collie. I loved the shadows behind him in the picture and the way his right ear drooped. This picture was my comfort when he died, as his was the first death I remember ever hurting so much. His picture somehow kept him in my heart a little longer.

This 'turning to pictures' for comfort was, and still is, a need I have. When a close relative, or pet (I become very attached to my pets) passes away, I need to know that they are somehow still visible to me. I need to assure myself that they really did exist. A photograph somehow fills a void for me.

Perhaps not all people feel this way. I guess I should keep this in mind, as I have often given pictures I have taken of others as gifts to their family. For example, I often take pictures of my girlfriend's little boy and later give them to her in a frame as a gift because I am afraid his growing up years will be lost to her. She does not take pictures, nor does her family, and it bothers me that they don't.

Another example: I came across a picture of my aunt and uncle from years ago. I had never seen it before and was sure my cousins hadn't either. I took it upon myself to have this picture mounted in an old-fashioned frame and gave it to my cousin for her birthday. She had lost her mother (my aunt) as a teenager, and I though she would appreciate an old memory at this point in her life. However I don't think the picture carried the same meaning for her as it did for me.

> *I have done the same over the years in my teaching. I have taken pictures of my students and displayed them on parents' night. However, I have not left them up, but have salted them away for eight years, until graduation night!* I seem to make it my business to stir upon some old memories in people! (emphasis added)

On the surface, Deborah's comments might appear to be purely nostalgic, especially her allusions to dead pets and lost youth. In this regard, her actions are in line with Carol Mavor's notion of 'collecting loss' introduced at the beginning of this chapter. At another level, Deborah is helpful and friendly, passing on the pictures to those who might want them, either because they are in them, or because they are connected to them in some way. However, the sentence 'I seem to make it my business to stir up old memories . . .' points to another level at work in Deborah's relationship with her photographs — one that appears to be a more radical act of taking charge or control. By making it her business (project) to pass photographs on to those whom she has deemed to be 'rightful owners', she is in effect stating that they *should* want to remember, and that it is her place to make them remember: her motherless cousin *will* see pictures of her mother, graduating students *will* see their curriculum vitae framed on graduation night. People *will* live historically. Deborah's 'mission' is an interesting one. On the one hand, it is important to recognize that the decision to live historically must rest with the individual. The value of a school photograph workshop lies in the willingness of participants to engage in this type of self-study. On the other hand, as we saw in the various responses to the workshop, such photography projects, while rich in terms of possibilities for reinvention through speculation and imagination, are not something that people necessarily engage in without some sort of prompt. Living historically does not just happen.

Another teacher, Carolyn, who has been teaching in early childhood and special needs classrooms for the last 10 years, uses Krisman's article to begin to examine what is voiced in her vast collection of school photographs taken in various classes over the years:

> *There are not many pictures of my students reading and writing. I used the camera mostly for trips and special days — Halloween, Christmas, end of year. I was able to see how I've changed the classroom setup. For the first three years, I had the students sit in pairs and I moved from there to having them in groups of four. Mostly all the pictures are posed and the children are smiling. I've always realized that pictures were an effective way of making the children feel they belong. At the beginning of every year, I take individual pictures of each student and make three copies. I use one picture for a class book, one for outside our room, and one to use when a child is the 'special person'. In the last two years, I have taken more pictures when creations are completed. Does that send the message that the product is more important than the process? Right now, I'm thinking I should take pictures of the children when they're mad, crying, etc. so that they have a 'complete' picture of*

who they are and perhaps they will then be able to understand more about being 'fully aware' of themselves . . .

Carolyn then goes on to reexamine the pictures that she has taken of her class in the context of her own family album:

When I look at my own pictures, I have very few pictures of me alone. I was the fifth of seven children. My parents obviously had their hands full. My identity was always that of being one of the seven and I fit into the group of 'the three little kids'. There's no damage, I would say, done to me, though it might explain why I like working in groups. I've worked in groups all my life. I can stand up on my own, though, and I think that's important too. It may be for that reason that I take the individual pictures at the beginning of the year. The students are part of a group, but first and foremost, they are people unto themselves and are responsible for themselves.

In her reflections on what she chooses to photograph, Carolyn echoes many of the ideas contained in *What Can a Woman Do With a Camera?* (1995). As Solomon writes in the introduction to that book:

In taking the simplest photograph we are choosing what to photograph and, just as importantly, we are deciding what to leave out. How often do we snap the messy rooms around our teenage children, or our babies amidst their clutter? . . . Sometimes we leave out what we think is too private or painful to share, or what would put our families in a bad light. So we follow conventional ways of presenting our families, ways learned from photographic magazines, on holidays, at weddings, on birthdays and other celebrations; ways which satisfy our longing for how we would like our families to be, loving and magically 'happy ever after'. Though no family is like this, there are enough fragments of fun caught by our cameras to present ourselves to ourselves in an idealized way. Thus family values are re-inscribed along very traditional lines. Women adopt these agendas and usually use cameras only to record events and capture surfaces. (p. 11)

In the same way that images in family photographs often represent an idealized version of family life, so do school photographs, contributing to ideal myths about what a class should be. While many of these are taken by school photographers who are outsiders to the school system, even the pictures we take as insiders (teachers) may be of idealized scenes. Carolyn's point about taking the 'complete picture' has important implications for reinvention: not only does it question how she contributes to the autobiographies of her students right now and for the future, but also how she sees her work as a teacher and her belief in an idealized 'perfect classroom'. We are reminded of Valerie Walkerdine's (1990) notion of 'pathological nurturance' in her work on child-centred primary classrooms — the sense that everyone has to be happy and learning all the time for us to think of ourselves as successful teachers. Walkerdine refers to the ways in which women teachers often 'buy into' the happy family mystique.

Staging Photographs Which Disrupt

In the same way that 'reconstructing the family photo album' projects can become ways of disrupting and contesting notions of the idealized family, the kinds of photographs that are taken at school can become a way of disrupting and contesting the fictional, non-existent ideal classroom. In looking at photographs in this more disruptive way, however, there are several points to consider: one is that what appear to be candid photos of our classrooms (as opposed to official school photographs) might be read as staged. What we see as 'photographic moments' may be governed by idealized notions of the classroom: those times when everyone is 'on task', people are smiling, learning, or giving demonstrations of having learned something (for example, students posing with their science project; students holding up their recently authored book, etc.). The converse of this idealization is that we never 'think' to take a picture if something worth being documented isn't taking place.

A second point concerns using the idea of staging as a 'disruptive' technique for self-study. For example, what would it be like to deliberately set up certain poses in our classrooms — not just the 'let's all be the perfect teacher and learners' pose, but rather 'let's engage in poses that are precisely what we don't want our classroom to be like, or poses in which we are uncomfortable, or poses that are inspiring'. As in Krisman's projects, these poses could be jointly constructed by a teacher and the students. This type of staging can be found in a relatively obscure book, written in the 1940s, called *Life in Schools: An Explanation of the Protestant School System of the Province of Quebec* (Percival, 1940). The book contains photographs submitted by teachers around the province of Quebec to help to explain the system of education generally, and provides what we think is a provocative example of the kind of staging we have in mind. Amidst the many photographs of the 'state-of-the-art' progressive schools of the time is a photograph labelled 'An old type spelling lesson: The boy walking to the foot of the class has just missed' (Figure 3.9). While this photograph could be real (in the sense that it depicts a real event — the kind that many teachers described in their memories of shame and humiliation in chapter 1), it seems to be contrived, and the use of the word 'old' in the caption suggests that the photographer wants us to see this as something that no longer happens. The photograph contests and disrupts: 'See — conditions in school have moved from old-type humiliation to more progressive forms of education'. While we can't know now who took the photograph, or why, or even if it was really 'staged', we mention it here as an example of how we might similarly think about reinventing our classrooms according to fantasy scenes.

Alternatively, two or more teachers might work together with staged 'poses', taking photographs of each other in positions where the 'subject' is demonstrating a particular 'look' or pose: being receptive to students' ideas, being more facilitative, adopting a less declarative stance, and so on. This kind of project has roots in some of the work on popular theatre of social change, for instance that of Auguste Boal (1995) in South America, or Zakes Mda (1993) in

An Old Type Spelling Lesson:
The Boy Walking to the Foot of the Class Has Just Missed

Figure 3.9   Old type spelling lesson

South Africa on 'people playing people'. In these forms of popular theatre geared towards social change, role plays, tableaux and 'freezes' are created as interventions which might contribute to thinking in a new way about a problem or issue, or 'imaging' one's self in a new role. Photographic staging through the tableau or 'freeze' would allow teachers to work with photographs as tangible texts which might, for example, be exhibited. Again, we see their potential as linked to telling new stories about our teaching.

Reinventing Ourselves: Creative Photo Memories

How might fantasy and imagination figure in self-study? Here are some examples of projects that teachers have either engaged in or imagined as possibilities for reinvention.

Ghosts

In this section, we examine the 'ghosts' in photographs — what is hidden, what never was, what lurks in the background, and, as in the case below, what is lost once the photograph is lost.

> *I remember giving her [her cousin's wife] the snapshot for safekeeping: only, when it was time for me to return home, it could not be found. This was for me a terrible loss, an irreconcilable grief. Gone was the image of myself I could love. Losing that snapshot, I lost the proof of my worthiness — that I had ever been a bright-eyed child capable of wonder — the proof that there was a 'me of me'. The image in this snapshot has lingered in my mind's eye*

for years. It has lingered there to remind me of the power of snapshots, of the image. (hooks, 1994, p. 45)

The term 'ghosts' seems to be particularly appropriate in our work as teachers/former students — there are always ghosts of our school pasts lurking in our present situations. As Gina, a beginning teacher, observes of her grade 5 class photo:

As I closely examined my grade 5 class picture and made a comment about each and every student, I could hear, if I looked closely enough, Jimmy's laugh, Stephanie's voice and Marg asking the teacher if she 'may go to the wash-room'. It really is an incredible feeling. As I looked through other elementary pictures, spooky feelings began surrounding me — I felt like I was coming in touch with ghosts — visible ghosts — breathing sighs of laughter, relief, fear . . .

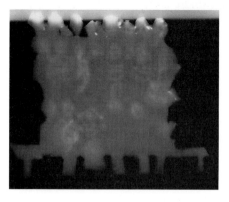

Figure 3.10   Impressionistic image

We are reminded not only of the ghosts in Margaret's grade 1 photo referred to earlier (the memory of the missing student who became her husband/ex-husband and the missing chocolate bar piece) but also of the ghosts that lie in the stories behind inscriptions. The potential of the ghosts in our school photographs to generate narrative and reflection is taken up by an art student, Sarah, in her construction of what might be described as 'the generic class photo' project. In her darkroom, she uses drawings to create impressionistic images such as the one in Figure 3.10.

As she writes:

I've always had trouble remembering the events and images surrounding photographs which no longer exist. I have almost no memories from the third and fifth grades, also years I haven't school photos for. Without them, I have nothing to remind me of my teachers or the people in my classes.

I began to think about this a few months ago while immersed in a photography class and far away from the pictures of home. I decided to try and recreate the ghosts and missing pictures from our photo box at home. Originally, I was just messing around in the darkroom, experimenting with the . ʾrious effects of shining light through simple drawings onto light-sensitive photo paper.

The technical premise is similar to that of a film negative. The dark images in the negative, as well as the dark pencil lines of the drawing, show up on developed photo paper as the light areas. Clear patches develop into black. Without having had any preconceptions about my photos, the results I found compelling. Lines blurred, the graphite lines became a mottled grey, and images seemed to appear out of the random.

> *Absentmindedly thinking of those lost class pictures, I sketched out a quick approximation of the shape and layout of a generic class picture, with three rows of students and the teacher standing to the right.*
>
> *The pictures which appeared were eerie and unsettling for me. What were previously mere scribbles and shapes became almost, but not quite, faces, and arms, and the personalities I began to remember from those years.*
>
> *As I looked at them, I saw Adam's perennial plaid shirt, the way 'those two' always stayed together, and then that girl in the front row who seemed to sit always the same, in a dress, with white socks and shoes, and yet who was every year a different girl.*

Sarah's description brings her ghosts to life, dressing them in white socks, the perennial plaid shirt and so on. The vividness of the personal details that linger in the surface structure of the generic line-up reminds us of the significance of what lies beneath the surface: the imprint of 'those two' and so on. Her project reminds us of how any class group photo (even, in this case, a set of blurred images) might evoke school memories, speaking to the potency of the ghosts in memory.

School Wear

Certain items of school wear are invested with meanings which can become central to self-study. In an essay entitled 'Phototherapy: The school photo (Happy days are here again)' Rosy Martin (1986) uses a series of photographs of herself in a project in which she re-examines her outsider identity as an adolescent schoolgirl. The photo essay features Martin now as an adult, clothed in a school uniform, and with school books and a cigarette. A key issue for Martin is the role played by class in a school environment. As she writes:

> The good schoolgirl, the academic achiever, was the part of me that sought solace in pleasing the teacher. However, I was constantly anxious, afraid both of failure and success, a perfectionist, who always managed to get something wrong . . . In 'learning to smoke' as a schoolgirl I was taking up the rebel position, and being 'adult'. I used to smoke when I was out with my working-class friends. (p. 42)

She goes on to note:

> Adolescence for me was a time of complex self-denial. Within each attempt I made to try on a particular identity, was the requirement to deny or not develop other aspects of myself. To negotiate my own position, within a set of conflicting demands, to try out various positions, and often to experience failure in these attempts, was part of the agony of adolescence. In creating these images [photographs of herself as an adult in various poses as a schoolgirl] I have been able to examine how much I still carry with me of those experiences. These images act as a reminder to me of my past, and whilst accepting the 'silenced' part of myself, I now know that behaviour is no longer appropriate. (ibid)

Inspired by such projects as Martin's, we are interested in how school-related clothing and photographs may be used to speculate and fantasize about our identities as learners and teachers. Consider for example Claudia's 'Prom Dress' fantasy.

Prom dresses

The first project involves high school prom dresses and prom pictures. The inspiration for such a project occurred to Claudia when she finally brought her prom dress to her home in Montreal after it had been hanging in her mother's closet in a garment bag for almost 30 years. It seemed like such a 'waste' to just put it into another closet, and yet what does one do with such an item? How does one get one's wear out of it? It is significant that her mother has so carefully looked after the prom dress all these years, storing it in a garment bag, moving it from her home to her apartment, never wanting to crease it. Claudia feels a great sense of responsibility in taking charge of the dress. What do other people do with these prom dresses? Are they like bridesmaid's dresses or wedding dresses? Does one ever get one's wear out of them? Not a 'saver' herself, Claudia regards the fact that the prom dress has been successfully preserved this long as indicative of the need to make its survival public.

For a time, she hung it on her living room wall, the dyed-to-match satin pumps artistically arranged on a table beneath. While there was some obvious aesthetic potential in that set-up, the dress being a solid shade of shrimp, clearly a more formal installation would be required to preserve it. Claudia imagines her project as one that would revolve around a photo proof, clearly stamped 'proof', of a formal portrait of herself in this high school prom dress. The project would also include forms of material culture — say the May or June 'prom issue' of *Seventeen* magazine from the year of her graduation. How do such garments still occupy our (mental) wardrobe? While prom dresses in a generic way might be seen to belong to the ritualistic practices of North American schools, they clearly can have personal meaning. In Claudia's case, the 'photo proof' of the prom dress has symbolic value. Proof of what? Graduation from high school? Being invited to the graduation dance? The imagined installation of the dress, the photograph and the pictures from *Seventeen* magazine represent just one entry from her curriculum vitae. It doesn't tell the whole story, but it is a piece of the history of being a learner and now of being a teacher. Claudia also thinks of all of the other 'proofs' that linger — the artefacts that teachers save — work from former students, thank you letters, lesson plans, worksheets and so on and how those too are part of the curriculum vitae.

While Claudia's interest in a prom dress installation follows from the particular rite of passage of high school graduations, there are other types of school rituals (along with the appropriate attire) which would lend themselves to the same kind of investigation. A former hockey player, for example, might recall and interrogate the experience of donning all the necessary hockey gear for the first time. The memory of playing on the soccer team and the recollections of winning and losing might be explored through an installation based on photographs of the school team, remnants of clothing or other artefacts, newspaper clippings and so on. In the absence of such artefacts, the rememberer might nonetheless be inspired to work now with catalogue images, contemporary newspaper accounts of school teams and so on. The links between the past and the professional identity of the rememberer could take a variety of interpretations. Indeed, the artefacts and photographs of the physical culture of a school may be some of the most probing in relation to body and self-study. Here we are reminded of the work of Judith Okely (1996) on gender and body, in which she has used school photographs. Focusing on girls' bodies and what is allowable in school sports — particularly in terms of kicking, physical contact and so on — Okely concludes that 'feminine dependency is learnt in the body' (p. 146). Winning and losing are also important themes that the rememberer might now want to investigate in the context of his or her teaching situation, or the idea of insider/outsider (belonging to a team/not belonging) and how this relates to the way he or she now organizes the classroom.

When I Look Upon This Photo

The use of material prompts in creative projects becomes central to a feminist autobiography project that Claudia embarks on, using a photograph taken during her first three months of teaching (Figure 3.11). As part of this project, undertaken with Susann, a researcher/ biographer, Claudia sorted through a series of photographs from her family album, including the one shown here, taken during her first year of teaching. One of the themes that Susann and Claudia investigate is ambivalence towards teaching. Claudia recalls that she had always sworn she would never become a teacher (*'Why did everyone assume I was going to be a teacher or a nurse?'*). Eventually this photograph is included in Susann's write-up of Claudia's life (Allnutt and Mitchell, 1994), with Susann's caption added to the photo: 'I've finally become a teacher'. When Claudia goes back to the photograph and its caption, she writes a short narrative:

Figure 3.11   *Claudia, first months of teaching*

When I look upon this photograph . . . I have no difficulty remembering the circumstances of the picture. It was taken by my brother at Christmas-time during my first teaching assignment, which was to teach English to 13-, 14- and 15-year-olds. It was the first time I had gone home in some sort of professional capacity. I had just turned 22, and wanted to look intellectual and somewhat literary or artistic — hence the octagonal horn rimmed glasses, the dark turtle neck sweater and the photograph in black and white, something significant at the time, since snapshots were supposed to be in colour. The year was 1970, and I remember choosing very carefully the very short jumper/dress that I am wearing — as some sort of statement about who I thought I was (young and radical) and who I thought I was not (conservative and part of the status quo).

Claudia then goes on to transform this first narrative description of a photograph into a poetic form, something suggested by Maggie Anderson (1992) in an essay 'In a dark room: Photography and revision'. Upon choosing a photograph (any photograph of interest), Anderson suggests narrating the photograph, describing it in as much detail as possible. Following this, the poet is advised to write at least three different poems, drawing from any of a number of positionings, and perspectives based on time (see box 3.5).

Box 3.5

'In a Dark Room' Poetry/Photography

Positions:
Speak the poem as the photographer.
Speak the poem as someone or something in the photograph.
Speak the poem as someone or something in the photograph addressing the photographer.
Address the poem to someone you know who has not seen the photograph.
Address the poem to someone in the photograph.
Address the poem to the photographer.

Time perspectives:
Write what happened just before the photograph was taken.
Write what happened just after the photograph was taken.
Write what happened as the photograph was being taken, outside the range of the camera.
Write the poem as if you have found the photograph years after it was taken.
Write the poem as if you were planning to take the photograph.
Write exactly the same poem in three versions: present, past, and future tense.

Following her description of the photograph of herself in her first year of teaching, Claudia writes the following poem:

Teacher: 25 years

When this photograph was taken:

> *My biographer constructs the myth in which the photographer and*
>   *me-as-subject also collude.*
>
> *'I've finally become a teacher' she writes of me.*
> *Why finally? I never wanted to be a teacher — or a nurse —*
> *I never even tried to become a teacher.*
>
> *When this picture was taken I had only been teaching for three*
>   *months.*
> *Teaching was only something to do 'for now'.*
> *Inside me is a novelist, an academic, a film-maker, a poet.*
> *Trapped inside and trying to get out.*
> *See — the turtle-neck, the glasses, the look.*
> *This is the look on the back cover of my first novel.*
> *No cat but at least the look.*
> *Why did I let her use the word 'finally'?*
> *Final. Tout fini. Finishing school.*
> *Do I get out for good behaviour?*

— I had only been teaching for three months.

With this poetic form, Claudia is able to take on her ambivalence about being a teacher, from the very beginning, and the kind of ambivalence that has remained with her during the more than 25 years she has been teaching.

Transforming a photograph into a poetic form is one version of 'when I first saw (look back on) this photo'. A mental image can also work as the starting point. Consider, for example, the following well-known poem by Margaret Atwood (1966), in which the speaker works with an imagined photograph:

This is a photograph of me

. . . The photograph was taken
the day after I drowned.
I am in the lake, in the centre
of the picture, just under the surface.
It is difficult to say where
precisely, or to say
how large or small I am:
the effect of water
on light is a distortion
but if you look long enough,
eventually
you will be able to see me.

(p. 11)

Charlotte Hussey, a Montreal poet and teacher, as part of a self-study course in teacher education, created a poem that draws on very vivid mental images of school. In that poem, 'Penmanship as a fine art', she investigates classroom transgressions:

Penmanship as a fine art

for Susan Andre

Seated, desk by desk, Susan and I scribbled
in blue-lined Hilroys, until one of us,
I can't remember who — deux jeunes filles
bien élevées — was braver. One of us started
drawing slight curves against the coarse
paper's grain, secretly fashioning
the c-shapes of our penmanship lesson
into bosoms. We tried to cover them as they grew,
pulling the page's edge like a bed sheet,
over breasts pendulous and weighted
with all our unvoiced longings.

Susan blushed, my breath quickened,
as I inked the nipples with tight,
circling strokes into sombre eyes
that too quickly became Mrs. Spiller's.
Marching her Stride-Rights up our aisle,
she rapped my nude with her steel-edged ruler,
slashing where a belly button might have been,
and ripped the book from my hand.

Stranded there on the bleached desktop,
the pen's shaft pressed against
a writing blister until it hurt
and hurt again, as I copied word
after word from Webster's Fifth Collegiate:
'Perverse — wayward, turned away
from what is right, good, or proper.
'Pervert — one who practices sexual perversion.
Perverted — misguided, abnormal, unnatural, wicked.

At a later point, Hussey writes about the poem and the images that she was attempting to convey:

It arose from an exercise done during a course on critical perspectives in teacher education. We were asked to free-write about an image or metaphor that was central to our notion of what a teacher is. The mental photograph, or emotional hieroglyph that began constellating in my mind's eye was based on an incident in fourth grade where I was punished for drawing the body of a nude woman during penmanship class.

> *Tellingly, I wrote my poem from the point of view of a shamed student, rather than of an empowered teacher. The persona of my poem appears in an early fifties-style classroom, complete with its puritanical, verging-on-sadistic, Mrs. Spiller. This visual scene floated up from that archive of childhood memories — that 'Now at all times' realm that Yeats (1973) wrote of in 'The Magi' (p. 141) where, as we travel further inside our emotions and imaginings, time itself grows more and more relative and the images found there tend to haunt and perplex us. Thus, 'stranded' in this stark, unforgiving classroom, the student and her friend are not idealized school girls, 'bien élevées', but more realistically drawn children hungry to express themselves, learn about sex, and explore their emergent female bodies.*
>
> *My poem, then, attempts to escape static depiction by capturing a moment of change — one of many subtle, or not so subtle, instances where these girls are learning how to lose their spontaneity, shut down their appetites, and close themselves away. It is when, as Sandra Lee Bartky (1990) writes, one experiences 'the cringing within, this felt sometimes as a physical sensation of being pulled inward and downward; the necessity for hiding and concealment'. (p. 86)*
>
> *What then, has this poem to say about my notion of a teacher? That they (we) can so easily betray their female students. As Bartky writes, 'women are more shame-prone than men, the cause is not far to seek: Women, more than men, are often made to feel shame in the major sites of social life,' (p. 93), at school and in their bodies.*

Charlotte's idea of the 'shamed student' is an important one in terms of self-study, speaking to the significance of the personae we carry around with us. Here it is the student speaking and not the teacher. Or rather, it is the adult speaking, but with the young girl still very much a part of that voice. Charlotte's project draws our attention to the significance of inter-generationality, particularly in terms of the links between women teachers and their female students, something we return to in the final chapter when we look at feminist nostalgia.

Discussion

In this chapter we have proposed that, as teachers, we appropriate the ordin-ariness of school photography to our own ends, to study ourselves and the ways we teach. Photographs — of our classrooms, and of ourselves as students and teachers — can be texts which both ask and tell. Rather than having them construct us in a certain way, we can use them to ask questions and tell new stories. These stories can come from an activity as simple as going back over our school photographs in a systematic way, to one where we embark upon particular artistic modes of investigation through essay, visual art, and poetry. Used in this way, photographs can take on what bell hooks (1994) describes as a 'decolonizing' function. As she writes:

The word remember (re-member) evokes the coming together of several parts, fragments becoming a whole. Photography has been, and is, central to that aspect of decolonization that calls us back to the past and offers a way to re-claim and renew life-affirming bonds. Using these images, we connect ourselves to a recuperative, redemptive memory that enables us to construct radical identities, images of ourselves that transcend the limits of the colonizing eye. (p. 53)

While hooks is talking about the ways in which photographs figure in the lives of Afro-American families — particularly those structured around patriarchal fathers-bearing-cameras — her point that the same visual images that have been used to colonize can also become tools for decolonization is an important one in our work as teachers. In many of our workshops, we were struck by how many teachers were still carrying around mental images of themselves in their third grade photo; they were still talking about having to stand next to so-and-so and how embarrassing that was; they still 'minded' that they had to stand in the back row or the front row or wherever it was that they didn't want to be. By engaging in their own photography projects, in any of the numerous ways suggested in this chapter, teachers can actively explore their identities and the ways in which they approach their students and their profession in order to reconsider and reshape what is already there, or create new constructions by taking their own pictures.

What *can* a teacher do with a camera?
What can a *teacher* do with a camera?
What can a teacher do with a *camera?*

Chapter 4

Undressing and Redressing the Teacher's Body

My grade 12 history teacher stands out very clearly in my mind, probably partly because of his 'unique' appearance. Before I had ever been taught by him, I had seen him in the hallways. I used to be very intimidated by his towering height, strange appearance, and his deep voice with a Russian accent. Once he became my history teacher, I grew to admire and like him very much . . . (Written on the back of a picture drawn by a female pre-service high school teacher)

In my first two years of teaching, I had little inkling of how my students viewed me — at least in the physical sense. I was their teacher and that was that . . . Under their innocent gaze I slid comfortably into the teacher mode — I felt safe, undefined, sexless . . . All that changed when I accepted a job at a high school. It was not long before I became aware of youthful eyes — male eyes — looking at me in a way that did not always suggest innocence or neutrality. Now what I decided to wear on a given day became the topic of classroom conversation . . . Now I felt as if I was being systematically undressed. (Excerpt from an essay written by a high school teacher)

My English teacher was a middle-aged single woman who dressed impeccably, always wore exquisite perfume, and greeted us each day with a cheerful hello. She made English come alive for us. (Excerpt from a teacher's journal)

Mr. Ryan was a mean, rotten slime ball. His yellowed teeth, the spit at the corner of his mouth, a few pathetic gray hairs slicked down with grease across his bald head, his sarcastic, menacing sneers — Ugh! I get shivers even now just thinking about him. I dreaded his classes, his taunts, his stick. We all did. I don't remember a thing he taught me. (Excerpt from a teacher's log)

When a teacher enters a classroom for the first time, it is not necessarily her or his ideas that first attract students' attention. It is the body and how it is adorned and clothed — how it looks, sounds, moves and smells. Whether or not we realize it, the image we project precedes us, introduces us, and inserts us into the communication we have with students. This applies to most teaching situations, from kindergarten to university.

It is not only students who notice the teacher's body. In examining accounts centred around school photographs gathered in the workshops we discussed earlier, we were struck by how frequently teachers were engaged in their own individual body project, even when involved in group work. Their smiles or the positioning of their mouths were very common sites for commentary. So was their hair. But what people were also saying was that much of the imagery they used as a point of reference was somehow 'out there'. They were very conscious of what others thought a teacher ought to look like, or of what they *thought* others thought! In this respect, the teachers were concerned with both the *personal* reaction to their own body parts and the *social* reaction to their body parts in terms of socially ingrained images.

Teaching necessarily occurs through the body. Although its presence is obvious, the 'teacher-body' is too often neglected, avoided, or taken for granted in an uncritical manner. There seems to be a social taboo that prohibits paying professional attention to the basic aspects of self that we all experience, teachers and non-teachers alike: appearance, dress, body shape, sensation, sensuality, sexuality, physical pleasure, pain, desire, fantasy, emotions. These fundamentally important aspects of human existence cross the boundaries of race, religion, class, sex, age, and all the 'isms' we use to identify ourselves in various social milieus. However, the way the body and its various features are conceptualized, manifested, interpreted, and lived depends very much on prevailing cultural norms. Are teachers thought to be exempt from all of this? Is the body not essential to both our basic sense of self and our teaching identity and practice? Crucial to self-study, the body provides vital information on who we were and who we have become. In the words of theorist Roland Barthes (1978), 'What I hide by my language, my body utters' (p. 45).

Teachers Have Bodies and Wear Clothes

Some years ago, my friend came upon her naked two-and-a-half-year-old son, Jonathan, climbing up onto the vanity over the bathroom sink. He was standing precariously on its edge and staring into the large mirror on the wall. 'Jonathan', she cried, 'what on earth are you doing?' He looked at her intently and replied, 'I want to see my whole *self'.* (Excerpt from Weber's journal, 1990)

This toddler acknowledges what should be obvious as far as teacher identity is concerned: the self necessarily involves the body — the *entire* body. Socialized into cultures of teaching which officially portray body, as opposed to mind, as secondary and not directly related to pedagogy, we may be tempted to dismiss Jonathan's concern with his body as superficial, a mere distraction from serious self-study. However, in a culture of teaching that ignores the body or regards it with suspicion, Jonathan's statement becomes all the more important. Studying or 'seeing' the self includes paying the body special attention, and recognizing it as integral to thinking, perceiving and feeling.

In her usual candid manner, bell hooks (1993) reminds us how the straitjackets of tradition and fashion keep the body in check by propagating deep-rooted stereotypes of what teachers look like and what they can be imagined to be doing, to the point that matters like going to the loo can be problematic for a beginning teacher:

> . . . individuals enter the classroom to teach as though only the mind is present and not the body. To call attention to the body is to betray the legacy of repression and denial that has been handed down to us by our professional elders, who have usually been white and male. But our non-white elders were just as eager to deny the body . . . When I first became a teacher and needed to use the restroom in the middle of class, I had no clue as to what my elders did in such situations. *No one talked about the body in relation to teaching. What did one do with the body in the classroom?* (ibid, p. 58, italics added)

But in spite of social customs, we are not very successful at ignoring our bodies and appearance entirely. Consider, for instance, the following reactions of a group of pre-service teachers to videotapes of themselves teaching:

> *'Gee, I'm really going* bald*!' 'I look like a* whale*!' 'Oh, would you look at my* hair*!' 'Look at me in this picture — no wonder my students say I look like a* mother*!' 'If that's what I really look like, I'm never leaving the house again!' 'Why would any one dress like* that *to teach?' 'What kind of guy would wear a* pink *sweater to class?! What's he trying to prove?'* (Excerpts from field notes and questionnaires, emphasis added)

As the above quotes illustrate, when confronted with visual images of themselves and others, teachers quite naturally home in on their appearance before anything else. In our previous book, *That's Funny, You Don't Look Like a Teacher* (Weber and Mitchell, 1995), we described just how preoccupied pre-service and beginning teachers can be with what to wear. The familiar adage, 'Don't judge a book by its cover or a gift by its wrapping' does not seem to apply to the public life of professionals. The comments some of the teachers included with the self-portraits they drew for us showed that they felt torn between the desire to express themselves personally, to be true to who they felt they were, and the desire to comply with perceived notions of how teachers should look. Their concerns call to mind questions raised by anthropologist Fred Davis (1992) regarding choosing what to wear:

> Whom do I wish to please, and in so doing whom am I likely to offend? What are the consequences of appearing as this kind of person as against that kind? Does the image I think I convey of my self reflect my true innermost self or some specious version thereof? Do I wish to conceal or reveal? . . . and so forth. We are all too familiar with the oscillations and *dis*-ease these identity uncertainties evoke in one's self. (p. 24)

Indeed, as Madeleine Grumet (1995) points out, an absorbing problematic in modern pedagogy (albeit one of the least discussed) is *what to wear.*

This statement applies even to those who say they don't care about their appearance, who wear 'any old thing'. The teacher's appearance and clothes catch students' attention and guide their perceptions. Some of the information that is transmitted silently from person to person by dress is not easily translatable into words. Much of what we say to each other concisely with clothes would be time-consuming or socially clumsy to communicate orally. Goffman (1959) and Eicher and Roach-Higgens (1992) underline the importance of dress to self-presentation, claiming that it usually precedes verbal communication in establishing an individual's gendered identity as well as expectations for other types of behaviour (social roles) based on this identity. Clothing signs make visible the structure and organization of interactions within a specific social context — for example, in schools where there is an official dress code. As we argue in the next section, the teacher body and its appearance need to be taken seriously.

Reconceptualizing the Teacher's Body: Seeing the 'Whole Self'

Traditional teaching involves some*body* inducting some *body* into a *body* of knowledge. The English language acknowledges the bodily component of teachers and teaching. Yet although we may talk figuratively of a student *body* or a *corpus* of knowledge, in order to cultivate the mind, we mistakenly feel we must 'get past' the physical, personal body which can be distracting or even dangerous. Learning environments have historically upheld clothing customs (academic gowns, strict dress codes, uniforms) aimed at hiding, disciplining, or covering up the body in order to focus on mind. However, even if we are all dressed alike, we still teach with and through our bodies.

And students learn (or fail to learn) through theirs! In classrooms around the world, students are made to sit for long hours on hard chairs, overcoming their physical discomfort through force of mind, ostensibly concentrating on their lessons. When they disobey or fail to learn, it is their bodies that traditionally bear the brunt of disciplinary action — whether it be having to sit still with their heads on their desks or on 'time out' chairs, or being beaten with a strap or cane, or having to copy out lines until their hands ache. Ironically, this 'pedagogical' punishment of the body is an unspoken acknowledgment of the intimate relationship between the body and mind, an admission that they *are* indeed connected to one another.

Since body and mind act together, the notion of *body* as *'mindful'* is of critical importance to professional self-study. Yet, as already noted, discussion of the teacher's body is almost taboo, perhaps because contemplating the body unavoidably leads to the awkward (for educators) territory of basic bodily functions and characteristics, including pleasure and sexuality. And once a 'sex' word is uttered, all kinds of associations and stereotypes rise to the surface — including images of abuse, immorality, perversion, and all things 'bad'. Mention eros, pleasure, desire, or love as potentially pedagogical in relation to teaching, and suddenly you're on shaky ground and subject to suspicion. For those very reasons, we were wary of including them in this chapter, but to avoid recognizing their crucial significance to teacher identity and practice would be a cop-out.

Our Bodies, Our Selves: Using Drawings of Teachers as Springboards to Self-study

Students and teachers have normative expectations of how teachers are supposed to look and act. Young children 'know' that teachers don't need to use the toilet, don't smoke or drink, don't remove their shoes and put their feet up, don't play, don't have sex, and don't even have a life outside of school! In fact, they barely have bodies!

The strength and longevity of such popular images explain the innocent delight children experience as they grow older in seeing these norms transgressed, either by imagining or actually spotting their teachers acting like real embodied human beings. Figure 4.1, for example, is an imaginative drawing taken from a children's storybook, *Miss Malarkey Lives in Room 10*, written by Judy Finchler (1995), that depicts how teachers might look if they really did live in school.

Children and teachers alike respond to the book's humorous take on culturally ingrained taboos and stereotypes of teachers. The humour becomes even more explicitly focused on the teacher's body in another drawing in the book — a two-page 'centrefold' of the teacher's bare feet, featuring bright red, freshly painted toenails! Teachers with bare feet? Teachers who paint their toenails? Miss Malarkey is very different from the images most people conjure up when they think of 'teacher'. She's certainly no Miss Grundy.

When asked to 'draw a teacher', the children and beginning teachers we worked with revealed just how much popular stereotypes of teachers can influence personal conceptions of what teachers do and how they look. One female pre-service high school teacher, for instance, wrote the following comment on the back of her drawing of a teacher:

> *The reason I drew Miss Grundy from the Archie comic book series is that I always thought that she was a good teacher. She has a good sense of humour but she is strict and well-respected. This is partly how I would like to be portrayed.*

In our lives as teachers, we see and act in the world according to what we have consciously or unconsciously incorporated into our evolving notion of 'teacher'. There are the real-life teachers we have known, seen, or heard about, the popular culture teachers we have encountered in movies, comic books, novels and television, and there are the teachers we imagine other people expect us to be. The range of possible images is wide and varied: dowdy old maids, middle-aged bachelors, dashing heroes, spiteful witches,

Figure 4.1 Miss Malarkey

guardian angels, mean tyrants, comforting mothers, inept buffoons, magicians and so on. Many of these images are so comfortable or familiar that we simply take them for granted, unwittingly submitting to the considerable influence they bear on our emergent professional identity and practice (see Britzman, 1992; Bullough et al., 1991; Giroux and Simon, 1989; Joseph and Burnaford, 1994; Provenzo et al., 1989; Weber and Mitchell, 1995).

Box 4.1

Draw a Teacher: Accessing Cultural Images

1 On a blank piece of paper, using *coloured* markers, crayons, or pencils, draw a picture or symbolic representation of a teacher — any teacher, fictitious or real. *Include as much detail as possible.* Do not worry about artistic ability — this is not an art activity. Even stick figures will do, or perhaps an abstract representation will be best suited to convey your message.

2 Examine your completed drawing and write about it, either around the picture itself or on the back of the paper. Write your thoughts and reactions to what you have drawn. The following questions can be of help:

(a) What did you think, feel, or set out to do when beginning this task?

(b) Who or what does the drawing remind you of? Who might this drawing be based on (for example, fictitious or real teachers, media images, a composite of past teachers, etc.)? How does the drawing relate to your personal life experience?

(c) If it is relevant to your drawing, comment on the teacher's sex, gender, age, clothes, props, physical features, expression, ethnicity or social standing.

(d) If it is relevant to your drawing, comment on:
   (i) the students (or their absence);
   (ii) the nature of the student–teacher relationship;
   (iii) the physical setting (for example, location, arrangement of desks, homework, etc.);
   (iv) teaching style and subject matter.

(e) Look for contradictory images. We are often of two minds about many things. What does this drawing say about your own views or experience or aspirations as a teacher?

3 How do you feel about your drawing? Tell or write a short story about it.

4 Display and discuss your drawing with a small group of colleagues who have also done the activity. Notice and comment on any commonalities and differences that emerge when comparing the drawings. Together, prepare a comment on the activity and its significance to your professional development.

Figure 4.2 'There is no particular reason as to why I drew the picture this way. I imagine it is from my own recollection of elementary school. I always had female teachers who rarely wore skirts and most had glasses. Whenever we sat on the floor we always had little mats.' (Female teacher)

Figures 4.2 and 4.3 suggest that drawings relate not only to cultural images, but also to personal experience. In addition, both excerpts include comments on the teacher's appearance. Drawings can thus be used in different ways and in a variety of circumstances to jump-start an interrogation of the significance of body and appearance to teacher identity and practice. (See Box 4.1)

To probe student and teacher expectations further, the drawing activity can be combined with any of the variations we suggest in box 4.2. The very act of drawing directs attention to teachers' bodies, and requires decisions regarding adornment, appearance, clothing, and accessories. Drawings often reveal more than we intend to and point to things we may not yet be able to put into words. As simple as that may seem, the results can help pinpoint important areas, often by highlighting the role of cultural images and stereotypes in shaping our appearance. Drawings may also point to contradictions or tensions in teacher identity and practice. For example, one student teacher drew herself unsmiling, in very business-like clothing (a suit), standing by the blackboard in a formal, erect position. At the bottom of the picture she wrote:

I don't know what made me draw the picture this way. This is not how I dress or how I want to look or teach. I have a much more relaxed and informal style of dressing and teaching. I started out to draw myself, but somehow I got carried away by what I thought teachers should look like. We are supposed to be serious and strict. Maybe I feel that I am not yet a real teacher? Should I be more serious? But that's not me.

Figure 4.3 *'I drew this picture because it reminds me of a teacher I had in Sec. 1. Prim, proper, patient, yet* strict*!' (Male teacher)*

The teacher seems to be wondering if her personal style needs to be re-worked, masked, or obliterated in order to firmly establish a sense of professional identity. Can the personal and professional be mutually exclusive? What happens when who we feel we are seems to be in contradiction with who we think teachers are 'supposed to be'?

Casual drawings are helpful to self-study, as they reveal, upon close examination, our hopes and aspirations as well as our fears, disappointments, or frustrations. Drawings sometimes hint at new directions a teacher may wish to follow, or confirm and celebrate aspects of his or her current professional activities. They help us get in touch with our imagination, while at the same time revealing the extent to which our vision is confined by ingrained social images. If we don't like what we draw ourselves into, we can try drawing ourselves out of that image as a rehearsal of sorts for more serious reflection and action.

Dressed to Teach: Using Clothing to Explore the Teacher-Body

In this section, we introduce the real-life cases of several teachers. What these cases or accounts have in common is their illustration of the significance of clothing in relation to body and teacher identity. The first two cases also present ways to study the embodied teaching self. Sandra's story exemplifies a

Box 4.2

> ### Variations on the Draw-a-Teacher Activity:
> ### Self-Study and Reinvention
>
> Adapt and use the guidelines in box 4.1 to do any of the following:
>
> 1 *Draw yourself as a teacher.* This can be done several times, (for example, before and after your teaching practicum, or at the beginning of a term and near the end) and is useful in clarifying tensions and areas of concern or contradiction. Repeating the exercise over time can provide insight into how your views and identity change.
>
> 2 *Ask your students to draw a teacher* and invite written comments on their drawings. Lead a discussion about the activity. This can be very revealing and is a way of connecting with students and uncovering their expectations, stereotypes, and mind-sets. This should never be done in a situation where the students are to be evaluated or graded.
>
> 3 *Draw your favourite teacher* of all time. Display and discuss as in box 4.1.
>
> 4 *Draw the teacher* you *would like to become.* Write extensively about your drawing, why you included the elements you did. Keep it on hand to consult anew after a couple of months, or at the end of an internship or teaching term.
>
> 5 *Ask your students to draw an ideal teacher.* Proceed as in Step 2.
>
> 6 *Draw a 'teacher' as an agent of change.* This can help you imagine yourself (or someone else) differently; it is a way of symbolically looking at or 'trying on' different ways of being a teacher.

'teacher body-photo essay' and Robert's serves as an introduction to a reflective activity entitled 'dressing myself as a teacher'.

Case 1: The way I was: Reflections on two class photos: Sandra's essay

It is hard to avoid the body in types of self-study that involve visual images. Unlike drawings, which can be used purposefully to express thoughts, fantasies, and feelings, personal photographs may confront us more directly with lived bodily appearance, something we explored in the previous chapter. Consider the following essay where Sandra, a former elementary school teacher, reflects on two photos of herself taken during her first year of teaching.

Oh my Lord — I'd forgotten what I looked like back in those days! It's 1971
and my first full-time teaching position. There I am, looking like a Joan Baez
wanna-be with my long, straight, parted hair. And my feet — bare feet and
sandals! Would teachers choose or be allowed to dress like that in today's
schools? The picture is so dated. And the necklace and belt — I remember
them well because I made them myself. Many of us were into crafting our
own things back then. The necklace I made out of wooden beads, and the belt
buckle was a copper enamelling project, shades of bronze and purple, as I
recall. And those comfortable beige corduroy jeans — I wore them until they
fell apart.

I look like some kind of hippie, especially in contrast to my stu-
dents who are dressed in the obligatory school uniform. Even beside those
grade 3 children, I don't look very tall. It's always a surprise to me to see how
short I am. (In my mind, I'm tall, because until grade 7, I was always the
tallest in the class. Then my classmates soared past me.)

Look at those children — my first group of students! After all these
years, I thought I had forgotten their names. But now, seeing their faces and
expressions, I can recall many of their names. There is David, the one with
the chubby rosy cheeks and big teeth. I adored him. And his friend Brian, a
real sweetie. And there's Karen and Amy, delightful girls full of enthusiasm,
and, yes, that's Tina, a bit shy, with beautiful blue eyes. Oh, and quiet Kevin.
I wonder if he minded being so short? And there's Darrell, that impossibly

cute imp who had always hated school according to his Mum. He and I had a special understanding . . . 'Scallywags', I called them (they loved that)! They were all so full of beans.

And Pamela, with her missing front teeth, sparkling eyes, and winsome smile. I remember her mother helping me out in class. Pamela is the only student I have had contact with as a grown-up. She came up to me after a presentation I made at a teacher conference 10 years ago in Edmonton to let me know that she had grown up to be a teacher. She thanked me for having inspired her. What a thrill! I loved that class, I guess that is why I still recognize so many of those faces, why I have such fond memories of them. It was my first and probably my best year of teaching.

There was another official picture taken that same year that I seem to have lost. It tells the story behind the picture I do have, the story of a teacher who was blithely unaware, for most of the year, that the other teachers considered her a bit of an oddball or rebel. The youngest new teacher on staff, I was the only one who wore jeans or sandals or 'wild' jewelry, and I was one of only two teachers in the school who let the children choose what they were going to do, work in centres, keep guinea pigs, and so on. Seated beside my conservative and older colleagues, all of whom wore dresses or skirts or pant suits, I stick out like a sore thumb in that missing photo.

For most of that year I was oblivious to the occasional disapproving looks and comments made behind my back. No one criticized me to my face, the parents were satisfied because their kids liked school and seemed to be learning, the Principal was satisfied with me because the parents were, and I was too engrossed in working with those children to feel embarrassed about being different. I don't remember trying or wanting to be different. I was simply being a 'good girl', taking seriously the progressive ideas my professors had said were the hallmarks of good teaching. I remember giving it my all, going home exhausted to fall into bed at the end of a long day.

My colleagues were nice enough, on the whole. I think some of them found me impossibly young and tolerated my eccentricities with some amusement. Although I was later told that they had been a bit perplexed and a little scandalized, to my face they were polite, even friendly — especially one older lady from Britain who was a bit of an outsider herself in terms of taste and culture. I did not try to change them or how the school was run (well, not too much!), and so they pretty much let me do my own thing, as long as it was mostly behind my closed classroom door. I'm quite sure they thought I would smarten up in time and stop experimenting with those 'new-fangled' and unpractical ideas I had picked up at the university. In that conservative, traditional school, I did some of my best and most progressive teaching. I was quite happy there.

I wish I could find that staff photo. Mostly, I wish I could find my way back to the kind of passion for teaching I had then, and the small but meaningful ways I bucked the system so easily and naturally. Is my 'rebellion' just a trick of memory that I nostalgically impose to mitigate my current conformity, a simple matter of wearing different clothes? . . . not entirely . . .

One day early that year, I brought home my students' uncompleted language workbooks, the ones their parents had been required to buy. Totally disenchanted with the mindless exercises they contained, I usually fell asleep correcting them. With some trepidation, I heaved them all down the incinerator of my apartment building. I never mentioned them to the children or parents again. No one inquired after them or seemed to miss them. Although I felt a little guilty about destroying school and personal property, I also felt relieved at not having to deal with those darn things . . .

Have I gotten off track? Who have I become? Why do I feel I have sold out the 'me' in the picture? Am I just mourning my youth? Is it the image rather than the essence of 'rebel' I miss? I wasn't really much of a revolutionary was I? I didn't change the school, after all. But I felt more 'me'. I was much surer of everything then, in my first year of teaching!

The above essay is an example of the sort of memory work we discussed in earlier chapters, a further illustration of how even lost or absent photographs can trigger reflection. But it is also an example of how, in examining her photo, the first thing that captures the teacher's attention is her appearance. Sandra focuses on physical features of her body (hair and height), as well as clothing (corduroy jeans) and adornment (wooden beads and belt buckle). Not only does she notice these features, she is prompted to use them as signs that symbolize aspects of both her teaching practice and her relationship with the rest of the school staff. Her essay illustrates how body and appearance can simultaneously reflect a teacher's personal identity, social position, philosophy of teaching, and even political stance.

The body-photo essay guidelines in box 4.3 show how photographs can be used to systematically examine the teacher-body in ways that complement the work on collective memory that we presented in chapter 3.

Not surprisingly, body and clothing are usually interconnected in body-photo essays. It is difficult to separate a consideration of posture, gestures and facial expressions from the clothes and accessories that accompany, hide or support them. Combined, body and clothing emit a number of messages, some of which we might only be partially aware. Attending to these images in self-study can contribute to how we think about who we are or could be — as whole selves — in the classroom, something the next case takes on explicitly.

Case 2: Wearing difference: Robert's pink sweater

Unlike most of the things that made Sandra feel she stuck out like a sore thumb in her school picture, some aspects of our appearance that mark us are not easily changed. For example, depending on geography, genetics, history, context and culture, there are times and situations when our appearance causes us to 'stand out', whether we choose to or not. Some of us cannot easily blend into the majority in the school staff picture, even if we want to: the lone male on an elementary school staff of women, the black teacher on a predominantly white staff, the large-size teacher among smaller colleagues, the sole female Principal on a male-dominated board, the teacher in the wheelchair, the one wearing the turban, veil, cross, or yamulka in a secular school, the new young

Box 4.3

Guidelines for Teacher Body-Photo Essay

1 Assemble at least two, but preferably several photos of yourself as a teacher. Staff photos, class pictures and candid shots on field trips or in the classroom are all suitable. A collection that covers a period of months or years is very valuable.

2 Examine and compare the photos, making written notes of what strikes you about them, and what each one means to you.

3 Write down or tape record the memories that looking at the collection of photos evokes. Be as detailed as you can, trying to remember how things looked, smelled, sounded and felt.

4 Examine each picture and comment on the following details, making comparisons between people in each photo as well as among photos:

    (a) clothing, jewelry, accessories worn by each person;
    (b) hairstyle, body posture, adornment or distinguishing features (scars, tattoos, body piercing) size, shape, features (for example, lips, breasts, physique, nose), colour, and position;
    (c) facial and body expression (body language);
    (d) relationships between figures in photo;
    (e) circumstances behind photo: purpose or motivation for taking the photo, place, time, point of view (gaze).

5 In small groups, 'work through' your notes and photographs. Each person should have an opportunity to talk about their experiences. What inferences can the group make about these photographs and the accompanying memories? What can you learn about yourself as a teacher? What can you learn about teachers or teaching that could be useful in the future?

6 Individuals might go on to write an essay; groups might want to use the idea raised in the previous chapter of creating a photography display or installation — in this case around the body.

---

teacher in a school where the majority are near retirement. Not all of these differences, of course, have the same consequences. The only male teacher on an elementary school staff does not occupy the same precarious position of otherness as the sole female Principal on a male-dominated board; and neither may experience difference in quite the same way as the black teacher on a predominantly white staff.

Sometimes it is hard to tell if our sense of being different is imposed from the outside or the inside. The following story about Robert, a pre-service primary teacher, is a case in point.

The Pink Sweater

One of the most gifted pre-service students I ever taught was a congenial young man, Robert (not his real name), who bucked tradition in that he wanted to teach kindergarten or primary grades. A gifted musician, artist, and athlete, he turned out to be gifted in the classroom as well. The children adored him, and were eager to meet the many challenges he set for them. He was well-liked by the staff and Principal, and was flooded with job offers even before graduating. In fact, the Principal (male) took him aside and said 'You don't need to teach young children, we'd prefer to see you in the upper grades. With your talent, you could be an administrator in no time'. That comment, along with a remark he had overheard in the staff room about his favorite fuzzy pink mohair sweater, made Robert raise some very important questions when showing us his self-video in our weekly seminar at the university, a seminar in which he was the only male.

He showed a video clip of himself wearing his pink sweater, sitting on the carpet and reading to the children who were closely gathered round. One child was leaning against him, another was in his lap, and he would occasionally stretch out a long arm to pat a shoulder or knee in order to redirect or catch a youngster's attention.

When the video was finished, Robert asked us in a subdued tone, 'Why can't a man like young children, wear pink sweaters, and touch his students to reassure or guide them without fearing he will be judged unnatural, or even labeled some kind of pervert? Why is it okay for women to touch young children but not for men? Why do men get recruited almost immediately as administrators, but women don't? I don't want to teach the upper grades, I don't want to be a school administrator! Why do I have to fight just to stay where I am?'

He then described the sense that some people were uncomfortable with his choice of sweater. 'Men who wear pink seem to be instantly labeled "gay". Women who wear pants or boots or business jackets are not so quickly labeled "lesbian" — most of the women in my school wear pants. I'm not gay, but so what if I were? What would be wrong with that? I am not going to stop wearing my pink sweater.'

This uncharacteristic outburst from Robert provoked a great deal of discussion, a discussion that made us aware that even though we were all raised in the same society, we had differing values, and belonged to different sub-cultures. Some women felt that it was nice to see the shoe on the other foot, for a change, to see a man experience what it's like to be trapped in society's stereotypes of how teachers are supposed to 'look' (in the case of early childhood, female; in the case of male teachers, heterosexual). Although most women sympathized with Robert's predicament, one said, 'Oh, you poor thing, offered a posh job, recruited by administration, while I haven't had even one job offer!' Another woman said, 'At least gays get noticed, even if negatively.

Being noticed confirms they exist! Lesbians are treated as invisible, as if they don't exist.'

Another student said that she didn't think homosexuals belong in the classroom, that schools should reflect the values of the majority culture. This inspired one usually quiet woman to ask Robert why he was upset at being labeled gay if indeed he thought gay was a normal and good thing to be. This provoked a flurry of comments, many to the effect that the values of a democratic majority should entail valuing diversity and showing children that whatever differences we may have in lifestyles, language, gender, race, religion, age, class, ability, and appearance, we are all human and worthy of respect, even love. There was debate over the harm caused by the irrational stereotypical linking of homosexuality and sexual abuse, and of gender and administrative skills . . . (Excerpt from Weber's teaching journal, May 1989)

Robert's case raises important issues about the male teacher-body in education — issues we will take up more specifically a little later on. Because there *is* a self-consciousness to his choice of clothing, we can use the pink sweater as an example of how teachers can dress their bodies to express both personal and social aspects of their identity. His insistence on continuing to wear his pink sweater suggests that we do sometimes have choices, that in some circumstances we can resist confining or false stereotypes of gender and sexuality by using or dressing our bodies in certain ways. In light of his self-study, Robert's choice of clothing is no longer accidental or unthinking; it is now part of his identity as teacher.

Sartorial subversion can be pleasurable. When circumstances warrant, we can experience a certain amount of satisfaction in refusing to act (dress) as others expect us to, or according to dominant images (Gotfrit, 1988, p. 133). However, whether we know the codes or not, and whether we wish to fit in or 'dress against the grain', dressing to teach is something we cannot avoid, and must therefore incorporate into self-study. The exercise described in Box 4.4 enables us to confront our clothed reality in a concrete manner without visual prompts.

Identity, Difference, and Teacher Appearance

Choosing to wear difference is not the same as being perceived by others as different. Difference is seldom a simple matter of making a fashion statement. As the next two cases illustrate, it is hard for some of us to *be seen* as teachers, no matter how we dress. Being visibly different in a particular teaching setting affects how we are perceived in our role as teachers. It is not our bodies per se but the cultural reading of them that is crucial to how we might come to find ourselves being perceived as other. How do we define other? How do we see others as other? We are referring less here to individual differences than to a *social relationship of difference* between a specific sub-group and a larger social group.

Box 4.4

Dressing Myself as Teacher

This is an activity to do by yourself, initially.

1   What did you wear the last time you taught? Picture it. How do you think you looked? Describe and list all your items of clothing, jewelry, body adornments (for example, tattoos), and accessories. How did you wear your hair? How did you feel about yourself that day?

2   Is getting dressed to teach problematic in any way for you? Does what you wear relate in any way to what you do as a teacher? Do you think of yourself as a teacher? Do you have 'a signature look'?

3   Why do you dress the way or ways you do to teach? Do you teach better if you are well dressed? How does your appearance conform to or differ from that of other teachers you have seen or known? What messages do you think your appearance conveys to students, staff, or colleagues? Is your appearance or way of dressing any different outside of school? If so, how?

4   Would you wish to dress any differently to teach? What, if anything, might you like to change? Why these changes? What might prevent you from dressing that way?

Case 3: You don't look like the teacher

In an article entitled *Caliban in the Classroom,* Karamcheti (1995) describes how Western culture reads the body made visible by ethnic or racial difference. She reflects on being positioned by others as racially different in the context of the predominantly white, upper–middle class college classroom in which she taught. Being perceived as 'different' in this context, as we shall see, is not merely a matter of contrasting skin colour or body features; it is much more centrally connected to the baggage, images, scripts, and stereotypes that are socially constructed and linked with racial or ethnic features. She writes:

> The entanglement of the personal — the facts of race and ethnicity — with the professional — a teacher's authority to speak with credibility, and thereby to educate, to lead out — came home to me when I first began teaching . . . I taught freshman composition in the English Department at a predominantly white, upper-middle class campus in Southern California. I realized pretty quickly that my person in the classroom was a bit of a shocker for some students. On the first day of classes, I would deliberately wait until a few

minutes into the class period to allow people time to locate a new classroom in a new school, and then make my entrance, walk to the table at front and center of the room and put down my books. It was interesting to have students approach me, and, speaking very loudly and slowly, inform me that that place was meant for the teacher. (p. 139)

That's funny, you don't look like the teacher! Simply because of her features and skin, Karamcheti was assumed to be a foreign student, not a university teacher. So strong was the assumption that people who look like Karamcheti could not possibly be teachers, it overrode the students' reading of her clearly visible teacher body language — walking to the teacher's place and putting her book down while standing. When others have difficulty seeing us as teachers, it may be hard for us to see ourselves as teachers.

The following case illustrates another difference that 'makes a difference' to teacher identity: social class upbringing.

Case 4: Shannon: Wearing class identity

Shannon is an experienced teacher who works in a high school with 13-year-old girls in a large industrial city. She began a conference presentation on girls' rights with the following statement:

> *I am working class, and every day that I go into school, I wear my working class identity. I am aware that I am entering a middle-class environment wearing this working class identity.*

As Shannon went on to describe in her presentation, for her, 'wearing' an identity is not only about what she looks like, but also about class socialization and the power structures of the system in which she works. Shannon stressed that she is only now learning how 'the system' can work for women instead of against them. For example, such tasks as making phone calls to people 'in authority' are not taken-for-granted skills acquired during socialization. They thus become an important part of learning to use the system in which she and the girls are involved.

But despite her determination to master 'the system', Shannon makes a deliberate choice not to wear what *she sees* as the uniform of the middle-class teacher. From the 'outside', what she wears (Doc Martens, casual pants, etc.) is not necessarily that different from the attire of other teachers, although obviously this could vary from school to school. Some might argue that there is no such thing as a middle-class uniform for female teachers in North America. What is important is that Shannon herself interprets her own dress in terms of class. Our point here is that, in making the statement about wearing her working class identity, Shannon herself is linking ideology and clothing, and has clearly worked out clothing as a symbol of difference that is significant to her in terms of understanding herself as a teacher.

While we know of no easy way to have the kind of discussions about wearing/living difference, particularly since difference here is mostly about (in)equity and power, the questions which follow (box 4.5) may be useful as a way in, along with the photo and drawing activities that we described earlier. However, they cannot instantly dissolve culturally induced beliefs and stereotypes.

Box 4.5

Prompt: Living our Differences

The following questions could be used to focus group work on difference.

1　How might one handle situations of difference? Have you ever been in a situation like Karemcheti's?

2　How have people positioned you as 'outsider', by virtue of some visible difference (age, sex, race, physical features including voice or accent)? When does such a positioning contribute to being 'other' so that you have felt belittled, embarrassed, misinterpreted?

3　Are there times when being visibly different does not place you in the position of 'other'?

4　How do you respond to the situations when you witness colleagues or students being singled out, unfairly stereotyped, picked on, or simply treated differently because of differences of class, race, ethnicity or gender?

Embarking on self-study projects does not mean we are all going to love one another or agree with each other. But it can force us to confront ourselves and others in ways that are conducive to professional growth. Robert's self-study, Karamcheti's questioning of her position in the classroom (who *is* the teacher here?), and Shannon's statements about working class identity and how clothing is part of her own interrogation of who she is as a teacher, are all part of this professional dialogue.

Case 5: Dressing the teacher at home: The green robe

It is not only at work that we are 'professionals'. Many of us do not take off our teacher hat when we leave school. We may absent-mindedly or deliberately wear it at home and elsewhere.

One of the most profound and articulate interrogations of the significance of clothing to teaching that we have encountered is a conference presentation and subsequent book chapter 'Scholae personae: Masks for meaning' (1995), written by Madeleine Grumet, author also of *Bitter Milk* (1988). Using the symbolism of clothing, Grumet reflects on the teaching personae evoked as she reads and responds to her students' work, a task inherent and essential to teaching. She describes the at-home, 'domestic' pedagogical relationship as one which coexists with the more distant and scholarly persona of her on-campus self. This duality is underscored by the neatly-typed notes she writes for each student whose essays she intimately savours in the comfort and warmth of a flannel nightgown, her old bathrobe, and her husband's socks.

Madeleine Grumet's Green Robe

I will start this discussion turning to the place I would avoid, the thing I would not think about and would not choose to show you, my green robe. . . . My robe is what some would call kelly green. I don't remember buying it. I could blame it on a relative, but that would be cowardly, and a betrayal. It is warm and thick, Orlon probably, often coffee stained, and it is good for writing in on cold Rochester mornings, and afternoons for that matter, if no one drops by. It is not a robe for entertaining.

It can go in the washing machine and dryer, its synthetic fleece indestructible, but it works best when slightly soiled, worn with unwashed hair, a flannel nightgown, clogs, and Gerald's grey socks . . . It is my robe, it has my smell . . . When I think about it I remember my body . . . It is a green cocoon. After a while words fly out of it.

Maybe if I were younger and thinner, the green robe would be jeans and a sweatshirt. But I grew up in the forties when mothers wore housedresses that were not really robes, but were not really dresses either. You wouldn't wear one to the store, but you were dressed if someone rang the bell. When I would come home from school for lunch, my mother would be wearing a housedress covered with small flowers, and I suspect that even if jeans suited me they would not surround me with morning light and kitchen smells.

When it was my turn to keep house, I would sit at the word processor in the green robe, until the school bus rolled down the block. Then, as I saw my kids coming up the walk, I'd dash for the shower, protecting them from the sight of my literary decadence, for, unlike my mother, I was not dressed if someone rang the bell.

Convinced in the mid-seventies that students of education required a greater selection than what was available to them in a field dominated by positivistic social science, behavioural objectives, and standardized tests, I started asking them to write autobiographical narratives of educational experience . . . facing rows of students at Hobart and William Smith colleges — all of whom wore clothing designed to conceal all ethnic and class stigmata, all attired so that they would look exactly like each other — I asked for . . . multiple narratives: seeking the specificity, the material, the lost shoe, the dead rabbit that would return studies of education and them and me to the world . . . multiple narratives (Sartre's approach of window shopping, Olney's wriggling out of self-representations as a snake sheds old skins) . . .

invite the range, the contradictions, and all the robes — silk brocade, Orlon, rayon (packs well), terry, seersucker, velvet, leather, feather — that students could find for this academic procession . . .

Then came the three-week winter break, and I took all the stories home to read. I can still see them, sitting there in the study, next to the computer, waiting for me. I couldn't pick up just one or two and stick them in between trips to the store, or dash off a few before going out to the movies. Each set of three held a green world, thick with vegetation, and the only way I could make my way through it was in my green robe.

Green robed, I would crawl under their leaves, feel the rhythm of their sentences, move to the places they skipped over. A semiotic reading, if you will . . . And then at the end I would surface with a paragraph suggesting the philosophical questions implied in the narratives as well as readings that might inform further pursuit of these issues.

I denied the intimacy of my reading by abstaining from writing on their papers. I would place a number next to the sentence or word to which my comments referred and type them on a separate sheet of paper, sequenced by corresponding numbers. I read them in my green robe, but I typed my responses on the word processor, deliberately interposing the machine, the type of our texts, between our bodies. We made ourselves up in typed face. Masking our handwriting in type endowed our exchange with formality, intended to bring student stories into the legitimated discourse that constituted the knowledge of this philosophy of education course.

. . . Do I work with other people's children to separate from mine or connect to theirs? The green robe is no negligee. I wrap myself as a maternal body as I relinquish my definition to its green indeterminateness, tactile and cozy, rounding off eroticism. Let my children go . . .

With words I am disrobed and articulated. As text, in the typed responses, . . . I re-present myself as the object of desire, dressed up in the words of the world. In the mise-en-scène of the classroom, scholae personae simultaneously conceals and reveals my leaks, my denied dependencies, my fantasies, my desires. The green robe stays in the green room. (abridged from pp. 36–44)

Like Robert's pink sweater, a simple green robe can speak volumes. Needing to respond to students in the scholar/mother's garment but also careful to change out of that garment before anyone can see her, Grumet raises the possibility of a multilayered teacher identity wherein one may repress the *appearance of domesticity* without foregoing its essence of caring. Further, by displaying and writing about the domestic robe in an academic context, she rehabilitates the domestic as she hides it, bringing it momentarily out of the closet and into the classroom. Her story reminds us that we do not cease teaching or being teachers once we leave the school. For many of us, teaching is part of who we are wherever we are and however we dress. Like Miss Malarkey in figure 4.1, our at-home teacher body/persona may be less known to others, but remains a very special and crucial part of our teaching self. Like Grumet, perhaps we need to bring it out of the closet now and then for inspection in order to more fully recognize our teaching identity.

Grumet's story, like the others in this chapter, reminds us that we are not disembodied creatures. We have basic desires, taking pleasure in being comfortable and warm, wearing the clothes of a loved one, being near certain objects, or finding that certain smells or physical surroundings enhance or impede our professional work. Physical and emotional pleasure (and pain) are integral to our lives as teachers. But, as we explore in the remainder of this chapter, it is the physical and emotional aspects of the teacher that are the most problematized, vilified or ignored.

Teacher Sexuality

How do you 'read' the picture (Figure 4.5), taken from the cover of the academic text by Barreca and Denenholz Morse (1997)? Can teaching be simultaneously sexual and intellectual? Is there a discourse into which we might enter that would allow us to include our own sexuality as a normal and essential part of self-study? Ursula Kelly (1997) points out that even today, teachers as well as students continue to be positioned within a discourse of desexualization. Yet, as Joseph Litvak (1995) contends, no matter how much we try to ignore sexuality, no matter how much we pretend and act as if it has nothing to do with teaching, sexuality is implicit in schooling:

> Homosexuality and heterosexuality . . . were not merely extracurricular activities. Rather, they were ways of being that our teachers carried into their classrooms and communicated to us, whether or not they wanted to, as much as if not more than they did the authorized subject matter of algebra, American history, English, and, of course, French. Ostensibly, sexuality was the most 'personal' thing about a person, not just a private matter but in some sense the very essence of privacy, that which is by definition 'nobody else's business'. It was becoming clear to me, however, that acquiring cultural literacy — as one is supposed to do in school — meant, to no small degree, acquiring sexual literacy, not learning how to exclude the private from the public but learning how to read the private as it is everywhere obliged to manifest itself in public.
>
> My point is that, if you grow up in this culture, you become remarkably sophisticated, well before college age, about the sexuality of your teachers — more sophisticated, perhaps, than about your own sexuality, which, as they say, is another story. This sophistication doesn't consist primarily in an explicit trading of information about sexual organs and practices, though it usually includes plenty of that kind of exchange. What defines it best is an acute, often merciless receptivity to the ways in which the sexual 'truth' about a person spreads out to suffuse everything he or she says and does, especially at the level of apparently nonsexual words and deeds and especially when he or she is unconscious of their 'true' significance. (p. 20)

Litvak's point is an important one: whether or not a particular teacher endorses a specific conceptualization of gender, or wishes to be seen as a sexual and sensual being, teaching and sexuality may be completely entangled as far as students are concerned.

One way in which teacher sexuality does attract serious attention is as the object of rules or legislation to guide 'sexual propriety'. A cursory glance at the history of schooling reveals a camouflaged but ongoing public and political interest in questions of sex and the regulation of teacher-bodies (Prentice, 1994). At the turn of the century in North America, for example, female teachers had to obey long lists of rules that prescribed every aspect of their dress and private lives, from how many petticoats they had to wear under their dresses (minimum of two), to hem and sleeve lengths (very long), hair styles (off the face and shoulders, or covered), their marital status (single) and where they were allowed to spend their time after school (at home or church, never in ice cream parlors and never in the unchaperoned company of males who were not relatives!).

Even today, in many faculties of education, female pre-service teachers are singled out and admonished to avoid jewelry, make-up, short skirts, low necklines, jeans, and so on. Although they may be instructed not to dress sloppily, male pre-service teachers are not usually cautioned to tame their sexuality through dress codes, although, as Robert's story illustrated, their bodies and clothes are also subject to censure. In Western societies, the male dress code for the workplace was until recently very rigid and monotone. That situation is changing, but progress is very slow, so that there is still little need to set up tight controls on how men should dress. As a result, dress codes seem, by and large, to be a language used to refer to female sexuality. In more recent years, school boards have referred more explicitly to teacher sexuality by adopting legal policies to protect children and teachers from physical violence and sexual abuse. There is a great deal of discussion and debate around the subject of abuse and the ways in which schools might either contribute to or combat systemic violence. Unfortunately, as Johnson (1997) makes clear, this concern has often been interpreted to mean that teachers are not supposed to touch children at all or have warm, close relationships with them. Male teachers, in particular, are frequently advised not to be alone in a room with a student (especially females) with the door closed and so on. While questions regarding sexual abuse in schools should indeed be given serious attention, there is a danger in oversimplifying or even pathologizing all sexuality, love, bodily functions, and touching. What are the ramifications of such oversimplification in classroom life? One male kindergarten teacher was quoted as saying:

> . . . as you probably all know, elementary students like to hug teachers, like affection, and do not want to be treated as though they have some dread disease. As a result of my fear [of the no-touch policy], I don't touch students, except maybe on the shoulder or the arm. (ibid, p. 101, brackets added)

Several points deserve consideration here. One is that public discourse on teacher sexuality is located almost entirely within a regulatory and

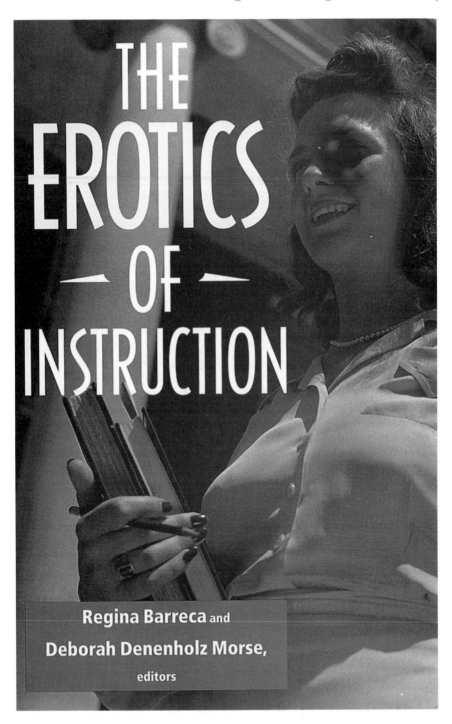

Figure 4.5 The Erotics of Instruction *cover picture*

pathologized framework which ignores its normal and positive aspects. A second point is that issues around sexuality are often problematized differently for male and female teachers, and are thus likely to emerge differently in the context of self-study. The third point is that current legislation and regulations regarding sexual harassment and sexual abuse acknowledge an important truth: sexuality is a part of human relations, including those that take place in schools.

Sex and the Female Teacher's Body

Jo's story, which follows, is a good example of the kind of ongoing regulation of women teachers' bodies that is likely to emerge in self-study. As noted by the high school teacher whom we quoted at the beginning of this chapter, the bodies of women teachers are frequently 'undressed' by students and administrators, or at least that is how many women feel. As a young teacher who enjoys the pleasures of dressing her body, Jo is a prime target for social regulation and a social discourse that casts women in the role of victim or object. In her account, we see ways in which many of the prompt questions offered in boxes 4.4 and 4.5 can be applied to a discussion around sex and the body.

Case 6: Jo: Breasts and jangly jewelry

'God! I'm all hair and boobs!' I am looking at my school photo taken in my third year of teaching when I was 26 years old. I have always been self-conscious of my body and how I look/dress: what to cover up (don't want to look fat), and, more importantly, what to reveal. I have this love-hate relationship with my body: There are parts of it I love, and parts I hate. Now, at age 30, the 'love' outweighs the 'hate'. I love my legs, I hate my ass, I am coming to terms with my belly, and I've always been ambivalent about my breasts. Ambivalent in that generally, I like the fact I have large breasts (though I've never liked what gravity does with them). However, there are times I see my breasts as a liability: they may add more pounds to my frame, I can't go braless in cute little tops and dresses, I have to psych myself up and devote an entire shopping spree to buying a bra, I get looked at by men, I am sometimes on the receiving end of cat calls and whistles. At one point in my life, I wanted a breast reduction; it would have meant freedom from the above-mentioned reality.

Now, four years after this picture was taken, I choose to wear clothes that accentuate my God-given attributes: body suits and jeans, short skirts and dresses . . . I am more at peace with my body; I actually like it; I want to celebrate it. Which poses a dilemma: How could a 'good' feminist like me want to wear 'sexy' clothes — the clothes of the 'oppressor'? But aren't I being a good feminist by being happy with what I've got? And then there's that other age-old taunt to consider: 'Well, what else does she expect, dressing that way? She asks for it.' I know this body politics is older than I am, but I'm learning, first hand, that it's not only how we dress, but also our body shapes — whether they are deemed 'ugly' or 'beautiful' by society — that can be a liability to us as women teachers.

As a young, female high-school teacher, I was conscious of the fact that I couldn't wear whatever I pleased, especially with my curves and nice legs. I like dressing — it is a way for me to express myself; it is a creative outlet. *When I was a student, the majority of my teachers looked dowdy, boring, or sloppy — especially the men. I had no intention of conforming to that dull stereotype of teacher. I liked looking good for my students. The girls, especially, complimented me on what I wore; my shoes were often of particular interest. Likewise, I'd ask them questions about their styles, clothes, where they got their nose pierced, and so on, just as I'd ask them how they were feeling, what was new in their life, what was important to them. That familiarity was just one aspect of my whole relationship with them; it was part of being human, of sharing our lives. It was about being known, being real.*

Because I was always conscious of my breasts, I didn't (couldn't — by whose standards?) wear body suits and jeans to school, clothing I find not only flattering on me, but extremely comfortable. If I did wear anything form-fitting, I always wore a blazer or loose shirt over it. I tried to downplay my breasts (not an easy task). It wasn't so much the thought that certain clothes might be considered 'inappropriate', but that somehow my breasts, in and of themselves, were inappropriate (God forbid a teacher should have large breasts). Somehow, my WOMAN-shape, my FEMALE sexuality would undermine my 'authority'.

On a couple of occasions during my teaching career, I was whistled at by male students while supervising in the halls. I saw each instance as a 'teaching moment' and went over to the young men in question and kindly told them their actions were inappropriate (because I was a 'teacher' which they could understand). I would then explain why many women are not flattered by being whistled at (at this they were confused and surprised). Finally, I would escort them to the VP's office to 'report the incident'. Why? Did I need a 'higher' authority to validate my own? Did I need the authority of a man *in a position of power? The VP was understanding but didn't really comprehend the social/political issues involved. It was just something you didn't do to a* teacher, *an authority figure. I think for him to have seen me — a woman and a teacher — as sexualized was disconcerting. As a teacher, in a hallway full of students, I'd been reduced to a sexual object. I knew I could not let these incidents go; it would undermine my authority (credibility) as a teacher. In the 'real' world, I would either have ignored the whistle, or shouted back some obscenity. But, as a teacher, I couldn't do that, and the young men weren't 'some assholes' on the street; they were kids, in a school, who thought they were complimenting me . . . Or perhaps they were politicized enough to know they were reducing me — and other women — to sex objects.*

In my third year of teaching, a friend and colleague who held an administrative position, suggested that my 'classroom management' might be better if I dressed more conservatively, tied my long curly hair back, and wore fewer jangly bracelets and dangling earrings, which were labelled 'distractions'. However, it wasn't until my fourth and final year of teaching that I really and truly understood just how much my woman-body and the way I clothed it could be a liability to me as a teacher.

Even as I write this, feelings of guilt/shame surface. What will readers think of me? Will I be seen as 'unprofessional'? I want to defend myself and remind readers that I didn't dress provocatively when I taught. I want to say that I didn't do anything to deserve what happened. Nonetheless, the same old question still arises: What did I do to bring on being stalked by a male student, one I'd never even taught?

This student had noticed me, noticed my breasts, my sexuality, but not in a healthy, sane way. I'd become a sex object in a sick boy's fantasy; I'd joined the ranks of all those other women who've been stalked by men; I'd become a statistic, a victim. I was human. I was female. I was vulnerable. It didn't seem to matter that I was and am strong, that I stand firm in my feminist beliefs, that I pressed charges, that I took our new sexual harassment policy — one I helped design — for a 'test-drive' and that I refused to see myself as 'victim' (I'd say, 'He's picked the wrong person to fuck with'). Why then, do I still wonder what I had done/shown to deserve this. (Written by Jo, a high school teacher)

In studying herself, Jo raises a number of key questions: How do we look at ourselves being looked at in a classroom? How do the conventions of the classroom preclude certain actions we might take in 'real life' (for example, wearing body suits and jeans)? How do deep-running emotions such as guilt and shame figure into our gendered and intellectualized self-images as women, teachers, or feminists? Are we complicit in the victimization of women even as we struggle against seeing ourselves that way? It is hard to overestimate the power of contradictory social mores to keep us in a perpetual state of dissonance!

Buried in Jo's story of being figuratively undressed and literally targeted because of her body, are other important notes, such as pleasure, desire, and sensuality. Jo enjoys fashion; it is a creative mode of self-expression for her, an extension of her aesthetic sensibilities and sensuality. In reaction to the dowdy teachers she herself had as a student, she 'dresses well', to please both herself and her students. Moreover, we see that it is not only the male students who notice and appreciate her appearance — the girls do too. A taste for fashion and style becomes a common meeting ground of desire that teacher and students share as part of a relationship. As Jo puts it, '*That familiarity was just one aspect of my whole relationship with them; it was part of being human, of sharing our lives. It was about being known, being real.*'

And the stalker? Even while her intellect is urging her not to see herself as his victim, Jo's emotions lead her to question and reproach herself. How are we to interpret and use Jo's story? Even more importantly, how will Jo use her own story?

The next case, about a university lecturer in commerce named Ellen, suggests that in light of restrictive social codes, there is very little Jo could have done that would have made a difference.

Case 7: Ellen: The day the heat went on: Double standards

[. . .] Ellen worked hard to prepare herself to make a good impression on the group. 'It sounds trivial,' she smiled, 'but women must worry about wardrobe in these public situations. If you look too frilly, you come across as an airhead;

but if you look too severe, you're a schoolmarm. There's another aspect to dress here, too. Most of the male teachers begin class by removing their jackets and rolling up their shirtsleeves. Women can't do that because shedding an article of clothing in front of sixty students in an amphitheatre might seem perilously close to some sort of striptease. I can't imagine any image less likely to bolster authority!'

The day the heat went on was a day in early April of her first year teaching at Fleming, during the third week of the Finance course. Ellen had worn a typically conservative outfit: dark skirt, high-necked white blouse, woollen tweed blazer. Unfortunately, by afternoon, the weather had turned unexpectedly warm. At 1:00 P.M. when she entered their classroom, Ellen noticed her LG VI students were all 'casually' dressed; several were in running shorts. It was instantly apparent to Ellen that somehow the heat in their classroom had been turned on by mistake. Ellen got about fifteen minutes into the discussion before beginning to feel extremely uncomfortable. She was putting a student's key points on the board when 'the temperature felt as if it had gotten up near 90°. The students were all slumping. I was trying to listen to the speaker, but I, too, was beginning to succumb to the incredibly cloying atmosphere. That room was always stuffy. Now it was dizzyingly hot'. As the student continued, Ellen stepped back from the board, shrugged out of her blazer as unobtrusively as possible, and turned to drape it over the chair that stood behind the instructor's desk near the blackboard. Then she turned to walk back to the board. As soon as her back was turned, the wolf-whistle rang out from the top row, where, Ellen knew, a bunch of drinking buddies sat together. (Hansen, 1995, pp. 134–5, italics added)

In the simple act of removing a jacket, a scholar and business professional finds herself reduced in her students' eyes (in her eyes?) to generic woman-as-sex-object, despite the high-necked blouse.

Flugel (1966) suggests that styles of dress and elements of appearance act to summon distinct feelings that enhance role performance and increase one's sense of importance. Accessories and choice of clothes can help project a visual image in which a person's appearance is augmented by elements that extend the body's reach. For instance, wielding a pointer, wearing glasses, or carrying a briefcase literally increase a teacher's physical ability to control the environment, and, according to Flugel's theory, enhance his or her sense of power and identity. Traditionally associated with a serious, professional, 'male' world, these items, when used by women, become borrowed symbols. However, the power they accord is likewise borrowed, and can be taken away as easily as it was assumed. Ellen had, in effect, chosen a serious, 'male' piece of clothing (her jacket) to ensure her students' respect. However, she soon realized that the apparent respect of some students was superficial. Had a similarly dressed male lecturer removed his jacket, it is highly unlikely he would have been subjected to catcalls. It's the undressing of a female that transforms the situation — the woman-body beneath the clothes is vulnerable.

Coming right after Jo's story, Ellen's is particularly telling. Would dressing differently have been of any help to Jo? Ellen's story features a female

Stone Soup

by Jan Eliot

Figure 4.6 Stone Soup

academic dressed very conservatively in a high-necked business blouse getting the same type of reactions from a few of her male students. Perhaps Jo could have experimented more with her style of dressing, removing the jangly jewelry or tying back her hair, but her curves are *her*. Moreover, Jo made it quite clear that although she was stylish, she did not wear tight-fitting clothes in the classroom. Ellen's experience suggests that changing one's style of dressing doesn't necessarily help to deflect socialized tendencies to ignore women's intellectual power by calling attention to their bodies. Even if their intentions were to compliment her, Ellen's students were able to negate her intellectual power (at least momentarily) by treating her 'whole self' as a sex object.

Female teachers' bodies are subjected to gazes that are filtered through ingrained prevailing stereotypes that suggest that one cannot be a woman (sexual) and a professional (intellectual) at the same time. While one could perhaps imagine an ideal culture in which an appreciation for people's sexual attractiveness does not interfere with respect for their intellect or 'whole self', the social reality that Jo and Ellen face makes such possibilities seem very elusive. Being a woman is too often a handicap to gaining professional respect because of the simplistic but deep-rooted images that depict the female body as a distraction or threat to the male mind. These ingrained images and associations are outdated but pervasive myths that won't go away easily.

Sex and the Male Teacher's Body

It is not only women who are the targets of cultural myths. Male teachers, too, are burdened with the 'excess baggage' of negative stereotypes associated with male sexuality and teaching. Unlike female teachers, whose bodies are more likely to be regulated through dress codes or abused both literally or figuratively, male teachers are more likely to be typecast as villainous perpetrators of sexual offences and perversions. Sexual abuse becomes equated with contradictory and false, but nonetheless ingrained, cultural attitudes that 'all male attention to children or women is suspect'. The following case demonstrates how such attitudes are perpetuated.

Case 8: The music teacher: Why Jennifer had to go to Switzerland

> *We all envied the girls who were in the senior high school band, not because of their instruments or because they got to miss boring study periods for band practice, but because they got to spend many long hours with Mr. Peterson, the drop-dead gorgeous (and married) young music teacher. Not only was he handsome and sexy, he liked to joke around a lot, and would flirt with his students and make them feel special, especially the girls. He usually had a 'favourite', someone he might even take out for a coke or something. But we all liked to drool (swoon) over him.*
>
> *One year, his favourite was Jennifer, a blonde-haired senior who was as smart as she was beautiful and popular. Rumours soon started that she was romantically involved with Mr. Peterson, that they had been spotted holding hands in a nightclub. In hushed and deliciously scandalized tones, it was whispered that they were sleeping together — this was the fifties, an era when 'going all the way' was a term whose meaning was still a bit vague for many girls who thought of necking as being the height of naughtiness. The rumours became more and more persistent, especially after Jennifer left the school abruptly 'to attend a finishing school in Switzerland'. It was said that Mr. Peterson had gotten her pregnant ('knocked her up') and that she had been sent away by her parents for an illegal abortion or possibly to have the baby and give it up for adoption overseas. I never learned if those rumours were true, and I quite forgot about them until many many years later when I read in the local newspaper that a music teacher had been accused of what today we label sexual harassment.* (Written by a female high school teacher just before her retirement)

We see in the above case how the onlookers, the tellers of the story, took apparent delight in viewing the music teacher and Jennifer through an erotic and luridly sexual lens. We don't even know if the story is true. It may be part of those naughty myths and speculations that young and old love to shock each other with, imaginative expressions of desire and possibility. Nonetheless, the story does raise issues of serious abuse of power and sexual misconduct. It supports cultural stereotypes of heterosexual males as potential sexual predators (a fate they share with gay teachers), of blondes as flirtatious sexpots who are asking for it, and of school girls as innocent prey who secretly enjoy being preyed upon. Such titillating stereotypes can provoke extreme reactions that make matters worse by condemning desire and sexuality *per se*, ultimately covering over the possibilities for discussion of what sexuality might otherwise mean to teachers and students.

The 'no touching' policy ostensibly applies to all teachers, but in practice, it particularly targets men. Even though there are incidents of female teachers also exploiting students sexually, it is the male teacher-body that is most often brought under suspicion in the areas of sexual misconduct and abuse. Moreover, as Robert's story suggested, it is male teachers of young children, in particular, who are subjected to severe scrutiny. This situation could discourage men from entering or remaining in elementary schools and can make life very stressful or tricky for those who do. What are the implications for children? Consider the following statement made by a male elementary pre-service teacher who is quoted in an article by Richard Johnson (1997):

> Children need the gift of touch, they need to feel wanted and most of all they need to feel valued. But I'm male, and part of my teaching code prevents me from showing the care that I often want to show . . . Recently, while I was on practicum, a young boy came up to me and gave me a hug. I just froze, my mind racing a million miles an hour. Do I hug him back? If I do, is that taking the student-teacher relationship too far? Why shouldn't I be able to give him a hug? Why should I even have to think about all this stuff? (p. 103)

The frustration this future teacher feels is not an isolated example, and might be taken as an indication of how social policies intended to protect children may in practice deprive both children and teachers of the very things they need to thrive in a learning environment: trust, caring and connection. But that does not mean that there is no need for teachers to question and reflect on their actions.

The next case, written by a male high school teacher, takes us further into the difficulties of negotiating questions of sexual propriety in the classroom, reminding us that sexual misconduct is not necessarily only a question of teacher-touch, and affirming the need for us to question our motives and our actions.

Case 9: When good intentions aren't enough

Her name was Rosa, and I was her teacher. Strikingly pretty, she struggled over texts easily managed by an able fourth-grader. But Rosa was 15, and a member of my Title I remedial English group in an inner-city high school in Northern California. She sat in my third-period class with a permanent scowl on her face, expressing her discomfort to Luis and Carlos, the two other native Spanish speakers in the group. To me, she said little except for curt inquiries about her grades and what she needed to do to avoid an F.

Rosa lived in a Spanish world. She spoke Spanish at home, at her job in a taqueria, with her friends, and, prior to her freshman year in high school, in her public school classes in Southern California. Rosa considered English an intrusion, a trial to be endured . . .

After my first few weeks at the school, I diagnosed the problem as one of relevance — what intelligent person in his or her right mind could get motivated by reading about the production of paper in British Columbia or the habits of beavers in Vermont? I asked my students what they were interested in, and their answers — Madonna, AC/DC, Kiss, Prince — made up my mind. I knew it! To hell with basal readers; bring on Rolling Stone,

Tiger Beat, *and, in a pitch of daring, the issue of* Time *with the 'Private Life of Michael Jackson' emblazoned on the cover.*

. . . As the year wore on, . . . I sensed that books and texts — indeed, the whole act of reading — were instrumental to them. They represented something to do to get something else, like a driver's license or a passport. Sneaking a book underneath the covers with a miniature flashlight and savoring the stillness of a house in slumber was a world foreign to my students. Most of all to Rosa. Nothing I did seemed to reach her. When I tried speaking Spanish, she muttered derisively, tortuga, *turtle.*

Undaunted, I kept trying. I brought in articles about Madonna, her idol, and I encouraged her as she stumbled over the simplest sentences. Sometimes she would really try, usually with a brush in her hand to let me know that reading would not get in the way of her grooming, but I didn't care. I was pleased by any sign of progress.

I have always valued teachers who are genuinely interested in their students, who learn their names quickly, who are aware of day-to-day changes in their students' lives. One morning, Rosa came to the group with a new hairdo. Instead of straight jet-black hair flowing down onto her shoulders, she wore it up, in carefully crafted curls.

What I said was innocent enough: 'I really like your hair, Rosa'. I wanted to let her know that she was not just any student, but an individual, someone I could compliment not just on her reading but on other things as well. It was a nicety, a social grace, a well-meaning way of letting her know that I noticed.

Soon afterward, Rosa began cutting class. In the hallways, she averted my eyes and pretended not to notice me. When I issued a 'pink warning slip' to her counselor, she showed up for class, but as soon as I asked her to read, she heaved her chair against the wall and dashed from the room in a huff. What had I done? Where had I failed? Beverly, my supervisor, also wanted to know.

Two weeks passed before Beverly told me that Rosa had been transferred to another reading group. Beverly said that she had a few questions to ask me. The Assistant Principal wanted to know whether I had ever said or done anything that might have led Rosa to thinking that I had any 'non-educational' (a delicate way of saying prurient) interest in her.

Me?! A pedophile? . . . Come off it! Beverly's questions became more pointed. Was it not true that I had mentioned to Rosa that I liked her hair, that I had said that I liked her blouse? Well, yes, but it was a ploy, part of an effort to personalize the classroom, to make it a more humane place. Was I aware, Beverly asked, of what it means for an older man to remark to a 15-year-old Roman Catholic Chicana from a traditional home that he 'likes her hair?' But I was only trying to . . . No, I didn't know. Given my background, how could I have known?

This story is true. Although I was unable to help Rosa, I did get a glimpse of the complexity of cultures in conflict. We bring to the classroom a freight of cultural assumptions — assumptions so deeply embedded that it can take an incident as unexpected as this to shock us into an awareness of our differences. 'Innocent' and 'well-meaning' are truly in the eyes of the beholder. (Wineburg, 1995, abridged from pp. 161–3)

The teacher who wrote the above account was willing to depict himself in an unfavourable light, if necessary, in an effort to increase and share his self-knowledge and professional understanding. This act demonstrates the sort of professional attitude that facilitates self-study. The case also reminds us that touching is not the only way teachers and students express and sometimes misunderstand each other's desires. Wineburg's experience is especially relevant in light of the worries voiced earlier by male teachers who may feel they are automatically under suspicion as potential abusers. Failure to acknowledge and examine these issues in professional self-study may increase the likelihood of misunderstanding and abuse.

'How could I have known?' Wineburg asks. It is important for all of us to ponder that question. Such a question cannot be posed in the absence of a consideration of both the social and legal implications of our pedagogy. Moreover, specific local context and cultural norms will weigh heavily in assessing appropriate ways to express teacher love. The answer may not be simple.

Constructed Sexuality

Litvak, to whom we referred earlier, tells this next story about a gay teacher whom he remembers from childhood. He recalls finding the story of this teacher's sexual orientation 'titillating' — being regarded as possibly gay automatically locates the teacher within an eroticized space. But then simply being a man or woman does that as well, as we have seen in so many of the stories cited in this chapter.

The French Lesson

Near the end of my career [as a student] in junior high school, I heard a mildly titillating story about a certain teacher — a French teacher — at the high school I was to attend in the fall . . . It seemed that if you took French, as I planned to do, you might well end up in the classroom of a certain Mr. Boyer. And it seemed — here's the titillating part — that Mr. Boyer, whose name was almost too good to be true, was famous at the high school for 'liking boys'. Though it's been a long time, I'm pretty sure my gleeful informant managed to embellish his tale with suitably lurid images of lechery and molestation . . . It wasn't long, then, before I was regaling my classmates with my wickedly acute rendition of Mr. Boyer — but of a Mr. Boyer who, despite my junior high school friend's ominous assurances, spent most of his time trying to pass rather than making passes. So what my routine consisted of, essentially, was a florid amplification of all the little ways in which the notorious French teacher revealed not so much his homosexuality as his closetedness; it was a question, in short, of ruthlessly bringing out his techniques for not coming out, techniques that were thereby seen repeatedly and delectably to backfire. (Litvak, 1995, pp. 19–21)

While the story his friend told about the French teacher seemingly focuses on homosexuality as a potential source for an abuse of pedagogical power, Litvak makes quite a different point: in a sensationalistic way, the story emphasizes that '*every classroom is an eroticized space*: eroticized in different ways and with different effects, depending on the sex and gender of the students, but eroticized nonetheless — *even or especially when the teacher goes strictly by the book and when nothing recognizably erotic takes place in that classroom*' (p. 19, italics added).

We have included Litvak's account of a gay teacher here for a variety of reasons, not the least of which is the fact that what happens on the margins is less familiar, often more discomforting, usually most easily ignored or denied — but at the same time more likely to be discussed, albeit in reductive terms. For example, Anna, a young lesbian teacher, told us about her experience of going to student services on campus for counselling about an issue that had nothing to do with her teaching. Upon learning that she was lesbian and a teacher, the counsellor's first words of advice were, '*You know you can't get involved with your students!*'

We agree with Deborah Britzman's (1995) contention that homosexuality and heterosexuality are each defined in terms of the other, and that *all* teachers could achieve a deeper understanding of both their students and themselves if they were more familiar with the fields of gay, lesbian, gender, and queer studies. As she notes:

> Educators would significantly benefit from acquainting themselves with the fields of gay and lesbian studies, not because it would access some distant other, but more immediately, reading gay and lesbian scholarship, representations, and expressions might compel a second look at *one's own constructed* sexuality and a different look at what it is that structures how the sexuality of another is imagined. (p. 88, italics added)

To the benefit of all teachers, a discourse community has emerged which has begun to closely examine (homo)sexuality in the context of teaching. Examples include Kissen's *The Last Closet: The Real Lives of Lesbian and Gay Teachers* (1996); Jennings' *One Teacher in Ten* (1994); Tobin's *Making a Place for Pleasure in Early Childhood Education* (1997), and Khayatt's *Lesbian Teachers: An Invisible Presence* (1992). The growing body of scholarship in this area could contribute to reducing the strength of heteronormativity and might encourage all teachers to consider how their sexuality is constructed and played out within their professional milieu.

Britzman's call for teachers to look at issues of constructed sexuality is particularly useful in that it offers a strategic entry point for investigating the significance of sexuality in teaching. In box 4.6, we invite teachers to consider hypothetical questions as guides to thinking about the ways that teacher sexuality is constructed socially and experienced personally.

Box 4.6

Constructed Teacher Sexuality

1 How does knowing that a teacher is straight enter into discussions about teaching? Under what circumstances?

2 How does knowing that a teacher is gay, lesbian or bisexual enter into a discussion around teaching? Under what circumstances?

3 What essential difference would it make to learn that a teaching colleague whom you had never thought of as anything but straight is gay, lesbian or bisexual?

4 What essential difference would it make to learn that a teaching colleague whom you had always thought of as gay, lesbian or bisexual is heterosexual?

5 Watch the movie *The Children's Hour* and the much more recent movie *In & Out*. What are your reactions to each? Who do you relate to? In what ways do these films address your professional milieu? Discuss them with other teachers.

When we first proposed the activities listed in box 4.6, some non-gay and non-lesbian teachers indicated that they did not like being referred to as 'straight' — they felt it made them sound as though they were 'self-righteous', or 'following the straight and narrow', whereas to be homosexual was to be radical, marginal or, in some social circles, avant-garde. When the term 'heterosexual' was suggested, they didn't like that much either. They admitted that they were not used to the idea of being defined in terms of their sexuality at all — regardless of what the appropriate term might be. Right away then, the prompt served to raise questions about the ways that sexuality is socially constructed. The questions were part of the answer.

The Body Electric: Eros and Teacher Love

'*You know you can't get involved with your students*'. What does it mean to get involved with your students? Can it mean loving them? Caring for them? Being concerned for them? Knowing them? What is teacher love? Is there any such thing? When is it too much? How do we separate teacher love from . . . what? Abuse of power? Pathological love?

We start with the idea of 'the body electric', a term that Marni Koerner (1992) takes from Walt Whitman's collection of poems, *Leaves of Grass* (1936). Whitman writes of singing the body electric, describing the individual body, what it means to be embodied, and how through our bodies we 'sing' feelings of intensity, depth, and possibility. Koerner (1992) extends Whitman's image to the collective body of the classroom:

> In my experience as a teacher, and in my role as parent/teacher to my own children, I know what it feels like to get to that special 'teachable moment'. I know what it is like to tell a story when people are listening with rapt attention. More than listening; they are understanding and are on the same wavelength . . . There is a feeling of being caught up in the moment, of being a part of a single experience that culminates in a light bulb turning on, a click sounding, a bell ringing — what some teachers describe as the 'uh-huh' moment. The teachers I talked with had these feelings too. I call this theme 'creators of the body electric.' . . . The metaphor of the body electric captures both the idea of the collective body of students and teacher and the rapport and communication that can flow among them. (p. 47)

Sandra's photo essay cited earlier in this chapter also evoked a little of this 'body electric'. In her memory there was a feeling of connection and excitement among herself and her students. Her recollections of her students were filled with affection, even love. Robert too expressed his fondness for his kindergarten students, one that extended into touching or physical proximity, such as letting them lean against him as he read to them and so forth. Madeleine Grumet's account was also infused with a deep caring for her university students — an emotion which shrouded itself in the comfort of her green robe. And what of the male early childhood teachers we have cited who would like to be able to show affection towards their students, but are afraid to? What kind of love are all these teachers expressing?

At their best, teaching and learning are grounded in and sustained by passion, pleasure, and desire. It is easy to 'read' the passion Sandra felt in teaching her grade 3 class. Her passion fuelled her desire to teach according to her convictions, and perhaps even blinded her to others' perceptions. Sometimes it is love that gets us into teaching in the first place. The following comments made by a beginning teacher underscore the positive impact of love and pleasure on learning:

> *My history teacher, Mr. S., truly was the catalyst for my interest in the teaching profession as well as the match that lit my fiery passion for European history . . . Mr. S. ran his classroom in a very organized fashion but the desks were not in rows. We sat in a circle . . . He was so full of knowledge (much of it first hand) about European history that he did not have to refer to notes or anything — he would just tell us stories off the top of his head. Mr. S. had lived in many countries throughout Europe, but I believe that he was born in Russia. He was the first teacher to ever make me feel as though I was as*

> *intelligent as the other students in the class. He used to encourage me to talk in class and he seemed to really value what I had to say . . . He was a very kind and intelligent man as well as an excellent teacher.* (Comments made on the back of a drawing done by a female pre-service high school teacher)

In his book *The Passionate Life* (1983), Sam Keen urges readers to remember that in its earliest conception 'erotic potency was not confined to sexual power but included the moving force that propelled every life-form from a state of mere potentiality to actuality' (p. 5, cited in hooks, 1993, p. 60).

As McWilliam and Jones note in *Eros and Pedagogical Bodies: The State of (non)affairs* (in McWilliam and Taylor, 1996), a teacher can display, through language, deed and gesture,

> what it means to be passionate about knowing, to desire to know, and a student who, having gazed upon this display, imitates but goes on to do much more, to develop her own passionate love affair with a larger body of knowledge . . . Teachers' anatomical bodies can be demonstrated to be so important as 'sights' or 'bodies' of knowledge. (McWilliam and Jones, 1996, p. 135)

Teachers in love with a subject, topic, or book exemplify for their students the intrinsic links between thought and feeling, mind and body. However quietly or subtly, body language communicates the excitement that ideas can generate, the passion that knowledge can instill, and what it means to learn through our senses. It can also let students know that at least some teachers are aware of the sensations, pain, and pleasure that our bodies afford us:

> When powerful teaching evokes exciting learning in confined spaces, desire is mobilized in both teachers and learners, and this is not contained as a purely intellectual response. The body is animated, elated by the experience of powerful pedagogical moments . . . If teaching-as-usual is unpleasant, dull and restrictive, then 'good', exciting, motivating teaching is erotic, passionate, dangerous, and evokes body-pleasure. (ibid, p. 128)

For many students, from kindergarten through university, a pleasurable aspect or phase of schooling is loving favourite teachers, developing a kind of romantic 'crush' on them, and according them great importance in their lives. There is an innocent (and sometimes not so innocent) sensual flavour to students' recollections of favourite teachers of both the same and opposite sex, and a pure pleasure of shared experience — sharing each other's company, ideas, viewpoints, knowledge, feelings.

Teacher–student love is not often one-sided. Teachers can and do develop close emotional bonds with some of their students. Consider this account from Grace, an elementary school teacher:

> *I love some of my students, not in a sexual way, really, but in a sensual or spiritual way. They have the power to brighten my day, break my heart, worry*

*or exasperate me, make me sad, or make me smile just because of who they
are. They matter to me. Sometimes I have a natural impulse to fondly tousle
a youngster's head, or pat on the back a kid who seems to need reassurance
or even hug a child as a sign of my affection or approval. Would it be wrong
to act on these impulses? Is part of why I became a teacher due to my need to
love and be loved, to feel and share the pleasure of relationship in learning?
Is that bad?* (Excerpt from a journal kept during a professional development
seminar)

The questions Grace asks of herself are hard to ask and even
harder to answer. For one thing, they are bound up in serious debates about
the appropriateness of teachers touching students, a concern we raised earlier
in different ways. Focusing on the positive aspects of love and pleasure does
not mean dismissing concerns about the dangers.

Distinguishing Pedagogical Love From Pathological Nurturance

Grace's journal draws our attention to issues around teaching such as nurtur-
ing and caring. The stereotype of primary teacher as maternal feminizes the
staffing of elementary schools, discouraging men who wish to teach at that level.
But women too suffer from the tyranny of this stereotype. Valerie Walkerdine
(1990), for example, explores what she calls the 'pathological nurturance' that
can evolve from women's enculturation into an ethos of self-sacrifice that
confuses caring with submission and self-effacement. Is Grace bordering on a
pathological form of caring? To address this issue, she would have to continue
her self-study to focus on the specifics of her situation, the frequency and
intensity of her feelings, how she interacts with her students, and how her
feelings are situated in the context of her whole life, important questions in
self-study.

Perhaps, however, Grace is simply voicing what many teachers
experience — moments of intense relationship that highlight the pleasure of
teaching and give impetus to student learning. Maybe her feelings are simply a
form of what Nell Noddings (cited in Johnson, 1997) calls a 'caring encounter',
a pedagogical touching of encouragement, warmth, and relationship.

Alternatively, perhaps Grace really *is* too needy, and too willing to
turn over to her students the power to control her happiness. Carolyn Steedman
(1987) reflects provocatively on a type of teacher love that can be viewed as
self-imprisonment. Starting with Simone de Beauvoir's famous statement that
the bearing of children is the quickest and surest route to a woman's enslave-
ment, Steedman writes of her own experience as an elementary teacher, showing how, like all aspects of pedagogy, teacher love is experienced bodily:

> I know that you do not need to bear children in order to have them. As in
> most primary school classrooms, they rarely left me. We stayed together in
> one room most of the day long . . . I didn't know what was happening to me.

My body died during those years, the little fingers that caught my hand, the warmth of a child leaning and reading her book to me somehow prevented all the other meeting of bodies . . . I never left them: they occupied the night-times, all my dreams. I was very tired, bone-achingly tired all the time. I was unknowingly, covertly expected to become a mother, and I unknowingly became one, pausing only in the cracks of the dark night to ask: what is happening to me? . . . Children make you retreat behind the glass, *lose yourself in the loving mutual gaze. The sensuality of their presence prevents the larger pleasures*: the company of children keeps you a child. (pp. 126–7, italics added)

Steedman then imagines an alternative scenario:

Or: there is the other way. She moves from her desk to the window, looks down at the yard, the gates, the streets, the fields beyond; *smooths an eyebrow with a finger, corrects the setting of a belt.* She thinks of: not being here, of love, a houseful of furniture, of marriage, *the meeting of bodies, a new winter coat.* The children's murmur rises behind her; she turns to quiet them, and they bow their heads to their books in obedience . . . She is a woman liberated, a woman who has escaped all our fate: she is a woman who is not a mother, *a woman who does not care: a woman who has refused to mother.* (p. 119, italics added)

Steedman speculates that one of the most interesting aspects of the history of classroom life may be 'an overt and bored resistance displayed towards a set of ideas — an official pedagogy — a resistance displayed by women who have refused to take on the structures of maternal thinking in the classroom' (ibid, p. 124). In other words, to some teachers, there is concern that the bodies of children can make the teacher body a maternal one exclusively, limiting and confining the teacher to a partial or stifling life dependent almost solely on interacting with students. Her words also acknowledge what we were discussing earlier — the sensual, embodied nature of teaching. Both confinement and liberation are felt with our 'whole selves'.

But as we saw in Madeleine Grumet's essay, teacher love does not have to be pathological. Indeed our contention is that more often that not, it takes the form of a pedagogical caring and concern — one that respects both students and teacher in mutually beneficial and satisfying ways, facilitating learning and growth for all. We are referring to the sort of caring and commitment that Nel Noddings (1984) describes in *Caring: A Feminine Approach to Ethics and Moral Education* or that Jane Roland Martin (1992) writes about in *The Schoolhome: Rethinking Schools for Changing Families* or the thoughtful tact that Max Van Manen (1986) evokes in *The Tact of Teaching.* These scholars maintain that love of students *per se* is not enough to make a good teacher — the quality, form and expression of that love matter a great deal. When it is 'pedagogical', a teacher's love includes enthusiasm for a subject or topic, a passion for learning, an ability to listen carefully, and a commitment to students, self and others. It is always embodied. Being able to identify and reflect on the way we 'love' as teachers is a signpost of professional commitment.

How do we have discussions about topics that have always been taboo? Who breaks the silence? What are the consequences of breaking the silence? Our aim is to encourage a discourse for professional self-study around the body, appearance, love, sexuality, and pleasure. Like the toddler Jonathan, quoted at the beginning of this chapter, we want to see (study) our whole selves, and agree with the following statement made by Tobin (1997):

> Suppressed desire, victimization, and heteronormativity characterizes contemporary research, theory, and practice in . . . education. Ignorance, inattention, fear and hostility to pleasure and desire are diminishing the quality of life for young children and their teachers. Scholarship . . . has failed to challenge the mean-spirited misinformed, morally panicked public discourses that are distorting how we care for and teach young children. To turn these dynamics around, we need to shift the terms of the argument. Pleasure and desire, now banished to the dark recesses of early childhood educational theory and practice, need to be brought to the fore. (p. 2)

Tobin's comments about early childhood education apply equally to other contexts for teaching. Where are the stories written by former students who feel that their teachers provided positive models or guidance for coming to terms with their own sexuality and identity? And what about current students? Is there any safe and appropriate context in which their views and stories can be heard? What of the body and its pleasures within the classroom? When and how can we include pleasure in the curriculum? Where are the acknowledgments that a slight but unmistakably erotic charge suffused a particular class, semester or moment with a pleasure that became integral to learning that neither student nor teacher would willingly forgo? Where are the stories about teachers or students struggling with inappropriate attractions, dealing with them, using them for good or bad purposes? When, where, and how will we tell those stories? In scanning the programs of teaching conferences and the lists of new publications, we are encouraged to see that these stories are not quite as rare as they used to be. We have only begun to take pleasure, desire, and sexuality seriously in self-study. We have barely begun to recognize, celebrate, and interrogate the teacher and student body electric.

In the next chapter, we turn our attention to one arena where teachers' bodies, clothing, love, and eros *are* on public display: the teacher movies and books of popular culture. Does the popularity of these texts depend on their ability to tap into and romanticize the real life desires and fantasies that people experience, but are not allowed to discuss, except in a fictional context?

Chapter 5

Reel to Real: Popular Culture and Teacher Identity

> You trying to figure me out? Here let me help you . . . I've seen the same fucking movies you have, man. (Emilio, a high school student to his teacher, Miss Johnson, in the movie *Dangerous Minds*, 1995)

Although we may not like his street language, the teenaged Emilio shows remarkable insight in recognizing what his teacher does not — the influence popular culture has on her efforts to 'save' him. Educated like most of us in the cultural school of popular images, he sees through her attempts to 'psych him out', and identifies the likely source of both her actions and his critical awareness: 'the same fucking movies'.

The knowledge and images embedded in popular culture might be taken as common ground, regardless if people agree or not on its value or significance. Studying it carefully might initially seem a safe enough detour from self-study since popular images offer the comfort of distance — they are not as closely personal, for example, as the school photographs we discussed in chapter 3. The perceived distance between what's 'out there' and our inner sense of self can be useful, enabling us to relax our guard. It is easier to be critical of a fictitious teacher than we could otherwise be of ourselves or our colleagues. And yet, if we persevere and probe the popular in the service of self-study, we eventually find that this initial distancing can be turned as a social spotlight on our private teaching selves, helping us to understand and even act on how we are shaped and situated by the popular.

Popular Teachers

I was only two years out of high school myself when I first saw *To Sir With Love* . . . I marvelled at the heady freedom Sir seemed to be offering: Rather than continuing to plod through the boring exercises of the prescribed high school curriculum, Sir suggested that they use class time to talk seriously about life. In a dramatic act of rebellion, he flung the school textbooks into the wastebasket, saying 'Those are out. They are useless to you.' Oh, how I wished I had a teacher like Mark Thackeray when I was in high school, someone who recognized the dull, lifeless nature of the official curriculum that was uncaringly and unrelentingly force-fed to us hour after hour, day after day . . . For me, at that time, the movie offered a seductive glimpse of

possibilities: schooling as meaningful, as connected with life, work aspirations, even love and romance — subjects much on the mind of adolescent
girls . . . I remember identifying with Sir as he battled with cynical teachers,
prejudice and ignorance, ultimately rejecting a much more prestigious career
as an engineer for the love of teaching, for the love of children. Romantic!?
Heady stuff?! Prior to seeing the movie, I had never even considered a career
in teaching, but I did not forget that film. It lingered somewhere in the sedi-
mentary collage of images that form the inchoate, primary material for thinking and feeling. (Weber and Mitchell, 1995, pp. 137–8)

The above excerpt was written by Weber reflecting on her reactions decades earlier to the movie *To Sir With Love*, a film that was based on
the autobiographical novel written in 1959 by engineer/teacher E.R. Braithwaite
about his first year's teaching experience in an inner city high school in London.
Almost 30 years later, we meet another beginner. LouAnne Johnson is hired to
teach English in a special academy program for underachieving teenagers in
an American inner city high school. Like Braithwaite, in her efforts to reach
and help her students, she has some very gripping and powerful teaching
experiences which she relates in a readable and moving book, *My Posse Don't
Do Homework*. The book sells enough copies to be widely available in paper-
back, read not only by teachers, but also by the general public. The writing is
clear and effective, featuring dialogue that helps you 'see' and 'hear' the characters, most of whom are probably dramatized and romanticized composites
from her real-life experience, although one can never be sure about such things.

Depicting her students and herself as fallible, uncertain, but highly
appealing heroes, Johnson describes the foibles and faux pas of her rather
unorthodox pedagogy. This includes buying things for her students out of her
own pocket, bailing them out of sticky situations with the police, ignoring
school rules when she finds them inappropriate, taking her class on unusual
field trips, finding out the hard way that she is ignorant of the 'street code' that
guides her students' actions, and giving them all an A to start the semester, an
A that is theirs 'to lose' or to keep.

Some teachers might shake their heads in disapproval at certain of
Johnson's actions. But many readers, especially prospective or beginning teachers,
cannot help identifying with the character 'Miss Johnson', empathizing with
her frustrations and cheering each triumph in her efforts to help students. She
is a flawed but tough and well-meaning hero for the 90s, one who seemingly
bucks the system for the sake of her students and struggles to survive in a
tumultuous and sometimes overwhelming personal and professional world.

Johnson's written account spreads further into contemporary popular
culture when the book is rescripted, embellished, and dramatized as a slick,
hip Hollywood movie, *Dangerous Minds,* featuring superstar Michelle Pfeiffer
as 'Miss Johnson'. To the beat of its 'cool' rap sound track, the film demonizes
school administrators who are portrayed as uncaring, mean, and cowardly
bureaucrats and bullies. The movie version of Miss Johnson is a neophyte — a
vulnerable, yet strong and determined saviour of her stereotyped black and

Hispanic students. The film increases and heightens the book's violence and eliminates some of its nuances, imposing a classic 'teacher story' narrative on the snapshot vignette format of the original *My Posse Don't Do Homework*. *Dangerous Minds* is widely discussed and reviewed. It has arrived.

The movie is such a commercial success that the book is reissued using the movie title, *Dangerous Minds*, to replace the original. Various spin-offs emerge. For example, the motion picture soundtrack sells well in CD and cassette versions. American television executives, always on the look-out for potential hit programs, buy a one-hour weekly television drama series, *Dangerous Minds,* as a vehicle for television star Annie Potts. The show is given a prime time evening slot and does well enough to last a year in the highly competitive (some might say vicious) rating wars that shelve or cancel most new shows after only a few weeks. Meanwhile, the movie version is released on videotape for both rental and purchase.

Thus, we have been describing how a teacher's *real experience* is filtered through her memory and narrative art into a book that shares her views and feelings about her teaching with a wide audience. The book is eventually adapted into several *'reel texts'* (movie, TV series episodes) that are consumed by legions of moviegoers, television audiences, record album buyers, and video renters. Consumption ('reading') of the *reel texts* becomes the *'real experience'* of prospective teachers, film buffs, teenagers, film critics, and the like. The evolution, mutation, and transposition of one teacher's experience from the text of her life to the lives of many continues. A few years after the release of the movie, many people who saw it have graduated from teacher education programs to start their own teaching career. Years from now, we can imagine them seeing the movie again, perhaps as a television re-run, and using the movie as a prompt for remembering. Perhaps this re-view will make them realize, as Weber did with *To Sir With Love*, how their perspective or 'take' on the movie has changed, or how certain of its images have silently coloured their views of teaching for years.

The Cumulative Cultural Text of 'Teacher'

The different yet connected versions of *Dangerous Minds* seep into what we call the *cumulative cultural text of teachers* (see Weber and Mitchell, 1995). A *cultural text* extends beyond the notion of written and oral texts to include artefacts, social activities, and people — all of which can be interpreted or 'read'. Some texts are broader, lengthier or more general than others. The term *cumulative cultural* text was originally coined as a way to describe the cultural significance of the longevity of such popular texts as Barbie (Mitchell and Reid-Walsh, 1995). We think it is particularly appropriate for describing the 'life' and 'after-life' of teacher texts in popular culture, providing a type of 'map' for considering how, as teachers, we 'insert ourselves' into the text of teacher, as well as how we separate ourselves from the conflicting images and stereotypes of teacher.

A series of varying Miss Johnsons blends into the multilayered repository of popular teacher images that is peopled by the generations of real and fictional teachers embodied in books, films, TV programs, comics, songs, and so forth. The composite representation of Miss Johnson takes its place amongst previous generations of film and book teachers — Miss Dove (*Good Morning Miss Dove*), Miss Brodie (*The Prime of Miss Jean Brodie*), Mr. Thackeray (*Sir*), Our Miss Brooks, Sylvia Ashton Warner (*Teacher*), Mr. Keating (*Dead Poets Society*), Mr. Escalante (*Stand and Deliver*), Miss Masembuko (*Sarafina*) to mention only a few. Mr. Holland of *Mr. Holland's Opus* joins the throng shortly thereafter. At least three other teacher films follow in the span of just one academic year. The next academic year begins with the release of yet another blockbuster, *In & Out*, about a fictional gay high school English teacher who is 'outed' to both himself and the entire television viewing world by one of his former students during an Academy Awards acceptance speech. And so it continues . . . A multitude of teacher images feeds into the popular culture into which we are born. These images overlap, contrast, amplify, address, or confirm each other as they compete for our attention. The cumulative cultural text of 'teacher' is a massive work-in-progress that embraces the sub-texts and counter-texts of generations of paintings, memoirs, novels, songs, toys, movies, software, stories, photos, and television. Although Miss Johnson is a cumulative cultural text in her own right, she is thus also part of the larger cumulative text called 'teacher'.

Like the character Miss Johnson, many teacher texts are based on the experiences of real-life teachers or former students turned authors. But popular images take on a face and life of their own that often overshadow the originals. When we picture 'Sir' in our minds, it is actor Sidney Poitier, not teacher/author Braithwaite we see. Similarly, it is Michelle Pfeiffer or Annie Potts or our own image of Miss Johnson that we see, an image that may not be true in some ways to the real Miss Johnson's original experience. Similarly, the pain of racial discrimination that Braithwaite experienced and expressed in his book is minimized in the film *To Sir With Love*. The fictional rewrites and rep-resents the real, becoming a different kind of reality for the reader/audience who experiences popular images.

The extended life enjoyed by many popular images of teachers is made possible through the same kind of variation and serialization that transformed and popularized the image of Miss Johnson into a cumulative cultural text, giving it presence, longevity, and power. Implicitly and sometimes explicitly, each television episode of *Dangerous Minds*, each portrayal of Miss Johnson, and each version of her story builds on, influences, contextualizes, and refers to the others. Together, they *constitute the cumulative text of Miss Johnson*. But this serialization into multiple texts only happens if there is something commercially viable in the initial representation — something that captures people's interest, that draws them in or addresses them in a meaningful way that sells. In other words, popular texts wouldn't *be* popular unless they managed to tap into the particular desires of many readers. In that sense, they serve as a kind of mirror for society, and have something very important to reveal to us about ourselves.

The layered sedimentation of past images is churned up every now and then by social events, permitting old teacher images to rise to the surface to be reborn and shared with a new generation. For example, some 20 years after the movie *To Sir With Love* was first released, a sequel movie was made for television, part of Hollywood's trend of recycling, rejuvenating, or revisiting images that were powerful in the past in the hope that they are still relevant and can attract new and old audiences. Contemporary popular culture subsumes not only the culture of today's children and adults, but also a myriad of images from the past which blend seamlessly and often undetected into our familiar, unquestioned everyday knowledge. And so, image-texts like *Archie* comics, television reruns (for example, *Welcome Back Kotter* or *Grange Hill*), new programs like *The Simpsons* that are watched by adults as well as children, and even toys (teacher Barbie dolls, Mattel and Playschool toys) connect generations of teachers (former children) and children (as students and future teachers), marking experience with codes and signposts that are casually shared, passed down, and assimilated in a sub-conscious, taken-for-granted manner. The resulting cumulative text is intergenerational, and gives members of a society a common frame of reference and a shared pool of expressive images to use.

In box 5.1 we identify three features of 'cumulative cultural text'.

Using Popular Teacher Images For Professional Development

What do popular teacher images have to do with teacher education or professional development? The success of books and movies like *Dangerous Minds* sets Miss Johnson up as a possible role-model for teachers, displaying, inserting, and enshrining her image in the cumulative text to be consumed by teens and adults, including practicing and future teachers. Some teachers recommend the book to each other, pass it around, and discuss it in the staff room over lunch. When the movie is available, they flock to see it, although some have told us that they are embarrassed to be seen consuming popular teacher movies, which they liken to being caught red-handed reading a tabloid. Aspiring and experienced teachers take messages of hope, fear, or scepticism from the film. Some identify with certain scenes, or question their own reality in the light of the book and movie 'fictions'. Others dismiss it cavalierly as Hollywood trash having nothing whatsoever to do with their teaching reality. But you cannot condemn what you have not noticed — negative publicity calls further attention to cultural texts. Movies and books about teachers accompany us throughout our lives whether we like it or not. They have much potential to influence:

> As a prospective teacher, I found inspiration for my practice by reading the
> popular teaching narratives of the time, books such as Sylvia Ashton-Warner's

Box 5.1

Features of Cumulative Cultural Texts

Cumulative cultural texts are:

1 *Multidimensional*: A single doll or movie or song or wedding or restaurant is a cultural text, but it is not cumulative until it has achieved the kind of popularity that leads to some sort of *spin off or serialization that gives it a multidimensional form*. As an example, the tragedy of the sinking of the *Titanic* is showing every sign of becoming a cumulative cultural text as the story becomes multidimensional: the original event, the newspaper and radio stories about it that captured the public's imagination, several movie versions, the search and location of the remains, the viewing of the relics, and so forth are multiple versions or chapters of its cumulative text. One could imagine further serializations with both cheap plastic or expensive detailed replicas of the ship becoming popular collectors' items, or Lego kits or toy series or animated cartoon or comic book versions adding their dimensions, too.

2 *Intergenerational*: Time, timing, and perhaps a kind of timelessness are required to establish a cumulative cultural text. The text must appear at a time (or within a context) that helps it capture or infiltrate the public imagination in a way that is so indelible it gets passed on by the generation that first wrote and read it to subsequent generations. This passing on can be deliberate ('Here is how to play this game') or casual and taken for granted (turning on a superhero cartoon program for the kids to watch, grabbing a coke for them from the fridge). The *abiding appeal* of some cumulative texts helps to ensure their longevity: generations laugh together at the antics of Charlie Chaplin, Monty Python, Donald Duck or Bugs Bunny. Striptease clubs, summer holidays, and fast cars are as much a part of today's scene as yesterday's. *Batman, Superman, Archie* comics, *Harlequin Romance, Sports Illustrated* and *Vogue* are still selling strong — so are Winnie the Pooh, Lego, Monopoly, Scrabble, and Paddington Bear. And of course there are the giants: the ubiquitous empires of Barbie, Coke, McDonald's, and Disney, just to name a few.

3 *Intertextual*: One good indication that a text is on its way to becoming a cumulative cultural text is when references to it are made in other texts. When a cartoon character refers to a cultural icon such as the *Titanic*, when a movie such as *Space Jam* refers to Disney characters, when one teacher character refers to another, the text of each amplifies or modifies that of the other, one popular image piggybacks on another, and both benefit from the other's notoriety.

(1963) *Teacher*, Clark Moustakas' (1963) *The Authentic Teacher*, or Virginia Axline's (1964) *Dibs*, as well as the classics, especially Plato's Socratic dialogues and some of Dickens' novels. These books were suggested but not required reading, an afterthought tacked onto course bibliographies but seldom discussed in class.

Like so many of my fellow education students, I found that some of these narratives spoke far more directly to my own pedagogical concerns as a future teacher than did the dry and often inept lectures and texts of my formal university courses. Not only did those stories inspire and engage me, they made me think. They made me ponder my own actions in a different light. They helped me understand the spirit, intent, and philosophical orientation that underlay the models and jargon of the time. (Weber, 1993, p. 73)

The cumulative text of teacher that we read in movies, books, and TV programs serves as a kind of informal curriculum or alternative Faculty of Education for adults who wish to become teachers. In the countless classrooms of fiction and film in which we all spend time, we are exposed to both right and left wing images of teaching, image-texts that can be agents of change and subversion, or conversely, unnoticed but powerful agents of reproduction and conservatism. The implausibility of some images and the juxtaposition of contradictory messages within the same image problematize our everyday conceptions of teacher. The cumulative cultural text of competing teacher images forms the background against which we struggle to clarify our professional identities.

Popular texts can be useful to teachers in discussing their work with non-teachers (Isenberg, 1994). Because so many people have read these books or seen these teacher movies, we can talk or write about our teaching in a way that is more accessible or intelligible to others by framing it in terms of popular images. Popular images may sometimes validate or legitimize what we do in the eyes of our families and the general public. Some of the sympathy they have for teacher narratives might rub off on us! On the other hand, we may feel pressured by these popular texts to construct a certain facade or identity we might not otherwise have imagined or chosen for ourselves, faking the hero, or even deluding ourselves. Popular culture is too powerful to be ignored. Ignorance of how it infiltrates the most elite curricula only increases its subversive powers.

What can teachers do with this cumulative text? There *are* ways to harness the popular to professional ends. Echoing the growing call by those who study popular culture in relation to teaching (for example, Brunner, 1991; Giroux and Simon, 1989; Joseph and Burnaford, 1994; McRobbie, 1992), our suggestion is that we unmask and use the collage of contradictory images, cliches, and stereotypes of teaching to advance professional development. But how might one do this?

The activities outlined in box 5.2 can be likened to walking or hiking paths that criss-cross each other, sometimes sharing a common section of trail. Some paths might lead to dead ends on some days, becoming blocked when unexpected mud slides or avalanches have made it difficult or impossible to

Box 5.2

Ways to Use Popular Teacher Images for Professional Growth

1 *Do close readings of popular texts*: Studying and comparing texts carefully can make us more critically aware of popular stereotypes of teachers' work and roles, and expose the political and social agendas and tacit messages that these popular texts support, critique, or reproduce.

2 *Use popular texts as cases*: By deliberately considering popular texts as cases of other people's experiences or possible experiences, we can more easily critique certain teaching practices (because they are someone else's) and articulate our own ideals and beliefs against the text, as a first step towards self-examination and self-expression.

3 *Use popular texts as 'conduits' to examining professional identity*: The goal here is to conduct specific interrogations of our own identity, practice, and beliefs by using popular stories to provoke or jolt us into authentic self-study. This involves carefully monitoring and honestly examining our own emotional reactions to the texts.

4 *Use popular texts from the past*: By revisiting films or books that influenced us in the past, we can uncover early motivations and images and evaluate them through the more dispassionate gaze that the passage of time provides. We can trace the influence they might have had or still have on us and re-situate ourselves through our current reactions and critique to a deeper commitment to professional growth.

5 *Use popular texts to develop an empowering sense of community*: Popular texts provide a ready-made pool of common images that we can use to compare and share our visions, fears, and personal experiences. Watching or reading or discussing these texts with colleagues has the potential to create a sense of community, to spark critique of the status quo, and perhaps even motivate collective action in the face of shared concerns or visions.

6 *Create popular texts of reinvention*: One way to influence the popular is to participate in it by actively putting one's own vision 'out there'. We need to envision our future and live it, not only in school, but also with popular culture. Writing a movie script or producing a video can be an act of imaginative and critical reinvention that projects us into the social arena. Teachers as authors or film-makers or script writers?

slog on. Sometimes, we set out on a journey inadequately prepared, or we choose the wrong route for that day's weather or time constraints. At other times, we are overly (or insufficiently) ambitious, attacking a trail that we are not ready for, or one that is too easy for certain of our goals. Easy walks and challenging hikes alike can provide pleasure or can prove disappointing. You can seldom be really certain ahead of time; a trail that disappointed yesterday may just hit the spot today.

Each trail has its own advantages, personality, and vistas, as well as its own dangers or traps. An example of a hidden pitfall that faces us when we examine popular texts is the *stereotype*. Dana Polan (1993) asserts that popular stereotypes and cliches contribute to the construction of the classroom:

> For many students, the teacher is not a conduit to knowledge that exists elsewhere: the teacher is an image, a *cliché* in the sense both of stereotype but also photographic imprinting that freezes knowledge in the seeming evidence of a look, where the image predetermines what the person means to us . . . The medium is the message, and the image of the professor often matters more than the ideas of the lesson. (p. 32)

Indeed, Alison Lurie (1990) accurately remarks that non-canonized (popular) texts are ideal for pushing cliches and stereotypes to the surface. In this regard, movies and novels can indeed be used like the drawings discussed in the previous chapter to expose the often contradictory stereotypes and desires that lurk behind professional veneer. It is almost fun to spot them. There may even be something entertaining about their blatant exaggeration. Therein lies the danger. Because stereotypes are so often caricatures, we may be too easily tempted to regard them as humorous images that have nothing to do with us or with the reality of schooling. We may be too willing to overlook the kernel or possibility of truth that may lie hidden within. In other words, we must be careful to take them seriously even when they seem innocuous or blatantly inappropriate. Left unexamined, popular images can be dangerous.

Close Readings of Popular Teacher Texts

There is seldom, if ever, only one definitive reading of a cultural text, but in any given situation certain readings are more robust or make more sense than others. Those readings that dig below the surface of the text, that ask critical questions, that try to read between the lines, and that contextualize the reading historically or politically we call *close readings*. In adapting this term from the field of literary studies, we include references to the primary text (the original film, television show, etc.), but we extend the idea of a close reading of teacher texts to include, where appropriate, references to 'spin-off' texts, as well as references to what authors, critics and fans might have to say about the particular text.

Box 5.3

Close Readings of Cumulative Cultural Texts

1 Describe the 'surface structures' of the text. What is the text ostensibly or explicitly saying? What are the details or minutiae that give it life? What is its 'look' or appeal?

2 Situate the text in terms of: Who created it? How and why? Who was it 'written' for? What is the political or social/historical context surrounding it? Common critical touchstones such as social class, age, race, religion, and gender may be important factors to consider.

3 How (and why) has the text become popular and cumulative? What are the spin-offs, serializations, or multidimensional features? How has it been repackaged, advertised, and 'sold?'

4 Describe and reflect on the 'deep structures' and 'counter-texts'. Re-read the text closely 'between' the lines. What are the implicit or hidden messages? Are there counter-texts that undermine the overt message (for example, does good triumph over evil using evil means)? What codes or conventions were used to tell the story in a way that makes it acceptable or popular (see box 5.4 below)? What images or stereotypes are created, contested, or perpetuated? What ideas or popular beliefs are challenged or reinforced? What room for ambiguity or interpretation does the text provide?

5 What do the critics, authors, and consumers (fans) have to say about it in articles, letters, interviews and so forth? In other words, analyse the texts that have been spawned by the primary one.

6 What special features might be important to a critical reading of this text? Features related to the medium in which the text was produced (visual imagery, soundtrack, camera angle, lyrics, packaging, etc.) can be especially relevant.

7 Relate the close reading to your own experience and observations.

Reading one text in the light of another helps throw each text into relief, and highlights details that may otherwise escape our attention. Comparing new teacher texts with ones we saw or read in childhood can provoke self-awareness and help us trace the evolution of our professional views within a changing social context. Since every text bears at least the faint stamp of the era that produced it, comparing teacher texts from different periods helps situate our personal reactions within an historical and political perspective.

Dangerous Minds: A Close Reading Against *To Sir With Love*

We began this chapter with an excerpt from an essay by Sandra (in Weber and Mitchell, 1995) in which she did a close reading of *To Sir With Love*, a film that had influenced her before she became a teacher. We continue here with her close reading of *Dangerous Minds,* which she contrasts with the earlier movie in order to ask certain questions. These questions are but a few examples of the many critical ones that can be used to read a text's deep structures, the ones beyond the obvious surface features of the story.

Although the movies *Dangerous Minds* and *To Sir With Love* were made some 30 years apart, many aspects of their surface detail and deep structure are remarkably similar, attesting to the long-standing appeal of the classic teacher narrative. Both films feature major stars and make very important use of popular youth music in their soundtracks. They are typical of the teacher-as-saviour/hero genre that dominates teacher movies.

In both films, the teachers and students are from disempowered social groups: Sir is black, from a working class background in a British colony; Miss Johnson was a battered wife. They both teach racially mixed classes in dingy inner city high schools. Although neither of them initially seems to relish the idea of teaching, they both have a romantic view of education as the light that will brighten the darkness of their impoverished students' daily lives. During the course of the films, they manage to reach children that others have not by dramatically rejecting and ostensibly changing the official school curriculum. They try to build bridges between popular culture and high culture, between knowledge and life, between youth and adulthood, between thinking and acting, between so-called working class failure and middle class success. One gets the feeling, however, that the bridges have a 'good' side and a 'bad' side, and that student traffic is supposed to go one way only!

We meet LouAnne Johnson (a.k.a. Michelle Pfeiffer) as she is heading into the school towards the Principal's office for a job interview. We learn that she has recently emerged from a painful divorce and needs a job. Although she has had a little teacher training, she has never before taught in a classroom. Hesitantly, she accepts, as a temporary measure, to teach underachieving inner city students in an old school with no paper and few books.

Like 'Sir', Miss Johnson is a teacher hero who cares about her underprivileged students and views education as the way for them to better their lives. Indeed, as several characters in the film point out, she wants to be a saviour. The parallel with Sir continues as we watch Miss Johnson use her physical defence skills (karate) and knowledge of warfare (she is an ex-marine) to get her students' attention and to demonstrate that she could keep them in line physically, if necessary. But, like Sir, it is their minds and lives as well as their behaviour that Miss Johnson seeks to influence. To achieve that end, she uses dramatic means to capture the students attention, rejecting the official curriculum as inadequate.

Her 'rebellion' against the curriculum includes substituting the poetry of Bob Dylan for the prescribed language drills. She takes her students outside the classroom, and offers them candy and other prizes as rewards for decoding the language of poetry. The explicit theme of her teaching is 'choice'. She believes every person has a choice of some kind and declares 'There are no victims in this class.' Her message to her students is embedded in the Dylan/Dylan contest that challenges her students to find a poem by Dylan Thomas that echoes the poem by Bob Dylan that they have studied together in class.

Near the end of the movie, Miss Johnson is still unsure if teaching is her calling and announces she is leaving. In a collective 'raging against the dying of their light', her students draw upon what they have learned from the Dylan/Dylan contest and Miss Johnson's teaching to resist her decision to leave, to convince her that they need her. And so, we know that she will stay, as Sir did, to rescue another set of kids in that dismal school which is somehow less dismal due to her presence. In the closing scene of the film, the friend and colleague who had got her the job, asks her 'How did they (the students) get you to come back?' To this she replies 'They gave me candy and called me their light.'

Comparing deep structures and surface structures

Despite the many similarities noted previously, these two movies are in some ways quite different. Unlike Sir, Miss Johnson is not a paragon of virtue and has faced many difficulties. We learn that despite her training as a marine, she was beaten by her husband whom she eventually divorced six months prior to her arrival at Parkmount High School. She confesses to a student that she once had an abortion.

Differences in the surface appearance of the two teacher heroes are not restricted to sex. Although both are very good looking (movie stars, after all), while Sir wears impeccably tailored suits, Miss Johnson deliberately dresses down, wearing huge sloppy sweaters, no make-up, jeans, leather boots, and the like. Her more upscale or 'proper' clothes are reserved for visits to parents, interviews, and dinners in fancy restaurants.

Even more pronounced is the range of social codes she uses in her speech. One minute she is carefully enunciating the language of poetry, the next, she is talking like the ex-marine she supposedly is, telling a student where to place his butt or telling another 'You guys don't know shit about karate'. Sir would probably not approve of LouAnne Johnson's dress and language, although there is one brief but memorable scene in which he feels comfortable (close) enough with his students to briefly demonstrate the spoken patois of his colonial boyhood.

In comparing these heroes, we should of course remember there are 30 years of history and different racial and cultural backgrounds separating them (not to mention the Atlantic Ocean!). Miss Johnson could be viewed as a white modern liberal, out to save the victims by convincing them that they do not have to see themselves as victims. Sir is out to save them too, but from the insider's perspective of the colonized, one who decides that the only way to lick 'em is to join 'em, by appropriating 'white' language and the culture of power.

Like most teacher films, including *To Sir With Love, Dangerous Minds* has several dramatic moments, many of them darker and less easily resolved than the situations that confront Sir. While Sir and Miss Johnson both experience failure and frustration in their efforts to get through to their students, Sir's problems are all at least partially solved by the end of the film. In contrast, some of Miss Johnson's failures are irrevocable — you cannot bring students back from the dead.

Sir has the advantage of a kind of social bilingualism: although fully fluent in the language, attitudes, and values of middle class respectability, he comes from poor working class roots and knows from personal experience the pain of racism and classism. He understands at least some of the social codes of his working class students' life on the streets ('Sir, you're one of us, but you're not like us').

Miss Johnson on the other hand is portrayed as naively middle class, ignorant of the power and specifics of the street code that runs her students' lives. She stumbles onto the code bit by bit and is sensitive and bright enough to recognize it, but only after she has unwittingly made things unnecessarily hard for her students. In her own eyes, she is responsible for the 'loss' of three and almost four of her students: two of the brightest boys (brothers) are pulled suddenly and permanently out of school by a female relative who angrily tells Miss Johnson:

> I know who you are — you're the white bread bitch who's messing
> with my babies' minds . . . I see what they bring home — poetry — I
> ain't raising no doctors and lawyers here . . . find yourself some other
> poor boys to save.

A third boy, Emilio, the class leader who it took Miss Johnson the longest to 'reach', is lost to her permanently. Miss Johnson had advised him to go see Mr. Grandey, the Principal, to report a drug pusher who had been threatening to kill Emilio for stealing his girlfriend. When Emilio followed her advice early the next morning, he was brusquely turned away by Mr. Grandey because he had forgotten to knock at the office door before entering. Almost immediately afterwards, he was shot dead three blocks away from school. As the Principal explains to Miss Johnson moments before we learn that Emilio has been killed:

> I'm trying to teach these children to live in the world. In this world, you don't just barge into someone's office, you remember to knock.

The fourth potential loss, in Miss Johnson's eyes, is her brightest student, Calley, who becomes pregnant and intends to respect the school's unwritten policy that pregnant girls withdraw and go to another school with a special program on mothering. These events sadden and trouble Miss Johnson deeply. Doubting her ability as a teacher, she decides not to return the following semester. But then, in a tearful scene, Calley shows up in class, Miss Johnson's loss is reversed, and she announces that she has decided not to leave after all.

Music as a mirror of change and continuity in comparing films

> But how do you thank someone who's taken you from crayons to perfume? . . . What is there for you I can buy?

The soundtrack of *To Sir With Love* launched the singing career of Lulu whose rendition of the title song rose high on the hit parade chart after the movie was released. Thousands of adolescents who probably hated school spent their money and perhaps even skipped school to watch a movie or listen to records about a teacher! Through the music, the film's traditional and conservative messages are flashily wrapped in a sentimental but hip package. The song reinforces the movie's message that academic knowledge, 'high' culture, middle class language, values, dress codes, and traditional gender roles are highly desirable.

The rap soundtrack of *Dangerous Minds* provides a 90s version of hip rebellion featuring several popular groups. But, on the surface, the music does not support the movie's essentially conservative message of hard work in school. Instead, the rap songs offer an explicitly contrived counter-text to the movie's content, wrapping the basically traditional teacher-movie text in a glossy defiance. In a sense, it is the rap (wrap!) more than anything else that gives the movie its surface cachet of danger. On closer inspection, however, it is this very cachet or counter-text that supports the film's traditional message by hiding or coating it in a veneer of rebellious chic that makes its conservatism easier to swallow whole. And there is more, when we dig deeper.

In the foreground of the movie is the popular culture of LouAnne's generation, the music of Bob Dylan, designated by the 60s teenagers as their poet/social critic/advocate for change. Significantly, it is not Dylan's current songs (poems) that are featured in the film, it is his work from three decades ago that weave in and out of the film as a sort of counterpoint to both the contemporary rap score and the revered canonical text of the 'real Dylan', poet Dylan Thomas. Bob Dylan serves as mediator from rap back to Dylan Thomas. Thus, in the same movie, we find:

Dylan Thomas: High culture; generation #1; perhaps low-brow stuff to LouAnne's grandparents' generation.

Bob Dylan: Started as rebellious low culture of generation #2 (LouAnne's); became canonized, as generation #2 became the gatekeeper of high culture, raising the status of its music.

Rap music: Generation #3; low culture, for now — but likely on its way up as this generation assumes power.

This multilayered use of music and poetry in *Dangerous Minds* provides intergenerational links. What starts out as rebellious and reviled low-brow youth culture can evolve into high-brow culture when those same youths grow up to become the mediators of taste. This co-opting of the popular facilitates cultural generativity, working to ensure that we will always be as we have always been. The generativity of many cultures is remarkably powerful, quite capable of absorbing rebellion and removing or using its sting to renew and perpetuate itself.

Thus far, this close reading of *Dangerous Minds* is but a first step into self-study. Initially, the critique offered is of the images of Miss Johnson and Sir, more than of ourselves. It is easier to see their flaws and strengths than our own. It is only when we apply the close readings honestly to our own lives that we are in a position to reinvent ourselves. To illustrate further, Sandra will continue the close reading in the first person, bringing it closer to home.

Teacher as agent of change: the personal and the social

Both Thackeray (Sir) and Johnson seem to view themselves as agents of social change, something I have always admired. Ostensibly, they both embody the romantic hope that dignity, morality and intelligence transcend class and race (and in Miss Johnson's case, possibly gender) to join us all together. Their styles, however, differ in significant ways. Sir seems to be saying: 'I will lift you up to my level through example and through polite discourse about real things. I will guide you to middle class language and to high culture. I will teach you self-control and respect for all people. I will show you that toughness is a quality of mind'.

Although she also preaches toughness of mind, Johnson seems to be saying: 'If necessary, I will try to bend down to your level. In order to reach you, I will speak your language, use your dress, go out with you, not as a chaperon but as a friend. I will show you that you always have a choice, even that means choosing to die with your head held high. You can choose to let me lift you up to my level, which is poetry. I want to arm you with words and ideas, to make you tougher so it will be harder for others in your world to knock you down'.

How effective are these film heroes? On close examination, I have to admit that Sir compliantly follows the school rules and submits to authority, making no fuss when permission for his class field trips is ultimately withdrawn. Sir takes serious steps to reform the academic lived curriculum in his classroom, but outside of the classroom is a different matter. He closes ranks with the other teachers who are bullying or rude, refusing to publicly entertain any criticism of other teachers from his students. Having worked his way up to the middle class, he seems, at times, to be practising a policy of exclusion, telling students they can accomplish anything they set their minds to, ignoring through omission the multitude of social and political impediments these young people have to face.

In comparison, Johnson's rebellion seems a little more courageous to me. She stands up to the Principal and lies to him on one occasion in order to defy school policy. Outraged by the Vice-Principal's policies of sending pregnant girls away, she urges a student to ignore them. She talks about writing letters to the newspapers if necessary to call attention to a board policy she finds unfair. And, more importantly, I sense less of a smug self-righteousness to LouAnne. She seems less sure of herself and her convictions — something I can identify with. Nonetheless, it bothers me that she still has the same conservative goal as Sir of the 60's — sell middle-class, heterosexual, white male 'high brow' culture-but she pursues this goal in a way that is perhaps more empowering for her students. At the film's end, her students take collective action, make choices, and resist her decisions in minor ways. Further, the film's message has more of a postmodern flavour: it is more ambiguous, students drop out or die, *suggesting that playing at saviour can destroy as well as save, that change is neither simple nor always for the good.* Ambiguity — now there's a state of mind with which I am all too familiar!

I was horrified at Miss Johnson's involuntary implication in Emilio's death. It scares me to think that not only are there students I fail to help, but maybe there are also ones who I unwittingly harm. In reflecting on all this, I am quickly losing whatever interest remains in 'saving' my students, and I am wary of my tendency to occasionally play the rescuer or rebel/hero. I think back now, for example, to my photo essay in the previous chapter with new insight, and laugh with a mixture of affection and embarrassment at my lonely rebellious act of throwing

> my students' workbooks down the incinerator. Was Sir's trashing of school textbooks somewhere in the back of my mind when I did that? I certainly don't remember it that way, but . . . I wonder, did I fancy myself a teacher hero? What kinds of actions would be more likely to transform or disrupt the curriculum in socially meaningful ways?

There is something 'dangerous' about playing teacher-hero, something condescending. Who can authoritatively label a group to be 'oppressed' or 'emancipated'? Who can declare with confidence they know how to empower?

> In our haste to embrace such attractive catchwords as empowerment and leadership, we have perhaps overlooked the real essence of hegemony. Empowerment is less than power. [. . .] to have authority delegated is not the same as to have authority. It is very clear that which is given may be withdrawn. (Cooper, 1988, p. 50)

But are we to dismiss out of hand the sincerity and authenticity of Sir and Miss Johnson's efforts? Flawed as they are, they do convey genuine pedagogical concern that could be helpful to their students or, for that matter, to teachers contemplating their teaching. In learning from their mistakes, we need not be smug — for we too are flawed and blinded by our social and historical contexts in ways we may only realize later.

Romanticized Images and Self-study

In addition to teacher heroes, popular culture is also replete with images of teachers as villains, the anti-heroes of teaching and schooling. Both sets of images are 'romanticized' — even when they are based on real people, they accentuate the virtues of certain teachers and the vices of others. Drawn with bold and dramatic strokes that make them stand out from real life, the mean teachers are meaner, the kind ones are kinder, the brave ones are braver, and the inept are even more so.

The significance of the study of these images to self-study becomes clear when we address the question: Why would anyone romanticize teachers' experience? Beyond literary effect, storytelling device, and commercial concerns, there are other meaningful possibilities: Romanticizing can be a safe way to voice a reaction or counter-text to everyday life. It is also ideal for expressing fantasies, fears, and desires that seem out of place in other genres. We can find evidence for this motivation in what Fiske (1989) calls 'secondary texts' of interviews and articles about authors of primary texts. For example, Francine Pascal, the author of the highly successful school-based novel series *Sweet Valley High*, said in an interview:

> I absolutely hated high school. Learning by rote made the whole system repressive. The 'Sweet Valley High' series draws a lot on my own high school experiences. Going to high school in the fifties, as I did, was not appreciably different from going to high school in the eighties . . . All of us think high school is wonderful for everyone else. The 'Sweet Valley High' series come out of *what I fantasized high school was like for everyone but me.* (Garrett and McCue, 1989, p. 194, italics added)

What is interesting is that Pascal has crafted a series where school is written as the *counter-text to her own everyday experiences* of schooling. Creating characters in reaction to personal school experience enables authors (former students or actual teachers) to voice the desires, fears, and images that are usually ignored or repressed as 'foolish' or socially unacceptable. When suddenly our fantasies, hatreds, or yearnings are projected full force onto a movie or television screen, catching us off guard, we may be inclined to laugh at them with embarrassment or quickly dismiss them as outrageous caricatures, distortions, and misrepresentations. But burying them gives them free reign to influence our rationalizations without detection. Perhaps instead, we should study them closely to glean the hidden messages they convey.

To better understand the stereotypes of popular teacher texts, it is helpful to interrogate them in terms of the codes and conventions that govern their use (see Box 5.4). As we illustrated in *That's Funny, You Don't Look Like a Teacher* (Weber and Mitchell, 1995), knowing these conventions makes it easier to recognize and expose them through critical close readings.

These codes and conventions all contribute to the generic structure of classic hero teacher texts, a structure whose prevalence is all the more evident when contrasted with those few image-texts that reveal the 'dark side of teaching', even for the hero. For example, *The Children's Hour, An Angel at my Table*, and *Waterland* all present dark images of teachers who are destroyed while teaching with little or no hope held out for their joyful return to teaching. These books and films serve as counter-texts to countless images of teachers as heroes devotedly working and winning against the odds.

How do popular romantic texts affect teachers and students? Robertson (1997) suggests that they may create unrealistic and potentially harmful expectations by encouraging teacher fantasy at the expense of reality.

> Dreams of love do not resolve the difficulties of teaching, nor do they increase the pleasures. In some ways, devotion fantasies help put into place a subjective reality that is bound to experience dismay. (p. 139)

The implication is that popular teacher images can set us up for disappointment, encouraging expectations that teaching should fulfil a deep desire to love and be loved, or a need to be needed or to save people, not necessarily the best motivations to take up or remain in a vocation where countless anti-hero images lead students to expect teachers to be mean and crabby, or inept and uninteresting.

In our fantasies, at least, we may like to think of ourselves as the exception, the hero who is not like the others. Hence the insidious power of romantic texts to feed self-delusion. As de Lauretis (1994) contends, popular texts offer spectators places in which to replay fantasies that are both in the text and in the viewer. We agree with Robertson's assertion that popular texts can function as the locus of a transfer that conceals and reveals what is taboo or cannot be easily spoken: teachers' real life desire for recognition and their wish to be the source of the knowledge (in fantasy, at least) that their students need in order for both teacher and students to feel complete. Are popular texts dangerously misleading, offering simplistic or fanciful answers?

Since we cannot make these texts disappear, our suggestion is to use the very elements that make these texts 'dangerous' to mitigate their power. In the types of self-study we and others propose, stereotypes are unmasked, at least partially, and fantasy and desire are more honestly acknowledged. As we illustrated with Sandra's earlier close reading, critical questions can be asked, making possible a reinvention of self as teacher who is a more savvy consumer or producer of popular culture. The hope, as Robertson (1997) says, is to find ways to disrupt fantasy's confines.

> Popular culture may be used within pedagogy to explore what fantasy hopes for and ignores when it imagines teaching. Screenplay pedagogy can work to disrupt those moments of feeling trapped in a history produced but unchangeable. Part of the lesson involves imagining how to teach in the absence of miracles. (p. 139)

For popular culture to assume this role in 'screenplay pedagogy', however, it must first achieve the status of being 'admissible evidence'. Because the general devaluing of popular culture has led to an isolated reading of romance texts (Moss, 1989; and Christian-Smith, 1990), we wonder if teachers themselves ever have a chance to question the ideologies that link romantic teacher-texts to their social context. Teachers are already isolated in their work as Lortie (1975) points out, and may be largely unaware of their role in the replication of the cumulative cultural text that they embody. Yet these non-canonized texts can shed some light on our socialization as teachers, expressing a variety of often contradictory popular views of who teachers are, what we do, and what we could *be imagined as doing.*

Popular Culture, Memory, and Identity

> Fact, fiction, and fantasy mingle together, and instead of trying to work out 'what really happened', I am beginning to see the place of the construction of all those fictions in producing me. (Walkerdine, 1990, p. 158)

Popular texts of teaching provide vicarious, emotional, and sometimes cathartic experiences which can help people realize they are not alone in their pain or

Box 5.4

Codes and Conventions of the Popular Teacher Texts

Most popular teacher texts are 'romantic', not necessarily in the sense of courtly love, but in that they provide all the ingredients of dramatic fantasy, including heroes and anti-heroes to represent the battling forces of good and evil. Writers and producers of teacher texts draw upon romantic codes, conventions, and recurring themes that have acquired common currency in the general culture. These conventions occur frequently in teacher texts written for children as well as adults.

1 Teacher heroes are usually outsiders who are teaching through circumstance rather than choice.

2 Teaching is natural, you do not need training if you've got 'the right stuff'.

3 Teacher heroes are rare and stand out in contrast to anti-hero teachers.

4 Teacher heroes liberate students by defying the official school rules and curriculum.

5 Real learning occurs outside of school.

6 Teachers become heroic through a turning point of sudden enlightenment, divine intervention, or the 'a-ha' experience.

7 Teaching is a heroic and solitary act. Teachers do not work collectively for reform.

8 Teacher heroes are devoted to their students and are rewarded with their undying love and gratitude in a dramatic scene.

---

predicaments. They provide a safe starting point for exploring and re-storying our own lives. Initially, for example, it may be easier to find the courage to condemn a mean or cruel act carried out by a fictional administrator than to voice one's rage at a feared or despised real-life one. It may be easier, at first, to recognize Miss Brodie's obsessive need to live her life through her students than it would be to recognize our own, or easier to condemn Marc Thackeray's addressing his female students as sluts than admitting to our own sexist language or actions. Words, labels, acts and images from fiction can be useful in retelling our own stories. Some may even transform our view of ourselves and others.

There is no obvious way to erase images which already exist (McRobbie, 1992): Miss Brodie, Miss Brooks, Miss Dove, Mr. Chips, Mr. Dadier, Mr. Keating, Miss Johnson, and Sir have become some of society's cliches for 'teacher' whether teachers like it or not. As Butler (1997), Brunner (1991), Giroux and Simon (1989), Robertson (1997), and others have demonstrated, popular teacher texts can be used as cases to stimulate discussion and reflection in the context of teacher education. How to use them? We have experimented with many different methods, one of which is outlined below.

Box 5.5

Using Popular Teacher Texts for Self-study

1 Choose a selection of popular teacher texts to study, either alone or as a group. Suggestions include teacher movies, books or television programs that you have not viewed or read before. Or you may wish to revisit some previously known texts.

2 View or read each text. If possible, visit each text twice, once for a global impression, the second time to pursue more detailed questioning. Make note of things that stand out, puzzle, shock, please, trouble, enthral or amuse you. In other words, keep tabs on what triggers your own emotional reactions.

3 Any of the following questions might be helpful to guide the second viewing (if there is one) and the subsequent writing.

   (a) Describe the scene or event that gripped or affected you the most. What is it about that particular scene that 'gets to you?' How does it connect to you or to your social or political context?

   (b) Describe the scenes or elements of the text that 'ring true' to you, and explain why they seem realistic or plausible. Do they remind you of any real life experiences?

   (c) In what ways does this text follow the classic teacher genre (heroes and anti-heroes) described earlier in this chapter? What are the implications?

   (d) What elements or scenes are controversial or dismay or worry you?

   (e) How are teachers portrayed in this text? What literary or film conventions are used to highlight the portrayal? How might this portrayal affect you, the profession, or the general public?

(f)   What images or stereotypes of teachers, students, or schooling are introduced or perpetuated in this text?

(g)   Why do you think this text has become popular? Whose point of view or gaze is presented or dominates? How does it speak to the past and the future?

(h)   How are power or cultural issues related to class, gender, race, ethnicity, religion, or age played out in this text?

(i)   What messages or images do you take away from this text and how might they relate to your professional life?

(j)   What other teacher texts or real life experiences does this text remind you of? How does it compare to other teacher texts you know or have seen?

4   Write up your reactions to the text, using whatever questions seem likely to take you deepest (those that will take you wherever you don't want to go are the ones you should choose!). Why is it that you responded the way you did? What can you learn about yourself as a teacher from the way you have responded?

5   Share as much of your response as you comfortably can in a discussion group. Later, reread and, if possible or helpful, rewrite your responses for yourself as audience, for your own personal and professional development.
    Alternative suggestion: Write a close reading of the film, video or book in comparison to another. Write this as a text to make public.

As we saw in previous chapters, self-study is often facilitated in group situations where not only shared images are highlighted, but differing views of teaching are also exposed. This holds true for critical self-examination using popular culture. Close readings of popular culture bring into focus the metaphoric stories that speak to our collective and individual experience. Through multiple readings of our own and others' reactions to teacher images, we enter into a dialectical relationship with the polarities, ambiguities, and tensions inherent to teaching. Consequently, interrogating popular teacher images becomes a sort of autobiographical investigation, inevitably including a deeper sense of the collective identity of teacher as well as some often un-expected insights into one's own individual history and identity.

The meaning of teacher education and actual teaching experience is filtered through the romanticized teacher images that constitute a good chunk of popular culture. Changing that reading means becoming aware of the filters we unwittingly use, and consciously adopting more suitable ones if that is what seems appropriate.

Reevaluating the Popular

Why do some teachers find themselves feeling uncomfortable admitting that they liked or were really moved by a popular teacher text? Robertson (1997) suggests it is because the texts contain elements of our secret fantasies and desires that are not socially acceptable in professional discourse. We are not that comfortable admitting narrative 'storying' texts into the curriculum of professional development. Perhaps it does not seem to be 'objective' enough. Yet *popular culture is not purely unreflective or superficial — it contains avant-garde elements, provocative ideas, even models for self critique.* We italicized the preceding to accentuate its importance. There are occasions when popular teacher texts demonstrate how to ask critical questions of ourselves. For example, Isenberg (1994) describes the inspiration for self-reflection that she found in the popular text, *Up the Down Staircase*, by Bel Kaufman (1964). She begins by quoting the main character, Sylvia Barrett:

> I had set out to tell you exactly what happened. But since I am the one writing this, how do I know what in my telling I am selecting, omitting, emphasizing; what unconscious editing I am doing? Why was I more interested in the one black sheep (I use Ferone's own cliché) than in all the white lambs in my care? Why did I (in my red suit) call him a child? (p. 43)

Isenberg uses the above quote to make a parallel with her own quest for self-knowledge:

> Here Barrett models the kind of reflection in which I needed to engage; her questions about her own motives and behavior as a teacher, a woman, and a writer were reassuring to me since I constantly asked myself similar ones. And I had no doubt that her responses to Ferone are indeed influenced to some extent by the fact that she finds him attractive and has unconsciously flirted with him. (ibid)

There are professionally legitimate reasons to admit to elements we like in popular culture: Not all teacher texts are unidimensional, and even those that are may be useful for the kinds of stereotypes they contain. There may also be a counter-text that can be heard, if one listens; some degree of meaningful complexity or depth or element of truth that makes these texts engaging. For example, Isenberg writes:

> Like that of Sylvia Barrett, Braithwaite's pedagogy is not especially revolutionary, but his personal involvement and investment in the teaching process

make it more meaningful than it would have been otherwise. By spending time and energy preparing relevant material, taking students on field trips, and openly explaining his own perspective, Braithwaite imbues his teaching with the caring that Nel Noddings (1984) advocates — caring that makes all the difference. In a sense, he himself becomes part of the curriculum, as his students study him for clues on how to live and learn in a difficult world. (ibid, p. 67)

Buried in the potentially dangerous and isolating romanticism of many popular texts are some useful messages.

At the very least, the popular stirs up controversy and debate in our profession. After all, at least some of these popular teachers are born of the lives of angry teachers who wish to critique the status quo. If we evaluate popular texts in the context of the lives of the teacher/authors who produce them, we may find that:

> Teaching narratives are plainly told by angry authors who describe the suffer-
> ing of a disempowered constituency in the hope of ending that suffering.
> They are structured around crises of literacy, identity, and control and operate
> within constraints and conventions that are politically determined . . . teacher-
> narrators are usually politically motivated; teacher authors use their own
> experience to bear witness to terrible, ludicrous, or simply counterproductive
> things that happen within schools . . . Their books are filled with descriptions
> of incidents that were detrimental to students. (ibid, p. 110)

Some teacher-writers try to represent a constituency that has not often been heard. The voices of teachers — along with the voices of children — have often been muted or stifled in the debates about schooling. For those who find popular texts dangerously misleading or reactionary, one course of action we can imagine is to start putting alternative popular images out there. Speak out, imagine, write, produce, and create. There is no medium more influential than the popular. Is that where teachers should continue to reinvent themselves — out in a broad public forum? The following is one way to explore this question.

Box 5.6

What if Teachers Were in Control of Popular Culture?

Alone or as a group, write an outline for a movie scenario or a novel about teachers, one that you think might put an important image out there, one that you write, perhaps, as part of your reaction to a popular text you have seen or read, or one that represents your own teaching fantasy, reality, or critique.

Scripts students and teachers have suggested include:

- A story about a group of traditional teachers who come to the defence of a new radical teacher. In the course of the film, the teachers oust the Principal, win over the parents, and begin to learn from each other.
- A TV sitcom series about an elementary school staffed mainly by men under a dynamic and beautiful female Principal.
- A movie about a group of disenchanted teachers who quit their jobs to start a new school of their own, and experience many ups and downs.
- Education's answer to the 'intern' medical movies about several very different students enrolled in a teacher education program and their exploits during practice teaching. The plot will involve troubled students struggling with their sexual orientations, their abusive home life, or racial discrimination and will feature dramatic confrontations at faculty meetings in the schools and the university. Two students will take their concerns to the mass media.

Even if we never get to 'play out' these scenes, in imagining them we begin to take charge of our own professional development in ways that are both pleasurable and inventive. In the face of the unrealistic and unflattering teacher images that bombard us from all sides, it is easy to be discouraged. But the sheer volume makes for a certain richness and complexity that may be more liberating than first readings indicate.

Writing, producing or directing documentaries, books, plays, and movies is one way to contribute to the wider social dialogue about what it means to be a teacher. But to be effective, we need to have something of import to say, we need to have a deeper understanding of our own local reality and our teaching selves, a challenge we take up in the next chapter.

Chapter 6

Turning the Video Camera
on Ourselves

Oh, no, I don't want to be filmed . . . I'll be too nervous, I'll panic, I won't be able to focus on what I am doing.

I don't think I could stand hearing myself on tape. And I know I'll look like a whale . . . they say the TV camera adds at least 10 pounds . . .

I KNOW all the dumb things I do while I teach . . . I don't need to have it rubbed in . . . I'm not exactly enthusiastic about having others see me either.

It's all too artificial. The kids will be distracted by the camera and will misbehave. . . . it won't be a normal classroom situation. (Excerpts from the journals of preservice students)

Figure 6.1   Teacher being videotaped

The opening quotes are the sorts of initial reactions that teachers may have when it is suggested to them for the first time that they videotape themselves in action. Yet, when they finally get around to doing it, the taping experience itself is usually a lot more positive than anticipated. What are we so afraid of?

At first glance, some of the approaches to self-study we have been describing in prior chapters may seem a little gentler, and less intimidating than videotaping. Doing memory work initially within the privacy of our own minds, writing down past events in words we feel we can control, gazing at hazy snapshots taken long ago, when we were young and had excuses, looking at movies about other teachers: these are very powerful tools for self-study, but for most people, they're not necessarily scary. Sometimes, in fact, they're very pleasurable. In looking back, we can filter our memories, censor our words, control our reactions, re-create images of ourselves before examining them closely (not too closely!). When the photograph is taken, we feel more able to compose our image by holding that smile or sucking in that stomach until the camera clicks. But video . . . to confront the evolving present, to face the moving image of ourselves, to be caught looking in the mirror . . . that enterprise might seem to be of another order, especially to people who are unfamiliar with the experience.

Even if we ourselves initiate the experience, knowing we are going to be videotaped means knowing we are going to be exposed (open) to the camera's unfaltering stare, to the cameraperson's or viewer's judgment, and perhaps most importantly, to our own uneasy stare. *And our students will know because they are participants too, with the power to make us as well as themselves look good, bad, or otherwise.* And we're not just talking about a moment's visual image. The wonderful (and some would say challenging) thing about video is that it picks up sound and movement as well as image, and it does so over what can be a long period of time. Further, being filmed drives home the fact that what we do is public and recordable, a jarring contradiction to the private intimacy we may usually *feel* in our classrooms. We might be uncomfortably aware of the camera's *listening* gaze, a gaze that forces us *to imagine ourselves simultaneously as we act with others.* And to have such immediate and limitless access to this record of our experience! How useful! But for some, how scary at first. Self-video necessarily involves facing oneself in ways that are anything but nostalgic!

We use the term 'self-video' to encompass a variety of activities: repeatedly videotaping and then viewing oneself teaching; reflecting, imagining, and acting on the basis of emergent video self-knowledge; experimenting and playing with pedagogical possibilities using video; sharing and critiquing videos (one's own and other people's); revisiting videotapes from the past to catch the fluidity, tensions, and contradictions of professional identity and growth (memory work); making videos to reinvent and express oneself anew as teacher. While much of this chapter is devoted to analysing conditions that facilitate or enhance self-video's potential, we also explore the tensions and dangers inherent to the experience.

The Nature and Characteristics of Self-video

The most objective image comes from the most personal approach. (Goethe)

Why do self-video? To learn what really goes on when we teach? To see other pedagogical possibilities? To see how we look in the eyes of others? To get in touch with ourselves? To get to know our students better? To answer specific questions we have about the way we teach? To imagine ourselves differently? For inspiration and new ideas? For fun? To explore these questions, we will present a series of cases based on our own personal experience and that of other colleagues.

Case 1: Caught on Tape: Calling my Bluff

I'll never forget the butterflies in my stomach when I was first 'forced' to confront myself on video. And to think I could have avoided the whole thing if I hadn't been so naive . . . let me explain.

It was my second lecture to a group of experienced teachers and principals who were taking an evening university course that I was teaching in their schools. The course was part of special university efforts to tailor professional development programmes to the milieu. This was more than 20 years ago (I mention this fact in light of the current ballyhoo about change and partnerships that we read so much about in the professional literature that makes it sound like it is something new!). Anyway, back to my lecture . . . there I was, a bit nervous because most of my 'students' were older and more experienced teachers than I. Did I have anything to offer them? Where did I get off trying to promote their professional development when I was just beginning my own in comparison?! Would they be interested in what I had to say, or just snore in my face (it was an evening lecture after we had all worked long days in the classroom)?

At first, things proceeded quite smoothly. They listened attentively and made comments that showed they were following. Encouraged, I began enthusing about the value of 'looking in the mirror', of confronting our professional practice and ourselves, of taking measures to facilitate self-study, such as journal writing, audiotaping, and, newly available in some schools, videotaping. I should have kept my big mouth shut!

Just my luck, we were in a school that had recently acquired a brand new, but large and cumbersome (by today's standards) video camera. The Principal of the school wanted to test both his new equipment and his new prof! With a challenging grin on his face, he politely interrupted my theoretical musings to call my bluff: 'I assume if you are so enthusiastic about the merits of filming oneself teaching, you would welcome my videotaping you right now while you are lecturing!' Caught by surprise and not wanting to lose face, I smiled and assented, 'Sure, why not?' Whereupon he rose with alacrity from his seat, disappeared for a few minutes to set up the equipment, and then quietly resumed his place with the others who exchanged amused glances. I tried to continue as if nothing out of the ordinary had occurred,

> *and after a while, to my surprise . . . it seemed as if nothing out of the ordinary had. Although I stumbled a bit at first, 'played up' to the camera, was conscious of it . . . eventually, I couldn't help getting back to my teaching. The material I was trying to get across and my students' reactions gradually returned to the foreground, pushing the camera's presence to the background, and for long periods of time, I really think I forgot it was there altogether.*
>
> *And so it was that I came to be sitting alone in a darkened classroom late one night watching myself on a special television monitor. Rolland, the Principal, was very discreet and professional, leaving me alone to view myself. I am not sure if I ever properly thanked him for pushing me into practising what I preached. The incident, however, seemed to seal the mutual respect we had for each other throughout the course. It was pivotal for me: giving me deeper insight into the nature of the self-video experience, and inspiring me to experiment with ways to use video in teaching and in self-study.* (Weber, reconstructed from two unpublished self-studies, 1977, 1997)

The phenomenon of being 'caught on tape', of being unexpectedly seen, of going instantaneously from the private to the public has important associations in Western culture. In North America, for example, we may think of O.J. Simpson's flight from the police in his white Bronco, shown live on TV, or the shocking assassination in Dallas of President J.F. Kennedy, or the brutal beating of Rodney King by L.A. police. Being 'caught' live on video camera is not exactly everyone's dream! It implies being under someone else's control. When something is caught, it is contained, held, fixed — not free, and certainly not private. The ubiquitous hidden camera in banks and convenience stores exemplifies the spectre of video camera as an Orwellian Big Brother, an unethical spy, a security device rather than a means of self-expression.

Unlike the case above where the teacher educator was, in a sense, suddenly thrown into the deep-end of video experience, confronted with an audience, an Other, she had not anticipated, in self-study, teachers usually know ahead of time that they are going to be filmed. And yet, sometimes, they still feel as if they are being 'caught', perhaps by themselves? Despite the element of surprise, the teacher in the above episode found the experience to be stimulating and ultimately very beneficial. And that positive assessment is one which many teachers share, *depending on the circumstances of the experience.*

What is the self-video experience, really? Box 6.1 outlines what we think are its distinguishing characteristics.

Seeing Ourselves: The Relationship Between 'I' and the Video 'Me'

Let's get this straight: a video tape of me teaching is not equivalent to me. As a student of Sefton-Green's once said of a photo, 'The "me" in the picture is *not* ME' (Buckingham and Sefton-Green, 1994, p. 98). It is a revealing but nonetheless partial representation of me that is based on what was visible or recordable via the camera's lens and microphone from a certain angle at a specific

Box 6.1

Distinguishing Characteristics of the Self-video Experience

1   **The sustained, listening, contextualizing gaze**: The video camera produces images *and* sound *and* movement over *time*. This yields a self-representation that is different from the still photo, one that appears *more fluid than frozen*, confronting us, not with a single slice or drop we can put on a slide under the microscope and decontextualize at our leisure, but rather with a running stream that presents multiple examples, variations, and complexities — perhaps even contradictions and tensions. In comparison with a photograph, video is a more complete and noisy text. Less edited and pared down to essentials. Less prone, some might say, to distortion, less likely, for example, to preserve a moment's smile in a lifetime of frowns. Viewing this self-representation may problematize the way we think of ourselves, challenging our idealistic mental snapshots. But it can also reassure us, providing a wider sampling of images and behaviour from which to choose the ones that we feel 'capture' us. In some situations, its evolution over time may seem more forgiving than the relentless restriction of a second's flash.

2   **A view from the outside**: If we have any image of ourselves at all as we teach, it is an internal, partial, and probably hazy one. We see our classroom life through the filter of our own perspectives and experience. A teacher movie might show the action through the teacher's eyes. Camera placement and movement would compel the viewer to see things as if she or he were the teacher. This is decidedly not the case with most self-videos. Camera placement and movement are often designed to showcase the student's or an observer's perspective, for example, taking in student activity that is outside of the teacher's line of vision or attention. In place of the look from within, we are offered a look from without. This is most helpful for self-study.

3   **Making (privately) public what is usually (publicly) private**: A sense of 'we' develops between the teacher and students in most classrooms. Although classroom life is a public experience in that individual actions are witnessed by others, it can also feel very private, something shared intimately as a single group. Even an unsupervised stationary video camera confronts the group and the individual with the possibility of an Other's gaze, making what feels private potentially very public, calling our attention to things usually taken for granted.

4 **Giving up control of the mirror**: It's harder to hold the pose for the video camera, to control what it sees. It catches us, not only within the pauses and silences, but also during the main event. No matter how much advance lesson planning and preparation we do, the text cannot be entirely known (written) in advance — this is classroom *life* we are talking about. *Because it is teaching*, because we can't be assured of the roles our students will play, we can't memorize and rehearse the entire script. In fact, doing so will often put us at a disadvantage — we may be so absorbed in delivering our rehearsed script that we are oblivious to the fact that it has become inappropriate or incongruous in the context of the spontaneous moments in the classroom. The only script that is captured, that counts, is the *lived script*! There is the distinct possibility that we will be confronted not with what we wish had happened, but with the unfeeling camera's version of what really occurred.

5 **Immediacy: experiencing the here and now**: The camera is rolling and we may not even know. Although we can cry 'Cut!', and try to redo a scene, the footage is there and our students were witnesses. And there is no forgetting or waiting period for film to be developed. No time to erase and redo the drawing, although we can later edit the text (tape). We may be dimly aware that any conscious attempt to represent ourselves to the camera, to construct what we want others to see, is doomed to fail. It's a long performance. However, the loss of control or of a certain authorship that this immediacy engenders is also a gain — an enhancement of authenticity and spontaneity, an incitement to *imagine as we act, to be aware of ourselves-with-others*.

6 **We can't ignore our students**: While our concern before filming may be with our self-image, the saving grace during and after classroom videotaping is our students. No matter how self-preoccupied we may at times be, after a while in the camera recorded classroom, we forget ourselves, *because we are teaching*: the importance of our work takes over and we center gradually more on them than on ourselves. And this produces a video that is worth watching. Similarly during the watching, after checking ourselves out, we become distracted by our students and learn a lot about them and how they 'read' us.

juncture in time and space. The videotape *per se* is not my view of myself. I watch the tape to experience and interpret this outside view of me, reconstructing or interrogating my self-image in the process. Buckingham and Sefton-Green suggest that

Figure 6.2 Teacher viewing self-video

> . . . part of the pleasure of photography is the play that it allows between fixity and flux between changing aspects of ourselves and the notion of an immutable identity. (ibid)

This applies perhaps even more aptly to video, which can capture change and contradictions because it involves motion, sound, image and time.

It is important not to confuse the videotaped 'teacher-and-students' with the much more complex and evolving reality of actual lived experience and professional identity. For example, one teacher educator wrote to us expressing frustration at the ease with which some of her student-teachers seemed to forget that what really matters is the quality of daily life and learning in their classrooms, not how wonderful or bad a videotape may seem. Caught up in their enthusiasm for self-video, some teachers may put too much emphasis on the video and not enough on what goes on and who they are every minute of every day in their schools when the camera is turned off. It is important to relate the video to the lived context of the teacher and students in question. A self-video CAN be highly effective or pivotal or meaningful. It can be a celebration or a wake-up call. But it is rarely the sum or essence of what can be learned or said about any class, school, student, or teacher.

Conversely, *a videotape is seldom unrelated or irrelevant to a better understanding of self-as-teacher.* Even if it's 'not me', it's me acting out an image, a role, a fantasy, or a stereotype. At times, when we don't like what we see, it is very tempting to equivocate or dismiss out of hand the possible implications of what the tape plainly shows. But discomfort can fuel the process of self-study. Dissonance between what we see and what we think or how we feel forces us to reflect critically and entertain other possibilities for ourselves.

Let's look at one teacher's experience that illustrates the potential of this activity more concretely.

Case 2: Dominique: A Videotape of a Teacher's Self-video Experience

Dominique! Dominique! *is the title of a videotape that was available (in French only) 12 years ago to primary teachers and produced by an early childhood consultant and a classroom teacher who collaborated to make the tape for the Quebec Ministry of Education. The tape traces the journey of a young kindergarten teacher through the initial process of self-video, and then visually documents her subsequent efforts to reinvent her practice in significant ways. In a cleverly designed shot, we see Dominique in profile, seated before the television monitor (which we also see clearly), viewing herself on camera for the first time. In other words, the tape enables the viewer to watch a teacher watch herself, evaluate herself, and change pedagogically. The intent was to give teachers a concrete example of how to use self-video for professional growth.*

The tape begins with long excerpts from Dominique's initial self-video. It reveals a pleasant and unassuming young woman, dressed comfortably in overalls, interacting with 5-year-old children in a classroom set up with colourful and well-equipped play centres, similar to those found in many kindergartens around the world. While some children are playing with the blocks or at the doll house or the woodcraft or painting centres, others are gathered at two large tables doing the day's craft activity. Seated at one of the tables in a low child-sized chair, Dominique is helping one little girl with the activity, while simultaneously fielding a torrent of requests from other children who come up to her or call out to her. The classroom is bustling and noisy. The teacher seems totally absorbed by the children and their needs. Her way of talking to them is direct, natural and caring. She seems down-to-earth, unpretentious, and unfazed by the camera's gaze. Things seem pretty normal for a kindergarten. Many observers would be impressed with Dominique's teaching depicted in this first segment. But not Dominique.

As we watch Dominique viewing this tape of herself in the company of the consultant, we see her growing discomfort. She cuts right to the chase. Laughing at herself with good-humoured dismay, she hones in on several incidents where she feels she helps children do things that they could do themselves if given the means and the opportunity. For example, the paper towels and equipment to clean up the messes so inherent to kindergarten work are not always easily accessible, and so Dominique finds herself helping children wash their hands. But most of all, Dominique is disappointed to see that she allows frequent interruptions from other children to prevent her from getting back to the child who had quietly requested her help in the first place. 'I can't believe it!', Dominique repeats over and over, watching herself on the monitor, slapping her cheek in surprise. 'I encourage them to be dependent on me . . . what I want to do is the opposite. Those children are perfectly capable of doing those things for themselves. And look at that! I forgot her, I never did get back to her'.

Dominique's observations remind us that in the heat of the teaching moment, we cannot be aware of all of our actions and those of our students. Nor do we usually have the time or ability to ponder their full significance while we're teaching. A videotape throws another view (representation) of classroom reality right in our face! And we can stand back and watch it repeatedly, learning from both our students and ourselves, reinterpreting and reconstructing our self-image as teacher. But we can only see what we are ready or able to see. Like all readers, we can only 'read' in terms of our own prior experience, values, and knowledge.

Perhaps the most significant aspect of Dominique's reactions to her videotape is the way she applies her teacher knowledge and personal philosophy to her situation. The tape evokes and taps into one of Dominique's fundamental purposes in teaching (to foster autonomy). Through her eyes (self as audience, teacher gaze), the central issue raised by the tape is how to best organize the classroom and interact with children in ways that make them less dependent on their teacher.

After seeing Dominique viewing her first self-video, we next watch her in frank discussions with the consultant who participated in the project. The consultant points out certain things on the tape that had captured her attention, but mainly, she listens and confirms, witnessing and supporting Dominique's attempts to identify concrete actions to bring her teaching practice more in line with her teaching philosophy. Among other things, Dominique decides to explain to the children that when she is working with a student, they should not interrupt and should go consult another child for help instead. She also wants to keep track of whom she interacts with, and plans to change the way some of the equipment and centres are set up. For example, everything needed to clean up spills at the art centre should be right there at the centre.

We then follow Dominique's efforts to modify her practice via excerpts from subsequent classroom videotapes. There is a noticeable change. The noise is not the same sort of noise as before, it sounds different. Things don't seem as frenetic. Everything just seems to flow. More of the children are engaged and busy in a focussed way. And Dominique! Her manner is just as absorbed with the children as before, but something has changed. She's calmer and more relaxed, taking more time to challenge children individually with questions and suggestions. Much less of her time is spent on 'housekeeping'.

She has indeed implemented her plans with very positive results. But the essence of what changes in the classroom transcends the measures taken. It is the very quality of classroom life and Dominique's demeanor that change. As Dominique puts it 'I notice things now that I didn't see before . . . I feel different too. I didn't just change my outward behaviour, I changed in here' (pointing to her head).

We have described the case of *Dominique! Dominique!* in detail because for us it posits certain conditions that seem to facilitate professional growth:

1 *Authenticity, commitment, and openness:* Whether Dominique is with the children, in conversation with the consultant, or viewing a tape of herself, it is very evident how genuine and deep her engagement with the self-video project is, and how committed she is to being a 'good' teacher, how open she is to critique, how natural and authentic she is in her struggle for growth. She is not afraid to be 'uncomfortable' with what she sees, using the resulting dissonance to imagine better ways of teaching. We wonder if these qualities underlie the changes we saw in her teaching. In other words, we argue that it is not only the specific measures Dominique implemented that made the experience so successful, but also the manner in which she lived the self-video experience.

2 *Open-ended dialogue (analysis):* Dominique did not use a previously defined protocol of analysis to interpret her video. Rather, she entered into a genuine dialogue with the video representation of her work, waiting to see what would strike her, what would emerge as important in the context of her experiential knowledge.

3 *Personal knowledge, experience, and self-reading:* Someone else viewing Dominique's tape or watching her teach might not have noticed or focussed on the question of student autonomy that seemed so flagrant to Dominique. We each use our own personal frameworks of analysis and philosophy of education to filter our readings of any text, including self-videos. Dominique's interpretation of her teaching self reflects where she is in her professional development and pushes her further towards her own vision of teaching. She did not merely find what she was looking for. She was surprised into a reflection she had not anticipated. The beauty of self-video is that it can pick us up from wherever we are and nudge us on in a new direction.

4 *Trust and sharing in community:* Like the work in previous chapters, Dominique's project implicitly makes the point that self-video does not have to be a solitary activity. It hints at the importance of having the support and point of view of some other trusted professional to facilitate and stimulate. Moreover, by making a copy of the videotape of the whole process available to other teachers, Dominique *makes the matter of personal professional growth a part of collective culture and development as well.* This is highly significant, suggesting a teacher who is open and secure in her professional sense of self, and who is aware that sharing the personal simultaneously strengthens the community and the self.

When the above conditions are not present, self-video may be less effective and less positive an experience. In fact, as the case that follows will demonstrate, under certain circumstances it can be unnecessarily painful or destructive. The case provides an important cautionary tale of what can happen when video is used insensitively and inappropriately, reminding us that *it is not self-video* per se *that guarantees professional growth; it is why and how it is done that is crucial.*

Case 3: I Can't Believe That's Me! A Cautionary Video Experience

Jane, a university lecturer in the history department, takes her teaching very seriously, wanting to do a good job, hoping to offer her students new and liberating ways of seeing the world. But, like so many of us, Jane finds that engaging her students meaningfully is not always automatic or easy, especially during certain 'compulsory' courses which some students take only because they have to.

She decided to sign up for a series of intensive workshops on improving one's teaching that was being offered by the university on a one-time basis for the professional development of interested faculty members. She was hoping to pick up some ideas that would be useful to her situation.

The sessions turned out to be boring, even painful, for Jane. She describes them as a series of dry and authoritative lectures followed by some prescribed small group activities. In Jane's view, teaching was represented in the workshops as something technical, almost mechanical. A matter of planning and objectives, one step leading automatically to another. No life! Little consideration of underlying philosophy! No organic growth to the process. No authentic teaching situations. Neither the workshop content nor the manner in which it was conducted appealed to Jane as a learner or as a teacher. Nonetheless, she persisted, dutifully taking notes, doing the assigned exercises, and engaging the instructors and other participants honestly but diplomatically with her questions and misgivings.

One of the 'special' features of the course was a video camera installed in a fixed position in the classrooms provided for small group work. The workshop participants were all asked to refine their mastery of certain didactic techniques by 'microteaching' a short prepared lesson to a small group of colleagues. Content didn't matter, they were told. It was just an exercise, a simulation. The fixed focus video cameras were matter-of-factly turned on when each person 'taught', and after a short discussion in class about how their lesson went, each participant was given their recorded tape. They were asked to take the tapes home and study or analyse them, using a simple guideline that had been distributed earlier. This protocol consisted of the following categories for organizing their self-critique: organization of the lesson; pacing; voice projection, eye contact, gestures, use of materials, interaction with students.

None of the categories or anything that had been said in class prepared Jane for what happened when she viewed the tape of herself. The image on the tape was shadowy, of poor quality, and slightly greenish, the lighting unflattering, the mechanical focus stationary and up close. 'That can't be me!! I look like a witch', Jane howled. 'If that's what I really look like, I am never leaving this house again'. She was badly shaken. It's not like she had never seen herself on video before or looked in a mirror . . . This tense sallow woman couldn't be her, could it? Is that what she is transformed into when she taught, she wondered? Or was it the artificial, strained situation of the micro teaching? Or . . . ???

Hours later, slightly recovered from the initial shock, she reviewed the tape according to the prescribed categories. They seemed simplistic and superficial to her. 'What about quality of discourse and ideas? Nature of engagement? Group dynamics? Level of inquiry? Space for and nature of student input and reaction? Implicit meaning or hidden curriculum — what's really going on here?' The questions that concerned Jane did not figure in the prescribed protocol. Although the purpose of the exercise had been to apply what she had learned about teaching, somehow the attempt to replicate or represent a 'real teaching episode' made the whole business seem fake and inauthentic.

During the next day's workshop, Jane soon realized she was not the only one who had experienced discomfort and difficulty. People wanted to talk about their video experiences, it had been powerful in ways the instructors had not anticipated. For example, the women, especially, had found the unflattering representations of their bodies unexpectedly hard to deal with. One hated her hair, another the way she moved. But the female workshop animators seemed to have little patience with or interest in this phenomenon.

'I look like a house', wailed one woman to one of the workshop instructors. 'Can't you get past your size?', the instructor responded impatiently.

There was not much time for or interest in hearing about people's self-analysis, and any comments about physical features in particular were dismissed with a laugh. Although self-video had been touted as a particularly significant and avant-garde element of the workshops, it was quickly dropped as a topic when it became evident that these might contain challenges and difficulties to the official workshop content. (Case constructed from interviews with 'Jane')

Jane's case raises many important issues, especially in contrast to Dominique's. It critically questions the use of simulated rather than authentic teaching situations, and illustrates how an insensitive or unsupported use of video can be counter-productive to professional development, and worse, cause *unnecessary pain.* Jane questions whose and what criteria should be used to analyse self-videos: important questions indeed. She feels that the self-analysis would have been much more useful to her had it been allowed to emerge from what was on the tape rather than forcing things into pre-determined categories.

Most compelling, perhaps, is the story's illustration of the importance of body image to self-esteem and to professional identity, especially for women socialized in a culture where emphasis on standards of female appearance is so pervasive. There is no mistaking that for Jane, as for so many, what she looks like as a woman/teacher is central to how she thinks of herself in relation to society in general ('if that's what I look like, I'm never leaving this house') and to students in particular. Jane's story echoes themes relating to body and appearance discussed earlier in the book, reminding us that self-study cannot ignore the teacher-body. How we dress and look *as teachers* to ourselves and to others can influence our identity and even our pedagogy.

Even alone in the privacy of our own homes, the viewing experience is never only personal or idiosyncratic. Personal views of self inevitably reflect outward to social constructions of self and the culture in which we are raised. As Ellsworth and Whatley (1990) point out, it pushes the viewer to see things from some one else's perspective. The video forces us to adopt,

> if only imaginatively and temporarily — the social, political, and ideological interests that are the conditions for the knowledge it constructs . . . the 'viewing experience' must be seen not as voluntary and idiosyncratic, but as fundamentally relational — a projection of particular kinds of relations between self, others' knowledge, and power. (p. 14)

Seeing Through the Video Body

Like the photographs and cases we examined in earlier chapters, Jane's story brings the importance of the body to teacher identity back to our attention.

Getting Past the Body

During a scholarly and articulate presentation at a national conference, a university professor of education described a self-study he had done by videotaping his classes over a semester. His focus was on evaluating how well his teaching practice reflected or applied his curricular beliefs and theories. In recounting how he had viewed and analysed his tapes, he remarked, 'Once I got past the body stuff, you know, bad hair days and that sort of thing, then I could really focus on my pedagogy'. (Notes from a session at the annual meeting of the AERA, Chicago, 1997)

In contrast to the toddler Jonathan in chapter 4 who sought out a mirror, the adult pedagogue seeks, not to see the 'whole' self, but to get past the body. Why is this so? 'Getting past the body.' That's the same phrase the instructor of Jane's workshop used and the type of dismissal of the body we heard in earlier chapters. But the video body is particularly difficult to 'get past' because it is bigger than the photograph. It moves and talks. Clothed and adorned and accessorized (for example, with pointers, glasses, chalk, or pearls), the teacher's body commands attention.

That teaching is an embodied function becomes immediately clear when we consider that one of the first things we notice about a teacher (after dress and sex), is the main instrument of instruction, the teacher's voice. Because it is so much a part of the serious business of teaching, however, we tend to forget that voice is a function of the body.

The Teacher's Voice

The sound of the voice (its pitch, its color, its intonational movements), the accent it speaks in, the amount of aural space it occupies and its general appeal are as much part of what creates gendered identities as the content of what is said or other aspects of material self-presentation. (Poynton, 1996, p. 109)

Is That How I Really Sound?

The first time I saw myself on videotape, what startled and shocked me the most was not how I looked, but my voice! *It didn't sound like me . . . my first reaction was 'Is that how I really sound . . . so high-pitched and little girlish?' How come I don't notice that when I am talking? Now that I think of it, I hate my voice when I listen to the pre-taped greeting on my telephone answering machine.*

After that taping, I tried modifying my voice, consciously lowering it when I was teaching or answering the telephone. But I'm not sure if that has really made a noticeable difference. Through video self-study, I have grown more accustomed to hearing my voice on tape, but coming to terms with this voice as 'me' is still not easy. It's not the voice I would choose or imagine for myself. I guess all these years I have been superimposing an ideal-ized 'vocal me' onto how I really talk. Unless, of course, all this technological registering of my speech distorts my voice, making it higher pitched than it really is? Wishful thinking! (Weber, excerpt from an unpublished self-study, 1992)

Although the term 'voice' occurs frequently in educational writing, the principal contemporary use of the word is as a metaphor for struggles for empowerment. *We are so caught up with the symbolic value of 'voice' that we risk forgetting to take seriously the very real and physical voices of teachers and students* that are integral to voice-as-power, voice-as-authority, voice-as-resistance, and 'multiple-voices'.

The materiality of voice, its presence and its forcible absence, is an essential aspect of the pedagogical experience. Think of the transgressive pleasure of 'calling out' and the unbearable frustration of not being allowed to speak, much less shout with my whole body, what I know, but having to wait my turn; the communal voice of the playground which can be rapturous . . . or hostile and aggressive towards those marginalized by dominant discourses; the classroom alienation of the adolescent, enduring yet another 40 minutes of yet another droning pedagogic voice; the abjection of students berated by the Principal, voice proceeding, as if the voice of God, from the box on the classroom wall . . . ; the pleasure of the improvization workshop and the scream-ing of barracking chants; the calming presence of one teacher voice, the teeth-setting-on-edge effect of another; and always the complex polyphony of the singleton voice of authority with its nominated soloists and the massed voice of the class, that bizarre collective entity. (Poynton, 1996, p. 105)

As we explore in the following sections, the voice is only one of the significant aspects of the teaching body as vehicle of communication. What we *do* with our bodies as we speak can change the meaning of what we say.

Speaking With Our Bodies: Paralanguage in the Classroom

When she is over-tired, a 3-year-old girl vigorously opposes being put to bed. 'I'm NOT tired' she says, stamping her foot, her eyes glazing over. What messages are being communicated here? Should we take her at her word, that she is not tired?

In answer to his partner's question, 'What's wrong, love?', a man replies with his jaw clenched, his voice angry, almost shouting, 'Nothing's wrong!' What are we to make of his message? Do actions speak louder than words?

It's not only what we say (content) that we communicate, it's how we say it (or don't) and what we do as we say it. If what a person says contradicts what she or he does, the savvy listener gives priority to the non-verbal message as more genuine or significant, as having greater truth-value and better representing the speaker's internal intentions and feelings (Watzlawick et al., 1967). These non-linguistic and non-verbal aspects of communication are referred to by linguists as 'paralanguage'. Although paralanguage is central to all spoken communication, the meaning ascribed to particular elements of paralanguage varies across cultures and from one individual to another. As Poynton (1996) points out:

> Voices, as embodied, participate in complex performances of gender, class, race, locale and sexuality using semiotic resources every bit as conventionalized as those involved in other forms of bodily performance. Even a phenomenon as apparently profoundly physiological as basic voice pitch can be demonstrated to be a complex combination of the cultural (the learned) with the biological (p. 109)

Both inside and outside the classroom, meaning is negotiated and is embedded in its situational and cultural communicative context. Making sense of this context requires a wide range of cues. Bruner and Haste (1987) argue that we all spontaneously use a culturally determined paralanguage or 'scaffold of meaning' to support, amplify, or even contradict our spoken words. Cues such as the elocution, gestures, and movements of a speaker not only direct attention to the particular context but also give information about the speaker and the degree of importance of what is being said and what is being left out.

Why should we focus on our use of paralanguage in teaching? A compelling reason can be found in *How Children Fail,* an account of closely observed classroom interaction published by journalist John Holt in 1964. His observations and analysis show how through gesture, tone of voice, and facial expressions, teachers can *inadvertently or deliberately* give the message that all that counts in class is saying the 'right' answer. 'Wrong' answers are bad and disgraceful, and the definition of 'right' is 'what the teacher wants to hear'. A complicity develops between students and teachers in which teachers help their students avoid humiliation by cueing them to the 'right' answer through use of paralanguage (for example, unconsciously mouthing the answer, nodding, or gesturing subtly towards a clue), and students learn to manipulate their teachers, how to play the 'good student' without the bother of actually learning the material. This encourages not understanding, but guessing, not independent thinking, but reliance on teachers for answers.

This view of classroom interaction is further supported by the research of scholars such as Delamont (1987) and Edwards and Westgate (1994), which provide many telling examples of how both teachers and students use paralanguage to control and direct each other's behaviour. Using detailed observations and videotapes of several primary classrooms, Weber and Tardif (1987) note specific uses teachers make of certain combinations of gestures, body movement, and intonation to support the management, routines and rituals of classroom life. Their paralanguage can be a deliberate pedagogical strategy to scaffold teacher communication, or it can be an unconscious counter-text that may help or confuse students in making sense of what the teacher really means or wants.

The following case describes how one teacher used self-video tapes to learn about her use of paralanguage in the classroom (Lavallee, 1990).

*Case 4: So That's How I Do It! A Teacher Reviews
Her Body Language*

Barbara Lavallee (her real name) is an experienced kindergarten and primary teacher. During the many years she spent as a second language immersion teacher, she spoke mainly in French to her English-speaking students all day long, whatever the subject matter or activity. Some parents were initially apprehensive that their children would be stressed or traumatized in some way by having to live in a new language at such a young age. They were relieved and then later delighted to note what a positive experience being a student in Ms. Lavallee's class usually was, how much French their children learned, and how the first language did not suffer (on the contrary, their first language flourished). As a result, Barbara gained a wonderful reputation, and many parents made specific requests that their children be assigned to her class. Other teachers and parents would ask, 'What's your secret? How do you do it?'

To give something back to the profession, and more importantly, to enrich her own development and the second language experience in her classroom, Ms. Lavallee volunteered to host and supervise student teachers from a preservice second language teacher education program. It was in this context that she first met two professors who were very interested in learning more about how young children make sense of a second language in an immersion classroom situation. This led to a two year ethnographic study wherein the two researchers observed, videotaped, and interviewed in Ms. Lavallee's class (see Tardif and Weber, 1987; and Weber and Tardif, 1991). The focus of the investigation was on the children's sense-making more than on the teacher.

Barbara became increasingly interested in the ongoing research, and kept a diary of her teaching for her own purposes. 'Why', she wondered, 'does it seem to work? Do I do anything specific that helps the children pick up a second language? Do I stimulate their growth and learning in other areas? What, if anything, am I doing right?! Do I have a secret? If I do, it's so secret that even I don't know it!'

These interrogations led Barbara to ask the researchers for the videotapes they had made of her teaching so that she could analyse them, focussing on her communication with her students. In a nutshell, what she found was that she used and modified paralanguage in many different and nuanced ways: to make the students feel at home and at ease (for example, smiles, comforting tone of voice, arm around a shoulder), to support the meaning of her communication (for example, gestures, miming, pointing), to encourage them to develop their own sense-making strategies (increasing silent wait time). She also noticed how her use of paralanguage changed in response to the children's progress. For example, she progressively reduced the number and types of non-verbal gestures and clues, forcing students to rely more heavily on the linguistic or semantic elements of her communication. 'So that's how I do it!', Barbara mused. Now that she was aware of it, she wondered if there were times when she could make better use of her paralanguage, if she provided too much or too little redundancy (scaffolding). And more and more, she wondered if she was too 'bossy', if she really needed to direct activities as much as she did.

Elements of Paralanguage in the Classroom

The term 'paralanguage' has continued to evolve since it was first coined by George Trager (1958) and encompasses the following elements.

1 *Paraverbal or paralinguistic elements (how we speak and how we are silent)* include: degree of intensity, rate and pitch, the use of 'non-words' ('ah', 'hmm', 'oh'), prosody (for example, whispering, drawing words out for emphasis) and the role of silence.

   Let's take as an example the use of non-words. Teachers often engage in a form of 'vocal dawdling' or pausing filled with non-words (for example, ah, oh, ah-ha) which allow time for new ideas to be absorbed or past ones to be reinforced. A powerful expression of ahh!! can confirm in children's minds that their guess was correct and an oh! oh! can challenge them to keep on trying as well as signal when behaviour expectations are not quite being met. Lavallee found that she used non-words for three basic reasons:

(a)   to allow time for collecting thoughts (teacher or students);
(b)   to deal with interruptions by students holding the floor;
(c)   to draw specific attention to features of content or language.

2   *Kinesic elements (gestures and expression)* incorporate the broad domains of (i) *facial expression* (smiles, frowns, grimaces, blank look, surprise, delight, worry, anger); (ii) *posture*; and (iii) *body movement*. Kinesic elements are similarly measured in terms of pitch, stress, and intensity as well as duration of movement. As an example, in her self-video study, Lavallee found that she made frequent use of such body movements as:

(a)   sweeping motions using hands and arms (special emphasis markers);
(b)   mimicking words and ideas using fingers, hands, arms and whole body;
(c)   pointing to child or object;
(d)   shaking or nodding her head;
(e)   holding up objects, moving objects.

3   *Proxemic elements:* These include touching behaviour (for example, tap on shoulder) and movements in social distance (bending towards child, walking about). As an example, Lavallee writes how touching children, physically moving them about, and bending over or pointing to them seemed to be her way to refocus student behaviour. Many of her proxemic behaviours revolved initially around questions of social distance and the establishment and control of the boundaries surrounding the open area (circle) of space between the children and teacher during group storytelling time. Whereas her teacher behaviours of touching and posture remained constant over the year, their functions changed from a stress on territorial control to simple manipulation of the available space in order to achieve pedagogical goals.

Analysis of classroom paralanguage helps us learn what we really communicate, to locate the counter-texts or 'mixed messages' we unwittingly send with our bodies. Compassion, revulsion, sincerity, nervousness, excitement, sensuality, approval, censure, bossiness, seduction — these are just a few examples of what we and our students communicate through paralanguage. Although largely taken for granted, non-verbal cues act as indicators of power relationships within the classroom and as cultural markers.

Because body language is cultural, like all aspects of language, its use can lead to misunderstandings and misinterpretations both inside and outside the classroom. For example, the body language of a student raised in a home-culture where showing respect for teachers and adults means looking demurely downward, NOT making eye contact, and not asking questions might be misinterpreted by some teachers as disinterest or rudeness. Similarly, some students might be mystified or upset by the informality or friendliness of some teacher's paralanguage, or conversely, frightened by what is interpreted as the cool distance and grimness of others.

That elusive 'certain something' (either positive or negative) that we may sense in viewing someone's self-video but cannot immediately put our finger on is often revealed upon analysis of the body's paralanguage. Understanding our use of paralanguage empowers us to communicate more deliberately. Pennycook (1985), for example, urges teachers to examine and refine their use of paralinguistic signals to convey information, thus permitting children to engage in communicative activities that would otherwise be beyond their range of understanding. We could actively teach our students how paralanguage supports or sabotages communication and expresses social and cultural etiquette. This becomes even more crucial in multicultural or second language classrooms.

Self-video in Teacher Education and Professional Development

Viewing the tape — that is when a self-video more clearly reveals its potential for good and evil. How do we use the tape? Where do we view it? Quietly, at home in our pyjamas with a diary close at hand? As a personal and private act of self-examination? In the classroom with our students? After school with a trusted friend and colleague, followed, perhaps, by an honest discussion over coffee? In our supervisor or professor's office, with a formal evaluation sheet or grid to fill out? Who views it and how? Through what lens is the tape perceived? In what circumstances or context was the tape made, and for what ends? Is our tape one in a pile of many to be quickly viewed by someone in a position of authority over us? Do we show it to our spouses and friends to give them a glimpse of our working life, integrating our personal and professional selves? Do we view it once, hurriedly, trying not to watch it through spread fingers as if it were a gory scene in a horror film? Do we watch it many times, eagerly, patiently? Do we systematically focus on specific elements or just sit back and try to 'get a feel of the whole'? Who does not get to see it? Do we share it with our students or their parents? Why or why not?

These were some of the questions we had in mind when we began experimenting with different ways to encourage and support beginning teachers to engage in self-study. We are painfully aware that the student-teacher/university–supervisor relationship is fraught with contradictions and tensions. No matter how collegial a relationship we may establish as teacher educators, our institutional affiliations cast us in a position of power and authority. The video camera can thus all too easily become an extension of the supervisor's eyes, and be perceived by student teachers as an evaluating gaze. To mitigate this perception at least partially, we do not evaluate the self-study video tapes

Box 6.2

Procedural Guidelines for Self-videotaping

1   What to videotape? When to videotape? How to videotape? Why videotape? These personal decisions are at the heart of self-study. Wrestling honestly with them and seeing what kinds of answers they provoke can be transformative in itself, before ever taping. These questions can also be useful in determining what camera placement and angles are needed. That said, just filming off the cuff or on a whim can produce equally wonderful material for self-study!

2   Obtain informed consent from students (and parents) before video-taping. Some teachers inform parents and children at the beginning of the school year that this will be a normal part of classroom activity.

3   Borrow the video camera and practise ahead of time to familiarize yourself with the equipment. Ensure access to an extension cord and extra lights in case the need arises. Use a tripod; the results are much more satisfying.

4   Someone should operate the camera. If you are being filmed, have someone else tape you rather than just plunking the camera on a tripod in the corner (although that can be done as a last resort). Videotaped material is much nicer and more useful when it features the moving gaze that only a camera operator can provide. It's so helpful to have a back and forth movement from the teacher to a child or group, with occasional appropriate close-ups of individuals, crucial objects or displays. We learn much more when we see our-selves through someone else's eyes. Paradoxically, the way to a more objective view is often through a personal viewpoint. The idea is to avoid what Annette Kuhn (1985) has described as the kind of camera placement typical of educational feature films from the early 1900s; namely, 'frontal "tableau" shots' that left narrative space undissected, keeping a distance from the action. (p. 108)

5   Don't forget to load the camera with a video tape *before* filming. (This had to be said!)

6   If you are acting as cameraperson, get some idea of what the teacher being videotaped is going to be doing. Reading a story to a large group? Moving about from small group to group? Is there something in particular that they wish you to follow or focus on? In other words,

figure out the best place to install the camera on its tripod. To obtain a decent quality of image, make sure that the *windows are behind* the camera. Don't shoot into them.

7 Set the video up in the classroom ahead of time and do a pilot tape *beforehand* in order to allow everyone to get used to the camera's presence and also to ensure that the equipment is working properly and the set-up is appropriate.

8 If it seems appropriate, show the videotape to your students soon after filming. Initiate a discussion about what happened (and didn't happen!). Enlist their aid in reflecting on life in the classroom. Ask the camera operator to film additional segments, focussing on the students, making sure that each and every child appears on the tape. Students are usually eager to see themselves and each other, and the experience can be one of self-discovery for them too.

9 If you feel comfortable enough with a supervisor or another colleague, you may later wish to share the tape with him or her.

that our students produce. Equally importantly, we try to make it clear that it is all right, even desirable, to 'screw up', to catch oneself or one's students on a bad day. The idea is to facilitate the use of video for self-study. A *self* study is just that, something that involves the self above all.

> *When I first heard we had to do a video, I was really nervous. But, it was really great . . . probably the single best part of my teacher education programme. Don't drop it as a requirement.* (Excerpt from student-teacher's journal)

> *If only we had done this earlier! I wish I had tapes from the beginning of my practicum. I learned SO much.* (Excerpt from student-teacher's journal)

The practicum set-up that provoked those unsolicited comments was as follows:

Student-teachers, even if they are placed in different schools and grades, pair up with a colleague of their choice. They visit each other's classrooms and videotape each other in action on at least one, but preferably two occasions. Each student-teacher keeps the master copy of her tapes and views them several times, using detailed guidelines or suggestions (an example follows later). They are encouraged (but *not* required) to share their tapes with their own students, their families, their supervising teacher, and each other.

This practicum thus provides time and opportunity for each student-teacher to visit another classroom or school, to see what others are doing, to share personal experience in a fairly protected and safe setting, and most important of all, to face themselves. Finally, they are asked to write a self-reflection based on the video experience, make a video, or find some way to represent their experience in a manner that integrates it meaningfully to their professional development. If a grade is required, it is this final representation or document (with supporting notes) that we evaluate, *not the videotape itself.* The students know that what interests us most is the depth of their analysis and their ability to articulate and reflect meaningfully on their experience.

Although initially most students balk at the very idea of being filmed, once they've done it, they demand to know why they weren't required to videotape themselves earlier on in the programme! Their enthusiasm is palpable — so much so that many of their experienced supervising teachers are inspired to do a self-video study for their own professional development! What begins as an individual endeavour soon radiates outward to the collectivity.

Box 6.2 contains are some suggestions that neophytes and experienced teachers alike may find useful, especially the first time they use video for self study.

After they have had the opportunity to 'live with' their tapes for a few days, our student-teachers meet in groups of three or four to show each other segments they have selected from their videos for discussion and feedback. They are invited to regard 'bad' moments as good opportunities for reflection, to ask each other questions, to share the joy and humour of teaching, to commiserate and offer support in facing the difficulties, to brainstorm and imagine possibilities for future growth, to notice and celebrate the nuances and finer points, and to respect each other's differences and preferences. The university supervisors do not attend all of these meetings, but make themselves available by invitation to participate in discussions, as teachers.

It is this *collective viewing* that students find especially helpful and enriching. It gives each of them a chance to view their teaching through at least two other teachers' eyes *and* allows them to see how others teach. They give each other pointers, spark ideas, and point out things that the person on tape did not yet notice. The more the experience is shared, the greater the range of possibilities for reinvention.

We have no formula to offer that fits all situations. What follows is the advice our own student teachers have found useful.

Reflections on Our Video Selves: Learning from the Videotape

After the teaching day is over and the first self-video completed, the real work of self-study begins. In privacy, view the whole tape straight through. Especially if this is the first self-video, it is perfectly normal to experience some nervous anticipation or shock (sometimes of pleasure — we don't always look or sound as bad as we think!) just at seeing and hearing ourselves on tape. Remember, it's *just a tape*. It is a representation of ourselves, yes, but it is not us. Videotapes often seem to be taken on bad hair days, or the day we develop adult acne or a run in a stocking, or a bad cold and a raw red nose! Dwell for a while, if you wish, on appearance, voice, and gestures. What is it that upsets or pleases you? How do your reactions relate to your experience and self-image both inside and outside of the classroom? Try not to gloss too quickly past the embodied self, because it is through it that we think, teach and live.

Important reminder: Viewing ourselves always involves emotions of some sorts. Rather than repressing them, we need to acknowledge them and examine their connections to other personal and professional events in order to be able to contextualize them appropriately. It may take a little time to come to terms with and get used to the video self. *How we initially view ourselves on video may have very little to do with the particular teaching episode and very much to do with our past experiences with other people outside of the classroom.*

Our experience suggests that it is useful to review the tape more than once: self-study needs to develop over time. What follows are *five specific ways to review, analyse, or follow-up a self-video*, some of which are more possible or helpful in certain situations than in others. We offer them *as possibilities and not prescriptions*.

First analysis (review): A silent movie — taking body language seriously

Rewind the tape, turn off the volume, and watch it once more *without any sound*. What does your paralanguage (body language) and that of the students say? Body language is usually the best (most accurate) indicator of student–teacher relationships and emotions. What is really happening on this tape? What kinds of relationships (including power relationships) can you see or intuit?

How do you 'come across' on the tape? How would you characterize yourself if you were writing this up as a script about a fictitious teacher (who is really you)? Box 6.3 is just one of many possible aids to get started. It can be used initially during a silent viewing (ignoring the adjectives related to voice), but is also useful to analyse how we sound as well as how we look and move.

Second analysis (review): Getting down to specifics —
some critical questions

Pose a few specific, significant questions to reorient this next viewing of the tape. As we saw earlier in the case of Dominique, these questions usually arise from our first review of the tape and reflect our own situation, knowledge and experience. Some of the following general questions may be helpful starting points for composing a more specific personal set tailored to your needs and context:

- What strikes you as most important or significant about the tape (for your own growth and benefit)?
- Tell a story about this tape. What is it about?
- How typical or atypical is this tape of your classroom life?
- What was it like to be a particular student in class during this episode? (Put yourself in a specific student's shoes as you watch.)
- Describe the mood and atmosphere in the classroom. Does it change, and if so, how and why?
- How do the people on the tape seem to feel about each other?
- What is really being taught and how?
- What is really being learned? What really happens?
- What, if anything, is 'teacherly' about the teacher? What makes her or him a teacher? What kind of teacher is she or he?
- How does the teacher 'teach'? Are any specific models, methods, techniques or philosophies exemplified?
- How is power distributed in the classroom?
- How are gender, class, race, religion, or other fundamental differences played out?
- What are the implicit rules that someone would need to follow in order to be a 'good' student in this classroom?
- What counts as 'good' and 'bad' student behaviour on this tape? What might that signify?
- What could the organization of time and space mean to the students? What does it mean to the teacher? (For example, what kind of messages are classroom routines, arrangement of furniture and materials, and the like sending?)
- Who does most of the talking (for example, teacher, boys, a small group, 'bad' students, privileged students)?
- What is the talk and action mainly about? What kinds of language and styles of interaction dominate?
- What kinds of questions are asked or comments made (including the non-verbal questions of glances, shrugs, facial expressions, etc.) by both teacher and by particular students? How are these questions and comments responded to (whose questions are dismissed or ignored)?
- What didn't happen that could or should have?

Important reminder: These are just examples of the kinds of questions that might be useful. The trick is to choose or compose just a few, the ones that are most appropriate to our own specific context and purposes. To be of any use, our reflections on the above questions must be *based on what is on the tape, and not on what we think we usually do.*

Box 6.3

How Do I Come Across? Possible Descriptors

Circle as many of the following words that apply to *the teacher who is seen and heard on the tape, not to who you usually think you are*:

Nervous   Warm   Confident   Scattered   Assertive   Soft

Organized   Calm   Unsure   Harsh   Dramatic   Perky

Mean   Humorous   Compelling   Understanding   Impatient

Casual   Strict   Supportive   Hesitant   Reassuring   Shrill

Animated   Droning   Energetic   Tired   Low key   Boring

Elegant   Jolly   Loving   Cold   Tender   Motherly

Solicitous   Radical   Friendly   Awkward   Cheerful   Tidy

Dignified   Rumpled   Lively   Shrewd   At ease

Harsh   Loud   Refined   Sloppy   Prim   Unkempt

Aloof   Uneasy   Engaging   Wandering   Busy

Caring   Sensitive   Intellectual   Bright   Funny

Distracted   Witty   Groomed   Stylish   Cool   Shy

Old-fashioned   Avant-garde   Confused   Impartial   Attractive

Engaging   Frightened   Uncomfortable   Competent

Insecure   Scholarly   Boorish   Rude   Nice

Young   Nagging   Sophisticated   Awkward   Wimpy

Embarrassed   Articulate   Mumbling   Business-like   Grouchy

Sarcastic   Detached   Discouraged   Stern   Frumpy

Reflect on the words you have circled and write about why you have circled them by relating them to the tape directly but also to any other relevant experience.

Third review: Integrating the professional with the personal

Is teaching an important part of who we are? Do we think of ourselves as teachers? One way to find out is to integrate the 'professional self' with the 'private self' by sharing the tape and our reactions to it with someone close to us, someone who is usually privy to what *is* important to us. The ensuing discussion may reveal some of the joys, hope, anxiety, ambivalence or fears that are associated with identifying ourselves as teacher. Writing an essay or making some personal journal entries after the experience can help consolidate and refine our reflections further.

Fourth review: Collective interpretation and reinvention

Show approximately 10 minutes of the tape to a small group of colleagues. Ideally, each person should have a self-video. Seeing how others teach increases our ability to imagine classroom life differently, to reinvent. Some tapes might inspire us to emulate. Others may confirm what we do not want to be or do. Reinvention is often facilitated by some undesirable situation that begs for a better solution or way of being. Lead a discussion, ask specific opinions on matters of concern. Make notes or tape the conversation; i.e. obtain some written form of feedback. Brainstorm together to imagine other possibilities. What would you do if you could go back and re-live the experience that you videotaped?

Fifth review: Reinvention through synthesis

One of the most significant things we can do after the initial taping, sharing, and analysing is to plan for and to do a *follow-up series of tapes*. As we saw in Dominique's case, the self-knowledge we gain from a first self-video needs to be fleshed out in pedagogical action. Subsequent self-videos facilitate, confirm, and renew our efforts to reinvent ourselves. But there are many other ways to follow-up the experience that facilitate reinvention. An article or report, for example, could include:

- description and analysis of the teaching self;
- what we would change and what we would *not* change;
- a description of our personal goals for future development as a teacher;
- what the video self-study has meant to us; what we have learned from it;
- appendices of the lesson plans or journal notes written for the activity and any of the review notes or students' and colleagues' comments that we wish to share.

Viable and valuable forms of synthesis include more literary or creative formats, for example:

- write a collection of poems about yourself, your life as a teacher, life in the classroom, or the self-study experience;
- write a story or poem or essay from the point of view of a student;
- write an article for a professional magazine or the school newspaper;
- make a collage that evokes the meaning and method of your self-study;
- reinvent the video: enlist your students to make a new video showing different outcomes;
- create or contribute to a web-site about self-video;
- do an improvizational drama or write a short play based on the experience;
- paint or sing what the experience has meant;
- make a video about self-study (maybe film ourselves *while* we are reviewing our tapes and make an edited collage).

The single most significant outcome is to take any new insight or awareness into our daily teaching. Truly listening to ourselves in the immediate past and reflecting on the significance of that experience to our practice, therein lies the key to changing our future.

Video Praxis: Resistance and Reinvention

Praxis . . . refers to self-creative activity through which men and women create (make, produce) and change (shape) the historical, human world and themselves. Praxis includes an element of critique of existing historical conditions and an element of possibility of reworking those conditions. In addition, the concept of praxis attempts to link or loop together theory and practice — in its strongest sense of '*practice as action*'. (Sholle and Denski, 1995, p. 11)

Video can be a highly effective form of praxis by providing us with the means to evaluate practical experimentations critically. In the case of Dominique, for example, we saw how she used repeated tapings to document her attempts to change the way she did certain things in her classroom. But video can be used in other ways too for professional development and expression.

In the previous chapter we posed the question 'what if teachers tried to influence popular culture?'. In chapter 3, we briefly described using a photo layout as a way to reframe or re-imagine ourselves as teachers. Here, we take up reinvention more concretely by asking: Can the video camera be used to reconceptualize or reinvent our praxis? We think so, for as Haug (1987) observes:

In an effort to make their lives meaningful, individuals attempt to resist the encumbrances of the dominant culture. It is however virtually impossible for them entirely to abandon traditional norms and expectations. On the other hand they can — and indeed do — find compromise solutions that extend the limits of their capacity for action. Thus we witness individuals searching for a meaning to life within pre-existing structures, yet at the same time negating them. (p. 44)

Could teachers stage some classroom plots that would allow them to critique and imagine new learning/teaching spaces? Two beginning teachers we discuss below did just that; they reinvented themselves as directors, producers and actors in a music video called *Dangerous Kids*.

Case 5: Dangerous Kids

As part of a university course on language and learning, two high school teachers, Ben and Gus (not their real names), produced, directed and acted in a short music video. Their initial audience was their colleagues — other beginning teachers who were struggling with their sense that the theories discussed in university seemed to have little to do with teaching practice in real classrooms. This is a concern of most beginning teachers, one that rightly finds its way into many university conversations and classroom discussions. As Weber (1990) points out, it is also one of those issues that never seem to be resolved; there is an ongoing tension that is often oversimplified or caricatured as a dichotomy between the academy (theory) and the field ('real life'). Is this tension necessary? Does this dichotomy really exist? Can or should it be resolved? Ben and Gus decided to tackle these questions in their own way by making a video 'spoof' of the movie Dangerous Minds.

The obvious gaps between 'textbook classrooms' and 'real classrooms' in Dangerous Minds *inspired Ben and Gus to invent their own version of a nightmare classroom — a place where teachers must wear hockey gear as armor for their own protection. For them, making the video was the point; it allowed them to 'play out' their worst fantasies and in so doing, talk about them more directly. The video also made it possible for their teaching colleagues in the audience to engage in a discussion they perceived as grounded in something 'real'. Here was a text they could sink their teeth into! The resulting dialogues helped the teachers and professors collectively recast the theory/practice dilemma in more meaningful ways.*

This first audience, however, was not all Ben and Gus had in mind when they made their music video. They were also targeting a second audience — the secondary English students with whom they would soon be working. Their particular interest was in the fact that one of the most 'everyday' genres that their students came in contact with was not novels, computers, textbooks or any of the other texts that we had looked at during the university course, but music videos. As they observed in the project log which accompanied their video, these three or four minute visual texts are really short narrative sequences that adhere to traditional dramatic principles related to structure, plot, character development, and so on, but which also have their own syntactic structure. Citing the artistic and commercial success of such early music videos as Michael Jackson's Thriller, *they go on to talk about the ways in which recent videos are artistic works that do more than just 'sell' the music. They express youth resistance and ideals, and reconceptualize their lives in a way that appropriates social norms for their own ends, creating their own culture. What are the implications for teachers? Ben and Gus say: We feel that if educators truly wish to bridge the gap between their students and themselves, they must overcome their initial reservations to music videos and treat them as a valid art form. In a sense this is why we decided to create our own low-budget independent music video. We wanted to demonstrate to our students that the music videos that they view daily on* Much Music *or* Musique Plus *can serve as valuable educational tools. Our video, appropriately entitled* Dangerous Kids, *is an attempt to poke fun at the highly successful but very melodramatic Hollywood film* Dangerous Minds *starring Michele Pfeiffer. By using the guitar-centered Guns 'n Roses song 'Welcome to the Jungle', we have created our own humourous interpretation of what it is like to teach in a deteriorated chaotic inner city school where teachers are forced to wear body armor to protect themselves. Our goal in the end was to make video making as exciting and as much fun as possible, to lose all pretensions and to fall under the medium's sway. To accomplish their goal, Ben and Gus had hijacked all the usual tools of American Billboard and Hollywood for their own project as teachers, one that they could eventually share with their students.*

Self-study is thus not only about ourselves. As many of the cases we have presented demonstrate, it serves other teachers and students, and can provide both the impetus and the blueprint for change, a point we shall take up more thoroughly in the next and final chapter.

Chapter 7

Theorizing Nostalgia in Self-study

No one ever told us we had to study our lives,
make of our lives a study, as if learning natural history
or music, that we should begin with the simple exercises first
and slowly go on trying
the hard ones, practicing till strength
and accuracy become one with the daring
to leap into transcendence, take the chance
of breaking down in the wild arpeggio
or faulting the full sentence of the fugue . . .
(Adrienne Rich, 1978, 'Transcendental Etude' in *The Dream of a Common Language: Poems 1974–77*, p. 73)

It's important to remember and record to set the record straight, to get the story out. But we cannot afford to make memorializing a fetish: the sign of desire once wounded and forever enshrined. Visiting hours are over. Wave good-bye. (Miller, 1997, p. 1013)

It may be tempting to wave goodbye to all of our school memories — once we've set the record straight. However, self-study, whether it refers to the distant past or yesterday, goes beyond getting the stories out, and into our continuing work as teachers. Remembering is not reserved for a time when we are no longer engaged in pedagogical acts. Remembering is a way of examining teacher identity as integral to professional development.

Back to the Future

Recently Claudia returned to the maritime village where she began her teaching career in the 1970s. Although it is close to 20 years since she left, not a lot has changed — the nine-classroom consolidated 'school house', as it is known, is still there along with the gas station and the two Baptist churches. The corner store has closed down but a new diner has opened where she stops for breakfast.

She notices a couple at the other end of the diner — a male in his late twenties or early thirties and a woman in her late fifties. The woman who is facing Claudia looks familiar — 'someone's mother' probably (as in the mother of one of her students), although it doesn't occur to her that the person sitting across from her would be a 'someone'. They both look over at Claudia and finally the man comes over, takes off his baseball cap, part of the 'uniform' for males in rural Canada, and awkwardly says 'Hey Ms.

Mitchell — *do you remember me?' As soon as he speaks Claudia can see that it is Larry Wright — and of course the woman with him, now even more familiar, is his mother. She immediately recalls the subject of Larry's report for a grade nine English project on the life of the New Brunswick writer Desmond Pacey. She wonders if he remembers who Desmond Pacey is. At the same time, his 'Miz Mitchell — Ms.' sends her into a flashback: Larry's class was the one that acquiesced with her request to be called 'Ms.'. One of the students even made her a t-shirt which she still has: 'call me Ms. Mitchell' is written on it. Larry too is having flashbacks, and asks: 'Do you remember that radio play we did on* Shane *in grade 8? That was great. Do you still have the tape?' Claudia answers that she probably doesn't but she also thinks to herself that it was made on a reel-to-reel tape; you probably can't even get one of those now.*

They chat on, reminiscing; Claudia asks after various members of the class of 1976. But later, what stays in her mind from the encounter is what has stayed in Larry's mind — the radio play. It is not as though Larry has gone on to become a playwright — although at least one student from that group, Catherine, has ('in case you don't remember me in 20 years').

This is not a sentimental recollection of a teacher's great kindness to a student. In fact, Claudia recalls that Larry was probably one of the students she was least kind to. What is poignant to her, however, is the fact that after all these years — in a section of the province that has high unemployment and dropout rates (especially among students from small fishing villages who would avoid going into the composite high school), and a life that could at best be described as harsh and rough (trailer homes, banking the house for winter with hay bales, seasonal employment, and a total absence of the cultural attractions of the city) — in all of this, a simple radio play that the grade 8 class of 23 or so students had scripted, acted out and orchestrated with the soundtrack from The Good, the Bad and the Ugly *still figures in someone's memory. She recalls that it was the kind of project that went on for weeks and, like most projects she has started in her teaching — both in school and university — at some point along the way she wished she had never started it — but it is always too late. She never remembers in time. In the case of* Shane, *there were so many scenes and it had been necessary to work out opportunities for more than one person to play lead characters like Marion or Shane so that everyone would get a chance to be something or someone.*

Claudia recalls that once the play was finished, students would never tire of hearing it; even when they had gone on to the ninth grade they would come back to her classroom at lunch hour and ask if they could listen to it. It wasn't something she owned. Rather it was something they owned jointly. And now all these years later here is Larry seeking custody — or at least visiting rights. Claudia knows that before 'visiting hours are over', it will be Larry's request to hear the Shane *audiotape again that she will remember and not the times in the middle when she wished she had never started the project in the first place. It is beyond nostalgia — but not so far beyond as to be forgotten.*

Studying this memory reminds Claudia of 'how she got here' and why she is still involved in teaching. It also gives her some insight into what it is that she wants to hang on to, what she wants to focus on in her work with beginning teachers; it gives her a sense of renewal and a way forward. Through this memory work she reinvents herself.

Some of the organizing principles and methods we have described may not seem that different from much of the current professional literature on autobiography (life history), narrative and reflective work. What is autobiography if not working with the past? Similarly, reflective practice, reflecting on that which has already happened, implies exploring a usable past. However, as Annette Kuhn (1995) notes, autobiography and memory work are not quite the same thing: 'I offer no life story organized as a linear narrative with a beginning, a middle, and an end'. (p. 3) Memory texts, as she goes on to write,

> . . . are driven by two sets of concerns. The first has to do with the ways memory shapes the stories we tell, in the present, about the past — especially stories about our own lives. The second has to do with what it is that makes us remember: the prompts, the pretexts, of memory; the reminders of the past that remain in the present. (ibid)

Like Kuhn, we regard memory *as a feature of* both conventional and alternative forms of narrative. The narratives we privilege in our work are multiple ones, more kaleidoscopic than linear because that, in our opinion, is how life is lived.

Towards a Theory of Practice: Reconceptualizing Nostalgia for Self-study

Because *how* we remember is as important as *what* we remember, the notion of nostalgia is important in and of itself. The term nostalgia leads us into an arena laden with competing ideologies and perspectives — from psychoanalytic approaches to the discourse of the Far Right on family values, getting back to the basics and so on. As Christopher Lasch (1984) puts it:

> In the vocabulary of political abuse, 'nostalgia' — along with 'elitism', 'authoritarianism,' and 'idealism' — now ranks near the top. No other term serves so effectively to deflate ideological opponents. To cling to the past is bad enough, but the victim of nostalgia clings to an idealized past, one that exists only in his head. He is worse than a reactionary; he is an incurable sentimentalist. Afraid of the future, he is also afraid to face the truth about the past. (p. 65)

Much earlier in this century, literary critic D.W. Harding (1934) wrote that the term nostalgia 'confers on the user a kind of aloof superiority . . . The word invariably conveys the same tone of slightly pitying disparagement, but what it implies beyond this vague attitude of the critic is seldom clear' (pp. 57–8).

Janet Zandy (1995), whose work we have referred to throughout this book, draws attention to the ways in which Western nostalgia usually refers to mainstream memories of happy, white, middle-class childhoods. Along with bell hooks, who rejects useless longing, post-colonial theorists such as Homi Bhabba, Trinh Minh-ha and Gayatri Spivak seek 'to radically destabilize the concept of tradition, as exemplified in Western nativist nostalgia for timeless, non-contradictory ethnic identities . . .' (Felski, 1995, p. 211). Nostalgia has a similarly negative connotation in some feminist circles, because of its attention to hearkening back to mother, the maternal and the feminine (and not the feminist). As Doane and Hodges write in their book *Nostalgia and Sexual Difference* (1987),

> . . . nostalgic writers construct their visions of a golden past to authenticate woman's traditional place and to challenge the outspoken feminist criticisms of it. *Nostalgia* is not just a sentiment but also a rhetorical practice. (p. 3)

For these authors, nostalgia can act as a mechanism of control, calling for the return to an earlier time, when everything — gender, race, class — was in its proper place.

Alternative Readings on Nostalgia: Feminist Nostalgia and Future-oriented Remembering

There are alternative readings of nostalgia, however, which place it in the context of looking ahead and imagining particular scenarios for the future. Nostalgia, as we use it, carries neither its medical association from the seventeenth century, when the term was coined by a Swiss physician Johannes Hofer to describe the homesickness of Swiss mercenaries, nor its association from the nineteenth century as a symptom of social malaise and pining or yearning for the past (Lowenthal, 1989). Our emphasis, rather, is on how the concept of nostalgia could be liberating. A similar view can be seen in the work of Christopher Shaw and Malcolm Chase (1989) who describe nostalgia in terms of imagination, noting that 'nostalgia becomes possible at the same time as utopia. The counterpart to the imagined future is the imagined past' (p. 9). Utopias, or what Roger Simon (1992) and others refer to as 'pedagogies of possibility' are much closer to our conceptualization of nostalgia in the project of self-study.

Cultural theorist Jackson Lears (1998) remarks that nostalgia can be regarded as an 'energizing impulse' or even a 'form of knowledge':

> The effort to revalue what has been lost can motivate serious historical inquiry; it can also cast a powerful light on the present. Visions of the good society can come from recollections and reconstructions of the past, and not only from fantasies of the future. (p. 66)

Much of what we have explored in this book has involved a reclaiming of the past that acknowledges the fact that it is gone and can never be relived in the same way. Indeed, it may never have existed in exactly the way that we think it did. However, as Annette Kuhn points out, this does not mean that it is of no use to us, for memories can evoke a utopia towards which we can work. The 'schoolhouse' to which we referred in the introduction, for example, might be seen to have a nostalgic-utopic function. For most of us, it never existed, and even for those who were educated in one-room school houses, the experience may have been less than idyllic. Yet the image of the 'schoolhouse' still holds an attraction that might be seen, for example, as a yearning for a close-knit domestic classroom where everyone feels they belong and are welcome and understood. Or perhaps it is the sense of order that we yearn for, the security of knowing where we stand. This evokes a pedagogic possibility.

In a sense, reinvention uses what we know now to inform and critique what *could* have been (*'that's not how it was but how I would have wanted it to be, and how I want to make it for others . . .'*). Drawing on the idea of the past being 'half-remembered and half-anticipated', a number of feminist scholars have rehabilitated the idea of nostalgia, terming it feminist nostalgia or 'future-oriented remembering'. Complementary to bell hooks' (1989) notion of a usable past, scholars such as Jane Flax (1987), Mary Jacobus (1987), Susannah Radstone (1994) and poet Adrienne Rich (1978) view nostalgia and utopia as significant to the act of working for change. Yearning for a past that never was can provide vision or impetus for future action. As Flax (1987) puts it: 'without remembered selves how can we act?' (pp. 106–7).

Alison Revisited

To illustrate what we mean by feminist nostalgia, we flash back to Alison, the woman we wrote about in the introduction, whose poignant letter about her third grade teacher provoked a wide variety of responses among the beginning teachers in our workshop, ranging from 'get over it' to nods of recognition. It is possible to read Alison's memory work as a type of feminist nostalgia that has a future-oriented dimension. For example, she reveals a sense of being 'rootless and dismembered' (Rich, 1978, p. 75), something that one of the workshop participants picked up on, commenting: '*Imagine a 48-year-old woman walking around still talking about the third grade teacher*'. While the reality of a 48-year-old woman walking around with this defeated child still within her is abhorrent to him, for Alison, this is the way it is! Like an itch that demands to be scratched, this rootlessness gives impetus to her self-study.

Moreover, in her memory-letter, there is an awareness of the incomplete — she knows that there are pieces and details missing. She knows this, because other people serve as witnesses, pointing out things which they remember that she does not. '*Mom was telling me recently that she and I went to a retirement tea for Miss R. but I don't remember'*. Her memories are partial and tentative, yet useful in their ability to point to the gaps.

Still later on in the same letter, Alison includes references to other episodes of school that are quite hopeful (and ones that the recipient of the letter had forgotten):

> *I am looking at a photo of our choir. The girls wore white blouses and (I think) black jumpers and the boys wore white shirts and black pants. We won two trophies for our singing in the festival. Do you remember that?*

This last remembrance suggests a sense of the half-anticipated, perhaps even the utopian. Does it mean that although there is that third grade child still walking around — defeated — there is also in this former teacher, Alison, a choir girl 'dressed to win' a trophy?

This sense of *a remembered self* is illustrated in *Sarafina*, a movie which is set in a South African school in Soweto during the apartheid era. The film explores how teachers like Miss Masembuko and their students led the struggle. 'What do you want, mistress?' asks the schoolgirl Sarafina of her teacher, Miss Masembuko. Aware that her teacher is under surveillance by the police and has an AK47 stored in her kitchen, Sarafina is struggling to work out what this political turmoil really means. Miss Masembuko's answer is filled with yearning:

> *Me, I want very many things. I want this war to be over. I want the hate to be over. I want my Joe back in my arms. I want quiet days and loving nights. I want babies. I want to come home to kindness.*

Miss Masembuko's words, the soft background music of the film as she says these words, and the sight of the AK47 that Sarafina discovers draw our attention to the rupture between the political life of Sarafina's teacher — the work that has to be done — and the ordinary world that she would like to have 'when all this is over'. At a later point in the film, after Miss Masembuko has been arrested and killed, we hear the teacher's words reframed by Sarafina, as she stands at the teacher's desk in a ravaged classroom. Standing at the front of the empty room (taking on the role of teacher), she recalls her teacher's words '. . . I want quiet days and loving nights . . . babies. I want my Joe back in my arms. I want blue skies'. This memory sequence might be taken as an example of future-oriented remembering. Sarafina is not so much yearning for a past that has been lost as she is fighting for a utopic future.

Sarafina's memories of her teacher embody both the personal and the political, serving a present and future tense function even though the raw material remains in the past tense. This is something that is central to the arguments of memory work advocates whose approaches we have described throughout the book. As Carol Tarlen (1995) writes:

> If memory is a past tense function, it plays no part in my working-class identity. If it produces nostalgia [as only a past tense function], then I have no use for it. If, on the other hand, memory enhances and informs the present, if it exists in a dialectical relationship to everyday life, then I can welcome it into my busy and activist working-class artist's life. (p. 20)

In this formulation, nostalgia complements the doing that we have proposed throughout the book, putting into practice Flax's idea that 'without remembered selves, how can we act?'. Alison's memory work and the film *Sarafina* are two examples of how we believe feminist nostalgia can serve to inform teachers' practice.

'Looking back — maybe! But feminist nostalgia?'

We see that a feminist formulation of nostalgia — one which seeks to *claim a history* — speaks to the lives of both male and female teachers. Indeed, on the occasions when men and women have participated in memory-work — both in our classes and in our lives around the kitchen table — we have been struck by how much Kuhn's (1995) notion of the 'abundance of raw materials' works for both males and females. Memory work should therefore not be viewed or treated as an exclusively female domain, even though we are also aware that men have typically been left out of nostalgic activities. As one of the women in a school photography workshop observed of her own family: '*The men were always in the living room watching the hockey game while we women sat around the kitchen table looking at photographs*'.

Our reconceptualization of nostalgia involves serious and committed study. Going back into history, working back through memories which might be painful, digging out photo albums, sitting down to deliberately consider issues of body and sexuality, watching and rewatching teacher movies, and putting ourselves 'warts and all' in front of a video camera are hardly activities for the fainthearted! It is only after undertaking self-study seriously that we become aware of the strength and hope we can derive from it. As Crawford et al. (1992) observe:

> Memory-work has changed our lives. In doing so, it has changed the way we teach, the way we interact with the professional associations of psychologists, the way we do research, the way we write. (p. 196)

Studying ourselves is really an act of commitment to personal and social change. It is not something that we can be 'willed to do'. We are the architects and the implementers of our own study. The impetus and motivation comes from within.

Crossing the boundaries between our professional and personal lives

Throughout the various approaches to self-study advocated in this book there has been a blurring of boundaries between the personal and the professional.

Some of this blurring is not new to the literature of professional development, where there is growing support for the role of personal knowledge and life history (see, for example, Ayers, 1993; Bullough, Knowles and Crow, 1991; Clandinin and Connelly, 1995; Cole and Knowles, 1998; Goodson and Walker, 1991). Beyond valuing the personal as part of the professional, we think that more attention needs to be paid to the crossover from the professional to the personal. How does what we do as teachers connect to our out-of-school life? As an example, after doing a series of workshops and writing several articles about the role of photographs in professional development, Claudia noticed that this experience was beginning to have an impact on her private, personal life. Going through a box of family snapshots with her mother, something she didn't think twice about in the past, is now experienced as 'a companionable feminist nostalgia activity'. She notices so much more now, the process of looking holds her attention as much as the photos do.

Each time they go through the pile, mother and daughter look anew at the same old photographs. Claudia notes that some that held no interest a year ago now take on new meaning. Now Uncle Harry is dead and pictures of him have a deeper significance. A granddaughter in her more grown-up state now resembles a photograph of a great aunt. Claudia, or perhaps her mother, wonders whatever happened to a particular outfit. Her mother declares that '*It would be right in style now — if only someone had hung on to it. Funny term, that — hanging on to things — whoever does? If only we would bother to anticipate the future*'. Each looks closely at certain photographs, looking for signs of themselves in the photographs from another generation. It was in the midst of such a conversation that Claudia and her mother Elsie discovered the photo of 'little Elsie' taken by Elsie's teacher, the picture we discussed in chapter 3. And so we come full circle: what started as a professional activity becomes a private mother–daughter moment which is then reinformed by the professional.

Revisiting Reinvention

> There may be no more pressing intellectual need in our culture than for people to become sophisticated about the function of memory. The political implications of the loss of memory are obvious. The authority of memory is a personal confirmation of self-hood. (Hampl, 1996, p. 211)

We posit that a pedagogy of reinvention through memory has a political agenda that involves a deliberate remembering — one which consciously 'uncovers' memory — and which implies a relationship to schooling that is anything but nostalgic in the usual sentimental sense. Here we refer to the particular humiliation and pain that individuals might have experienced, and also to how those experiences are linked to inequalities based on class, race, sex or religion.

There is nothing sentimental, for example, about the memories of children who have been abused by teachers, or young gays and lesbians for whom school has been a particularly unsafe space, or children who have been made to feel different or humiliated because of the religious or political beliefs of their families, and so on. For those who have no reason to be nostalgic about their own schooling, our notion of 'beyond nostalgia' valorizes a type of social memory, in contrast to what novelist Milan Kundera (1981) refers to as 'willful political forgetting'.

While much of the work that we have advocated in this book has centered on group work and the significance of remembering in a collective way, this should not overshadow the value of individual remembering and acting. One of the tensions that exists in at least some of the professional literature on teachers' lives is around this notion of the personal and the social. We have been particularly drawn to memory advocates whose work has not only made room for both, but has been grounded in the idea that a public framework for education necessitates both. As Annette Kuhn (1995) writes:

> . . . as an aid to radicalized remembering, memory work can create new understandings of both past and present, while yet refusing a nostalgia that embalms the past in a perfect, irretrievable, moment. Engaging as it does the psychic and the social, memory work bridges the divide between inner and outer worlds. It demonstrates that political action need not be undertaken at the cost of the inner life, nor that attention to matters of the psyche necessarily entails a retreat from the world of collection action. (p. 8)

'*Negotiating the Past*' (Nuttall and Coetzee, 1998) is not just about remembering privately and publicly, it is also about confessing. Something that infuses the discourse of many teachers is a confessional mode that accompanies the discovery of some new approach, pedagogy, or child psychology. For example, in the 1980s, when teachers were first exposed to the 'whole language' approach and philosophy of teaching, some came forward with admissions of feeling guilty about what damage they might have done to children using traditional methods. Similar confessions arose about making left-handed children write with their right hands, or making children read aloud even though they were awkward, halting readers and so on. The cruel quality of such practices now colours the professional literature (as many of the narratives in this book indicate). We need to examine how teachers can move forward from under the shadow of guilt.

To return to Naomi Norquay (1993), whose work on remembering difference we cited in chapter 2:

> In order to move forward, we must not be stifled by fear or guilt. Contextualizing our memories . . . does not absolve us of our actions on the other side of difference, but it helps us to understand them. My struggle is not simply a matter of 'taking sides', it is a matter of naming my privilege and

understanding how it works on my behalf . . . Through memory-work, I can interrogate my history so that the invisible practices of my privilege are disclosed. From that painful place, I can begin to reclaim and rename the past in order to envision a future that is shared, not restricted and not donated — a future that for me begins with the acknowledgment of my privilege as the place from which I speak when I speak about racism. This is where I must begin. (p. 250)

It is not unreasonable to speculate that whatever classroom and other social practices are now in vogue will at some later date be found to have had a harmful quality. Years from now, how will we think back, for example, on the significance of contemporary classroom practices such as group work, journal writing, student authoring, computers and so on? Our point is not that every innovation in teaching is inevitably 'tainted' or that we should avoid change. Rather, we ought to be prepared to think that we may have unwittingly done some harm — as well as some good — in our work as teachers. Our point is not to seek justification after the fact; 'I did the best I could'; 'I couldn't know . . .'; 'I'm sure that X knew it was for her/his own good. And I did lots of other good things'; 'Oh, they'll get over it'. Our confessional reference is really one of being transparent to ourselves.

The idea, however, of how we relate to our memories of those teachers from our pasts whom we now (or still) regard as having contributed to abusive treatment is another matter. How would Alison, for example, feel about a confession from her third grade teacher, if that were possible? What did Dale, whose memory work we described in chapter 2, really expect when she went to visit Miss T., her third grade teacher, the one who maintained the 'black hand' and 'white hand'? Would they be able to see them in a new light?

Being Present!

Much of what we have written about in this book has been in relation to a 'now' that includes a great deal of 'then' — schools from 5, 10 or 15 years ago, and in some cases up to 40 or more years ago. What about 'right now'? Will school occupy a different place in the memory of today's students when they become teachers?

We are drawn to Stanley Fish's (1980) now famous title, 'Is there a text in this class?' to raise our own question: *'Is there a teacher in this class?'* We speculate that as more of the learning experiences of our students are carried over into new learner-centred teaching spaces — including virtual classrooms — we are contributing to opening up new memory spaces. *'What about classrooms without teachers?'* scribbles one of Claudia's colleagues in a note during a department meeting. The chairperson of the department has just announced that with reduced budgets, there may not be enough regular staff to cover all the required courses. What roles might teachers occupy in classrooms? In relation to what kind of learning? Consider the following case.

Shor's Utopia

The notion of classrooms without teachers — at least without transmission model teachers — has been taken up in a particularly compelling self-study narrative written by Ira Shor (1995) entitled *When Students Have Power: Negotiating Authority in a Critical Pedagogy*. In this work, Shor provides a 'semester in the life of' narrative in relation to a course on Utopia that he was teaching at City of New York University. In that course it was his intention to decentre his own role as the teacher by involving the students actively in their own learning. What he had to confront was the resistance of the students to this approach based on their histories of more traditional models of teaching. As he starts out:

> *My story begins in a wretched basement room packed with stressed-out working-class students who have come for a required study of Utopia, of all things.*
>
> *These students found themselves in the curious position of being compelled to study Utopia while enchambered underground in an airless cinder block room too small for the overenrolled class. I found myself in the peculiar situation of teaching an allegedly 'empowering' and 'liberatory' course to people who were more or less forced to be there and wishing they weren't. I suppose this bizarre arrangement could be considered a sanity test to find out just how much teachers and students will put up with or can take. Then again, I'd like to think of this strange experience as a tale of two cities — two cities at war, really, a culture war in an age of conservative restoration, I'd call it, with one city old, familiar, neurotic and controlling, while the other appears new, unpredictable, risky and transformative. I see myself and the class traveling between the two warring towns, sometimes in both at the same time, sometimes split into groups inhabiting one town or the other, sometimes outside of the walls of both, wandering the heath at night, like Lear in the storm.*
>
> *The students, waterproof veterans of culture war and the irrational disciplines of schooling, were used to the unreasonable but were not expecting the unexpected. They had become resilient experts in the skill most taught by mass education — spitting out and spitting back the official syllabus force fed to them year after year. While waiting once again to swallow and expel knowledge like tasteless pumpkin seeds, they were ready to knit yet another teacher's name (mine) into their long sweaters of remembrance.* (pp. ix–x)

Continuing in this genre, Shor goes on to describe the 'Siberia zone' — the space the students chose to inhabit figuratively and literally 'at a distance' — in relation to being knowers. The narrative might be taken as a type of memory work which operates in several ways. First, it is an example of his own self-study (a recent looking back, but in the context of 20 years' worth of 'remembered' student-centred courses). The topic of Shor's compulsory course, Utopia, seems to be more than just a passing coincidence! Second, like other pieces of literature, it can engage readers in a form of memory work in the same way that reading/viewing other teachers' school narratives in film or literature invite us into a type of 'life amplified' (Gold, 1990). Finally, Shor's work is future-oriented, and he ends his self-study narrative on a note of 'see you in the future'. Referring to a discussion with Angela, one of the students who insisted that she is going to become a change-agent, he writes:

> I asked her if she could keep it up for 20 years or more because it isn't easy to make important social changes. Would the desire for change run out with her youth, after the routine problems of adult life and the unavoidable setbacks on the road to the future slowed her down? Absolutely not, she declared without hesitation, her sharp eyes fixed on me. So I made an appointment with her in 20 years. I asked her to meet me in my office on a specific date in the twenty-first century, so we can compare notes on how we kept trying to change the system. She said she'd be there, and I've kept her sign-in sheet with its address so that I can find her and keep the appointment. That year is approaching. I hope her desires for social change stay warm, bright and alive, and so do mine. (p. 221)

And so, a course on Utopia ends with a pact reminiscent of Cathy's inscription noted in chapter 3: 'To my two bestest teachers . . . In case you don't remember me in 20 years . . .' The present projects itself into the future — utopic visions.

Self-study: Resistance, Change, Renewal?

Are we 'slouching towards' a new Utopia? Whose utopia? What are the implications? To get to a utopia, we have to change, don't we? Do we have to change if we don't want to? What do people mean by 'change' anyhow? We speak of changing our clothes. Is changing our ways or changing our minds of the same order? And what kinds of changes are we talking about? For whose benefit?

It is tempting to think that we can easily change what we do; however, it is usually easier to change the way we talk about our work than how we actually do it. Remember, for example, Dominique who was taken aback by her first self-video and shocked into the realization that her teaching practice was not completely consistent with how she talked about teaching. The professional discourse of education suggests that a certain element of wishful thinking is endemic to the culture of teacher education (Weber, 1990). Do we invest unrealistic hopes in certain changes? Do we mistake the appearance of change for the essence of reform? Suddenly, we are all 'reflective practitioners' or 'cooperative learners'! Hierarchical supervision has evolved to 'collaborative feedback'! Journals will solve everything! And if they don't, school-based research will! The revolving door of education faddism is always in motion (phonics is 'in', then 'out', then 'in' again, and so forth) simultaneously expressing professional hopes and commitments while at the same time highlighting the difficulty or impossibility of implementing, actualizing, or living up to many of them.

Change in itself has no particular virtue or meaning *per se*. It is dangerous to read it at face value. Take Robert of the pink sweater from chapter 4, for example. After critical reflection, he affirmed his choice to *re-main as he was*, to continue teaching kindergarten and, figuratively speaking, to keep on wearing that sweater. Robert's refusal to conform to the status quo was paradoxically manifested by refusing to change, an act that in a sense reinvents the status quo.

More often, the status quo has a remarkable ability to coopt reform efforts so that significant change does not occur. Aronowitz (1981) notes this paradoxical ability of resistance to feed indirectly into dominant social expectations while apparently subverting authority. One classic example is Paul Willis's research, *Learning to Labor*. In studying working-class teenaged boys in Britain, Willis noted how in order to fit in both with their peers at school and with the expectations or mores of their families and communities, working class youths detested, protested, and disrupted schooling which they derided as useless elitist trash. In other words, in a number of subtle and not so subtle ways, they rebelled and refused to be 'good little students' (skipping class, not doing homework, disrupting class, fighting). But as Willis also points out, in the very way they rejected the system they felt was exploiting them, they also denied themselves the very tools (education, literacy, and so forth) they might have used to really challenge or change the system more effectively. Their actions simply replicated those their fathers had taken before them and assured that their place in the working class social order would remain unchanged.

Being told we should change or even telling ourselves that we will change can have the unintended consequence of provoking a firm entrenchment or resistance, for better or for worse. Teachers like Ben and Gus, for example, may initially deny their own emotional baggage from childhood, resisting the social pressure of their peers or professors, and avoiding introspection by instead admonishing others to 'get over it'. As Steedman (1987), Goodlad (1984) and many others point out, teachers are very good at quiet refusal and resistance to imposed policies or curricula that they do not view as beneficial to themselves or their students. Change can be easily subverted or deflected by disguising or covering over fundamental differences in a fuzzy blanket of what Hargreaves (1994) has called 'contrived collegiality'. Dressing old ways in the garments of new language does not fundamentally change anything.

Identity and Reinvention

In the course of doing the activities suggested in this book, seemingly paradoxical views and conflicting feelings may sometimes emerge. Student teachers in particular may feel torn in their identity. For example, in chapter 4, we saw how some of them struggled while engaging in the drawing task, wondering whether they could be true both to who they felt they were and who they thought they were expected to be. On one hand, they are considered and treated as university students; on the other, they are expected to march into other people's classrooms and act and think like teachers, that is, until they are supervised, in which case they are expected to act simultaneously as students and teachers. Some teacher educators, as another example, may be in the paradoxical state of wanting to be professors of education, yet hating the school system or particular state-mandated curricula. Overeducated or miseducated, others may have grown very weary of schooling, seeking to demolish the system altogether. And then there is Britzman's painful but unanswered question — can one be a teacher and yet hate school? There are times when the answer for some teachers is 'yes', but at the same time, they do not really want to leave teaching. Is it necessary to resolve these tensions in order to grow or change? As Britzman (1992) contends, this matter of identity is neither static nor easy, and quite naturally involves ambivalence and contradiction.

Moreover, student teachers, teachers and teacher educators may feel torn in terms of whether the enterprise of reinvention is around the individual and personal or the social and political. Studying ourselves (multiple selves), as we have noted in previous chapters involves a 'whole self'. It thus speaks directly to the heart of our identity, to who we think we used to be, who we think we are, who we wish we were, and who we hope to become — with the 'we' containing some 'me', 'us' and 'you'. We have no easy way of separating the individual from the social, nor do we have a straightforward way of separating the kind of 'hyphenated self' that is at the centre of collective action. De Lauretis (1986), however, offers an important reminder:

> . . . *identity* is not the goal but rather the point of departure of the process of self-consciousness, a process by which one begins to know that and how the personal is political, that and how the subject is specifically and materially engendered in its social conditions and possibilities of existence. (p. 9)

Reinvention as Change: Some Concluding Remarks

We are always evolving and growing in some way, but the movements may be subtle, slight, and so natural or regular that we are not aware of them. Many of the changes that occur in our bodies, identities, knowledge, viewpoints, and actions are small and incremental — unnoticed until they have a significant or detectible cumulative effect. Some of these changes we welcome. Others we resist or deny, suppressing them from awareness. Often, we don't know that or what we want to change before we are well into self-study. A good example is the case of Dominique who discovered during her self-video project that she wanted to change or modify her practice to make it more congruent with her beliefs. Reinvention does not always involve major change. Like Sandra who rediscovered what she valued in teaching through reflecting back on her school photo, we sometimes need to renew a sense of purpose or commitment that is similar but never quite the same to one we once had.

We have used the term 'reinvention' to refer to deliberate attempts to become more aware of unnoticed or neglected aspects of personal and social development and to harness that energy to our own professional growth. In many cases, reinvention is akin to a renewal that is chosen — enrolling in teacher education, for example, or wanting to feel more satisfied in our work as teachers. Reinvention can also be triggered by a sense of urgency or crisis, for instance, the kind that is provoked by unexpected occurrences or changes outside or inside schools, and sometimes even mandated. The kind of reinvention we have discussed in this book is not synonymous with mandated or imposed school reform or social change, although it can be a process sparked by such events. Especially when undertaken voluntarily, authentically, and collectively, reinvention can indeed lead to major change at an institutional or even a broader societal level (for example, leading to a restructuring of schooling).

Because the term 'change' is often used in contexts that make us uneasy, we prefer 'reinvention' as a more precise invocation of the kind of pedagogical projects we have in mind that take the past as well as the future seriously. Our contention is that one of the best or surest places to start a project of educational change that will be significant and effective is the teaching self. Especially when they are shared, small projects of teacher reinvention take on social and political as well as personal meaning, outlining pedagogical possibilities of hope through action. To return to a point that we raised in the introduction to the book, self-study might be regarded as a type of research-action — It is unlikely that we can engage in this kind of work in any systematic and conscious way without being changed.

Reinvention through self-study can be a powerful and highly effective means of self-transformation and a catalyst for professional growth. It can strengthen or weaken hidden bits of self, challenging us to incorporate certain ignored elements into our professional identity, or forcing us to wrap our imagination around a different image of ourselves in action. It can be wonderfully motivating in its ability to bring home a painful or a beautiful truth, and help us appreciate and even bring about our most meaningful moments as teachers. Studying ourselves does not always involve major change; sometimes it is just about revaluing what was already there and using it in new ways that are informed by both the personal and the social. Like Claudia who needed the reminder from her former student, Larry, of what it is she has always valued in her teaching, reinvention can even be about which parts to 'hang on to': hearkening back to the words of her mother, *'It would be right in style now — if only someone had hung on to it. Funny term, that — hanging on to things — who ever does? If only we would bother to anticipate the future'.*

PostScript

Hang on to things? Can the final paragraph of a book meant by its authors to be a radical reformulation of nostalgia and memory contain a line that might on the surface be read as a conservative imperative? Struggling with such a question takes us beyond nostalgia . . .

References

ALLNUTT, S. and MITCHELL, C. (1994) 'Double vision: Exploring principles and practices — Gynography in teacher education'. Paper presented at the annual meeting of the American Educational Research Association, New Orleans, April.

ANDERSON, M. (1992) 'In a dark room: Photography and revision', in BEHN, R. and TWICHELL, C. (eds) *The Practice of Poetry: Writing Exercises from Poets Who Teach*, New York: Harper Collins, pp. 231–5.

ANTZE, P. and LAMBEK, M. (eds) (1996) *Tense Past: Cultural Essays in Trauma and Memory*, New York: Routledge.

ARONOWITZ, S. (1981) *The Crisis in Historical Materialism: Class, Politics and Culture in Marxist Theory*, South Hadley, MA: JF Bergin.

ASHTON-WARNER, S. (1963) *Teacher*, New York: Simon and Schuster.

ATWOOD, M. (1966) *The Circle Game*, Toronto: Contact Press.

AXLINE, V.M. (1964) *Dibs: In Search of Self*, London: Houghton Mifflin Co.

AYERS, W. (1993) *To Teach — The Journey of a Teacher*, New York: Teachers College Press.

BAILEY, C. (1997) 'A place from which to speak: Stories of memory, crisis and struggle from the preschool classroom', in JIPSON, J. and PALEY, N. (eds) *Daredevil Research: Recreating Analytic Practice*, New York: Peter Lang, pp. 137–60.

BARRECA, R. and DENENHOLZ MORSE, D. (eds) (1997) *The Erotics of Instruction*, Hanover, NH: University Press of New England.

BARTHES, R. (1978) *A Lover's Discourse: Fragments* (trans. R. Hurley), New York: Hill and Wang.

BARTKY, S.L. (1990) *Femininity and Domination: Studies in the Phenomenology of Oppression*, New York: Routledge.

BARTLETT, F.C. (1932) *Remembering: A Study in Experimental and Social Psychology*, Cambridge: Cambridge University Press.

BOAL, A. (1995) *The Rainbow of Desire: The Boal Method of Theatre and Therapy*, London: Routledge.

BRAITHWAITE, E.R. (1959) *To Sir, with Love*, London: Bodley Head.

BRITZMAN, D.P. (1992) 'The terrible problem of knowing thyself: Toward a poststructural account of teacher identity', *Journal of Curriculum Theorizing*, **9**, 3, pp. 23–46.

References

BRITZMAN, D.P. (1995) 'What is this thing called love?', *Taboo: The Journal of Culture and Education*, **1**, Spring, pp. 65–93.

BRUNER, J.S. and HASTE, H. (eds) (1987) *Making Sense: The Child's Construction of the World*, New York: Methuen & Co.

BRUNNER, D. (1991) 'Stories of schooling in films and television: A cultural studies approach to teacher education'. Paper presented at the annual meeting of the American Educational Research Association, Chicago, April.

BUCKINGHAM, D. and SEFTON-GREEN, J. (1994) *Cultural Studies Goes to School: Reading and Teaching Popular Media*, Bristol, PA: Taylor & Francis.

BULLOUGH, R.V. Jr., KNOWLES, J.G. and CROW, N.A. (1991) *Emerging as a Teacher*, New York: Routledge.

BUTLER, F. (1997) 'From reel to real: Film narrative in a Bahamian teacher education program'. Paper presented at the annual meeting of the American Educational Research Association, Chicago, March.

CHALFEN, R. (1987) *Snapshot Versions of Life*, Bowling Green, OH: Bowling Green State University Popular Press.

CHALFEN, R. (1991) *Turning Leaves: The Photograph Collections of Two Japanese American Families*, Albuquerque, NM: University of New Mexico Press.

CHRISTIAN-SMITH, L. (1990) *Becoming a Woman Through Romance*, New York: Routledge.

CLANDININ, J. and CONNELLY, M.F. (1995) *Teachers' Professional Knowledge Landscapes*, New York: Teachers College Press.

COETZEE, J.M. (1997) *Boyhood: Scenes From Provincial Life*, London: Secker and Warburg.

COLE, A. and KNOWLES, J.G. (1998) *Researching Teaching: Exploring Teacher Development Through Reflexive Inquiry*, Boston, MA: Allyn & Bacon.

COOPER, M. (1988) 'Whose culture is it anyway?', in LIEBERMAN, A. (ed.) *Building a Professional Culture in Schools*, New York: Teachers College Press, pp. 45–54.

CRAWFORD, J., KIPPAX, S., ONYX, J., GAULT, U. and BENTON, P. (eds) (1992) *Emotion and Gender: Constructing Meaning from Memory*, London: Sage Publications.

DAHL, R. (1989) *Matilda*, London: Puffin Books.

DAVIS, F. (1992) *Fashion, Culture, and Identity*, Chicago, IL: University of Chicago Press.

DE LAURETIS, T. (ed.) (1986) *Feminist Studies/Critical Studies*, Bloomingto, IN: UP.

DE LAURETIS, T. (1994) *The Practice of Love: Lesbian Sexuality and Perverse Desire*, Bloomington, IN: Indiana University Press.

DELAMONT, S. (ed.) (1987) *The Primary School Teacher*, London: Falmer Press.

DEWDNEY, A. (1991) 'More than black and white: The extended and shared family album', in HOLLAND, P. and SPENCE, J. (eds) *Family Snaps: The Meaning of Domestic Photograph*, London: Virago.

DEWDNEY, A. and LISTER, M. (1986) 'Photography, school and youth culture: The Cockpit Arts Project', in BEZENCENET, S. and CORRIGAN, P. (eds) *Photographic Practices: Towards a Different Image*, London: Comedia, pp. 29–52.

DOANE, J. and HODGES, D. (1987) *Nostalgia and Sexual Difference: The Resistance to Contemporary Feminism*, New York and London: Methuen.

EDWARDS, A.D. and WESTGATE, D.P.G. (1994) *Investigating Classroom Talk* (2nd edition), London: Falmer Press.

EDWARDS, J.O. (1995) 'Class notes from the lecture hall', in ZANDY, J. (ed.) *Liberating Memory: Our Work and Our Working-class Consciousness*, New Brunswick, NJ: Rutgers, pp. 339–57.

EICHER, J.B. and ROACH-HIGGINS, M.E. (1992) 'Definition and classification of dress: Implications for analysis of gender roles', in BARNES, R. and EICHER, J.B. (eds) *Dress and Gender — Making and Meaning*, New York: Berg, pp. 8–28.

ELLSWORTH, E. and WHATLEY, M. (eds) (1990) *The Ideology of Images in Educational Media: Hidden Curriculums in the Classroom*, New York: Teachers College Press.

EWALD, W. (1985) *Portraits and Dreams: Photographs and Stories by Children of the Appalachians*, London: Writers and Readers Publishing Cooperative Society Ltd.

FELSKI, R. (1995) *The Gender of Modernity*, Cambridge, MA: Harvard University Press.

FINCHLER, J. (1995) *Miss Malarkey Doesn't Live in Room 10*, New York: Walker and Company.

FISH, S. (1980) *Is There a Text in this Class?: The Authority of Interpretive Communities*, Cambridge, MA: Harvard University Press.

FISKE, J. (1989) *Understanding Popular Culture*, Boston, MA: Unwin Hyman.

FLAX, J. (1987) 'Remembering the selves: Is the repressed gendered?', *Michigan Quarterly Review*, **26**, 1, pp. 92–110.

FLUGEL, J.C. (1966) *The Psychology of Clothes*, London: Hogarth Press (original work published 1930).

FRAME, J. (1961) *The Lagoon and Other Stories*, (2nd edition), Christchurch, New Zealand, Caxton Press.

FRAME, J. (1991) *An Autobiography: Volume One: To the Island*, New York: George Braziller.

FRIEDEN, S. (1989) 'Transformative subjectivity in the writings of Christa Wolf', in PERSONAL NARRATIVES GROUP (eds) *Interpreting Women's Lives: Feminist Theory and Personal Narratives*, Bloomington, IN: Indiana University Press, pp. 172–88.

GARRETT, A. and McCUE, H.P. (eds) (1989) *Authors and Artists for Young Adults*, Detroit, MI: Gale Research.

GILLIGAN, C., ROGERS, A.G. and TOLMAN, D.L. (eds) (1991) *Women, Girls and Psychotherapy: Reframing Resistance*, New York: Haworth Press.

GIROUX, H.A. and SIMON, R. (1989) *Popular Culture, Schooling, and Everyday Life*, Toronto: OISE Press.

GOFFMAN, E. (1959) *The Presentation of Self in Everyday Life*, Garden City, NY: Doubleday.

GOLD, J. (1990) *Read for Your Life: Literature as a Life Support System*, Markham, Ontario, Whiteside.

GOODLAD, J. (1984) *A Place Called School*, New York: McGraw-Hill.

GOODSON, I. and ANSTEAD, C. (1995) 'Schooldays are the happiest days of your life: Memories of school', *Taboo*, **2**, fall, pp. 39–52.

GOODSON, I. and WALKER, R. (eds) (1991) *Biography, Identity, & Schooling*, London: Falmer Press.

GOTFRIT, L. (1988) 'Women dancing back: Disruption and the politics of pleasure', *Journal of Education*, **170**, 3, pp. 122–41.

GRUMET, M.R. (1995) 'Scholae personae: Masks for meaning', in GALLOP, J. (ed.) *Pedagogy: The Question of Impersonation*, Bloomington, IN: Indiana University Press, pp. 36–45.

GRUMET, M.R. (1988) *Bitter Milk: Women and Teaching*, Amherst, MA: University of Massachusetts Press.

HAMPL, P. (1996) 'Memory and imagination', in McCONKEY, J. (ed.) *The Anatomy of Memory: An Anthology*, New York and Oxford: Oxford University Press, pp. 201–11.

HANSEN, A. (1995) 'The day the heat went on', in KLEINFELD, J.S. and YERIAN, S. (eds) *Gender Tales: Tensions in the Schools*, New York: St. Martin's Press, pp. 131–7.

HARDING, D.W. (1934) 'A note on nostalgia', in LEAVIS, F.R. (ed.) *Determination: Critical Essays*, London: Chatto and Windus, pp. 57–78.

HARGREAVES, A. (1994) *Changing Teachers, Changing Times: Teachers; Work and Culture in the Postmodern Age*, London: Cassell.

HAUG, F., and others (1987) *Female Sexualization: A Collective Work of Memory* (trans. E. Carter), London: Verso.

HOFFMAN, E. (1989) *Lost in Translation: A Life in a New Language*, New York: Penguin Books.

HOLLAND, P. (1991) Introduction: Memory and the family album', in HOLLAND, P. and SPENCE, J. (eds) *Family Snaps: The Meaning of Domestic Photograph*, London: Virago.

HOLLAND, P. and SPENCE, J. (eds) (1991) *Family Snaps: The Meaning of Domestic Photograph*, London: Virago.

HOLT, J. (1964) *How Children Fail*, New York: Bantam Doubleday Dell.

hooks, b. (1989) 'Choosing the margins as a space of radical openness', *Framework*, **36**, p. 17.

hooks, b. (1993) 'Eros, eroticism and the pedagogical process', *Journal of Cultural Studies*, **7**, 1, pp. 58–63.

hooks, b. (1994) 'In our glory: Photography and black life', in WILLIS, D. (ed.) *Picturing Us: African American Identity in Photography*, New York: The New Press, pp. 43–53.

Isenberg, J. (1994) *Going by the Book: The Role of Popular Classroom Chronicles in the Professional Development of Teachers*, Westport, CT: Bergin & Garvey.

Jacobus, M. (1987) 'Freud's mnemonic: Women, screen memories, and feminist nostalgia', *Michigan Quarterly Review*, **26**, 1, pp. 117–39.

Jennings, K. (ed.) (1994) *One Teacher in 10: Gay and Lesbian Educators Tell Their Stories*, Boston MA: Alyson.

Johnson, L. (1992a) *Dangerous Minds*, New York: St. Martin's Press.

Johnson, L. (1992b) *My Posse Don't Do Homework*, New York: St. Martin's Press.

Johnson, R. (1997) 'The "no touch" policy', in Tobin, J. (ed.) *Making a Place for Pleasure in Early Childhood Education*, New Haven, CT: Yale University Press, pp. 101–18.

Jones, L. (1990) *An Angel at my Table: The Screenplay: From the Three Volume Autobiography of Janet Frame*, London, Sydney: Pandora.

Joseph, P.B. and Burnaford, G.E. (eds) (1994) *Images of Schoolteachers in Twentieth-Century America: Paragons, Polarities, Complexities*, New York: St. Martin's Press.

Karamcheti, I. (1995) 'Caliban in the classroom', in Gallop, J. (ed.) *Pedagogy: The Question of Impersonation*, Bloomington, IN: Indiana University Press, pp. 138–46.

Kaufman, B. (1964) *Up the Down Staircase*, New York: Hearst.

Keen, S. (1983) *The Passionate Life*, San Francisco, CA: Harper & Row.

Kelly, U.A. (1997) *Schooling Desire: Literacy, Cultural Politics, and Pedagogy*, New York: Routledge.

Khayatt, M.D. (1992) *Lesbian Teachers: An Invisible Presence*, Albany, NY: State University of New York Press.

Kissen, R.M. (1996) *The Last Closet: The Real Lives of Lesbian and Gay Teachers*, Portsmouth, NH: Heinemann.

Koerner, M.E. (1992) 'Teachers' images: Reflections of themselves', in Schubert, W.H. and Ayers, W.C. (eds) *Teacher Lore: Learning From Our Own Experience*, New York: Longman.

Kotre, J. (1995) *White Gloves: How We Create Ourselves Through Memory*, New York: The Free Press.

Kozloff, M. (1994) *Lone Visions, Crowded Frames: Essays on Photography*, Albuquerque, NM: University of New Mexico Press.

Krisman, A. (1986) 'You shout at us one minute; you take photographs the next', in Holland, P., Spence, J. and Watney, S. (eds) *Photography/politics: Two*, London: Comedia/Photography Workshop, pp. 122–4.

Kuhn, A. (1985) *The Power of the Image: Essays on Representation and Sexuality*, London: Routledge & Kegan Paul.

Kuhn, A. (1995) *Family Secrets: Acts of Memory and Imagination*, London and New York: Verso.

Kundera, M. (1981) *The Book of Laughter and Forgetting* (trans. Heim, M.H.), Harmondsworth: Penguin Books.

LASCH, C. (1984) 'The politics of nostalgia: Losing history in the mists of ideology', *Harper's Magazine*, **269**, 1614, pp. 65–70.

LAURENCE, M. (1974) *The Diviners*, Toronto: McClelland and Stewart.

LAVALLEE, B.E. (1990) 'Teacher talk: The role of language and paralanguage in a French immersion kindergarten'. Unpublished master's thesis, University of Alberta, Edmonton, Alberta.

LEARS, J. (1998) 'Looking backward: In defense of nostalgia', *Lingua Franca: The Review of Academic Life*, **7**, 10, pp. 59–66.

LITVAK, J. (1995) 'Pedagogy and sexuality', in HAGGERTY, G.E. and ZIMMERMAN, B. (eds) *Professions of Desire: Lesbian and Gay Studies in Literature*, New York: The Modern Language Association of America, pp. 19–30.

LORTIE, D. (1975) *School Teacher: A Sociological Study*, Chicago, IL: University of Chicago Press.

LOWENTHAL, D. (1989) 'Nostalgia tells it like it wasn't', in SHAW, C. and CHASE, M. (eds) *The Imagined Past: History and Nostalgia*, Manchester: Manchester University Press, pp. 18–32.

LURIE, A. (1990) *Don't Tell the Grown-Ups: Why Kids Love the Books They Do*, London: Avon.

MANKE, M.P. (1994) 'The sentimental image of the rural schoolteacher', in JOSEPH, P.B. and BURNAFORD, G.E. (eds) *Images of Schoolteachers in Twentieth-Century America: Paragons, Polarities, Complexities*, New York: St. Martin's Press, pp. 243–57.

MARTIN, J.R. (1992) *The Schoolhome: Rethinking Schools For Changing Families*, Cambridge, MA: Harvard University Press.

MARTIN, R. (1986) 'Phototherapy: The school photograph (Happy days are here again)', in HOLLAND, P., SPENCE, J. and WATNEY, S. (eds) *Photography/politics: Two*, London: Comedia/Photography Workshop, pp. 40–2.

MAVOR, C. (1997) 'Collecting loss', *Cultural Studies*, **11**, 1, pp. 111–37.

McROBBIE, A. (1992) 'Post-Marxism and cultural studies: A post-script', in GROSSBERG, L., NELSON, C. and TREICHLER, P. (eds) *Cultural Studies*, New York, Routledge: pp. 719–30.

McROBBIE, A. (1994) *Postmodernism and Popular Culture*, London: Routledge.

McWILLIAM, E. and JONES, A. (1996) 'Eros and pedagogical bodies: The state of (non)affairs', in McWILLIAM, E. and TAYLOR, P.G. (eds) *Pedagogy, Technology, and the Body*, New York: Peter Lang, pp. 127–36.

McWILLIAM, E. and TAYLOR, P.G. (eds) (1996) *Pedagogy, Technology, and the Body*, New York: Peter Lang.

MDA, Z. (1993) *When People Play People: Development Communication Through Theatre*, Johannesburg: Witwatersrand University Press.

MILLER, J. (1996) *School for Women*, London: Virago.

MILLER, N.K. (1997) 'Public statements, private lives: Academic memoirs in the nineties', *Signs: Journal of Women in Culture and Society*, **22**, 4, pp. 981–1015.

MITCHELL, C. (1988) 'The art of making do', *Canadian Journal of English Language Arts*, **11**, 3, pp. 16–18.

MITCHELL, C. and REID-WALSH, J. (1995) 'And I want to thank you Barbie: Barbie as a site for cultural interrogation', *Review of Education/Pedagogy/ Culture Studies*, **17**, 2, pp. 143–55.

MOORE, M. (1994) *Reinventing Myself: Memoirs*, Toronto: Stoddart.

MORRISON, T. (1981) *Tar Baby*, New York: Knopf, Distributed by Random House.

MORRISON, T. (1987) *Beloved: A Novel*, New York: Knopf, Distributed by Random House.

MORRISON, T. (1996) 'Memory, creation, and writing', in McCONKEY, J. (ed.) *The Anatomy of Memory: An Anthology*, New York and Oxford: Oxford University Press, pp. 212–18.

MOSS, G. (1989) *Un/popular Fictions*, London: University of London Press.

MOUSTAKAS, C. (1963) *The Authentic Teacher*, New York: Ballantine.

NEILL, A.S. (1970) *Summerhill: For and Against*, New York: Hart Publishing Co.

NODDINGS, N. (1984) *Caring: A Feminine Approach to Ethics and Moral Education*, Berkeley, CA: University of California Press.

NORQUAY, N. (1993) 'The other side of difference: Memory-work in the mainstream', *Qualitative Studies in Education*, **6**, 3, pp. 241–51.

NUTTALL, S. and COETZEE, C. (eds) (1998) *Negotiating the Past: The Making of Memory in South Africa*, Cape Town S.A.: Oxford University Press.

OAKLEY, A. (1994) 'Women and children first and last: Parallels and differences between children's and women's studies', in MAYALL, B. (ed.) *Children's Childhoods Observed and Experienced*, London: Falmer Press, pp. 13–32.

OKELY, J. (1996) *Own or Other Culture*, London and New York: Routledge.

O'REILLY SCANLON, K. (1992) *Tales Out of School*, Carp: Creative Bound.

PENNYCOOK, A. (1985) 'Actions speak louder than words: Paralanguage communication and education', *TESOL Quarterly*, **19**, 2, pp. 259–82.

PERCIVAL, W.P. (1940) *Life in School: An Explanation of the Protestant School System of the Province of Quebec*, Montreal: Herald Press.

POLAN, D. (1993) 'Professors discourse', *A Journal of Theoretical Studies in Media and Culture*, **16**, 1, pp. 28–49.

POYNTON, C. (1996) 'Giving voice', in McWILLIAM, E. and TAYLOR, P.G. (eds) *Pedagogy, Technology, and the Body*, New York: Peter Lang, pp. 103–12.

PRENTICE, S. (1994) (ed.) *Sex in Schools: Canadian Education & Sexual Regulation*, Toronto: Our Schools/Our Selves.

PROVENZO, E.F., Jr., McCLOSKEY, G.N., KOTTKAMP, R.B. and COHN, M.M. (1989) 'Metaphor and meaning in the language of teachers', *Teachers College Record*, **90**, 4, pp. 551–73.

QUIGLY, I. (1982) *The Heirs of Tom Brown's School Days: The English School Story*, London: Chatto and Windus.

RADSTONE, S. (1994) 'Remembering ourselves: Memory, writing and the female self', in FLORENCE, P. and REYNOLDS, D. (eds) *Feminist Subjects, Multimedia: Cultural Methodologies*, Manchester and New York: Manchester University Press, pp. 171–82.

RAND, E. (1995) *Barbie's Queer Accessories*, Durham, NC: Duke University Press.

RICH, A. (1978) *The Dream of a Common Language: Poems 1974–1977*, New York: W.W. Norton.

ROBERTSON, J.P. (1997) 'Fantasy's confines: Popular culture and the education of the female primary school teacher', *Canadian Journal of Education*, **22**, 2, pp. 123–43.

SALAMAN, E. (1970) *A Collection of Moments: A Study of Involuntary Memories*, London: Longman.

SEITER, E. (1993) 'Buying happiness, buying success: Toy advertising to parents' in *Sold Separately: Children and Parents in Consumer Culture*, New Brunswick, NJ: Rutgers University Press.

SHAW, C. and CHASE, M. (1989) 'The dimensions of nostalgia', in SHAW, C. and CHASE, M. (eds) *The Imagined Past: History and Nostalgia*, Manchester: Manchester University Press, pp. 1–17.

SHOLLE, D. and DENSKI, S. (1995) 'Critical media literacy: Reading, remapping, rewriting', in MCLAREN, P., HAMMER, R., SHOLLE, D. and REILLY, S. (eds) *Rethinking Media Literacy: A Critical Pedagogy of Representation*, New York: Peter Lang, pp. 7–31.

SHOR, I. (1995) *When Students Have Power: Negotiating Authority in a Critical Pedagogy*, Chicago, IL and London: University of Chicago Press.

SIMON, R.I. (1992) *Teaching Against the Grain: Texts for a Pedagogy of Possibility*, Toronto: OISE Press.

SPENCE, J. (1995) *Cultural Sniping: The Art of Transgression*, New York: Routledge.

SPENCE, J. and SOLOMON, J. (1995) *What Can a Woman Do with a Camera: Photography for Women*, London: Scarlet Press.

STANLEY, L. (1992) *The Auto/biographical I: The Theory and Practice of Feminist Auto/biography*, Manchester and New York: Manchester University Press.

STEEDMAN, C. (1987) 'Prisonhouses', in LAWN, M. and GRACE, G. (eds) *Teachers: The Culture and Politics of Work*, Philadelphia, PA: Falmer Press, pp. 117–29.

SUTHERLAND, N. (1997) *Growing Up: Childhood in English Canada from the Great War to the Age of Television*, Toronto, University of Toronto Press.

TARDIF, C. and WEBER, S.J. (1987) 'French immersion research: A call for new perspectives', *Canadian Modern Language Review/La revue des langues vivantes*, **44**, 1, pp. 67–77.

TARLEN, C. (1995) 'The memory of class and intellectual privilege', in ZANDY, J. (ed.) *Liberating Memory: Our Work and Our Working-class Consciousness*, New Brunswick, NJ: Rutgers University Press, pp. 20–6.

TOBIN, J. (ed.) (1997) *Making a Place for Pleasure in Early Childhood Education*, New Haven, CT: Yale University Press.

TOMPKINS, J. (1996) *A Life in School: What the Teacher Learned*, Reading, MA: Addison-Wesley.

TRAGER, G.L. (1958) 'Paralanguage: A first approximation', *Studies in Linguistics*, **13**, pp. 1–12.

TUROW, J. (1989) *Playing Doctor: Television, Storytelling, and Medical Power*, New York: Oxford University Press.

VAN MANEN, M. (1990) *Researching Lived Experience: Human Science for an Action Sensitive Pedagogy*, London, Ontario: Althouse Press.

VAN MANEN, M. (1991) *The Tact of Teaching*, London, Ontario: Althouse Press.

WALKER, A.L. and MOULTON, R.K. (1989) 'Photo albums: Images of time and reflections of self', *Qualitative Sociology*, **12**, pp. 155–82.

WALKERDINE, V. (1990) *Schoolgirl Fictions*, London: Verso.

WALTON, K. (1995) 'Creating positive images: Working with primary school girls', in SPENCE, J. and SOLOMON, J. (eds) *What Can a Woman Do with a Camera? Photography for Women*, London: Scarlet Press, pp. 153–8.

WATZLAWICK, P., BEAVIN, J. and JACKSON, D. (1967) *The Pragmatics of Human Communication*, New York: W.W. Norton & Co. Inc.

WEBER, S.J. (1990) 'The teacher educator's experience: Generativity and duality of commitment', *Curriculum Inquiry*, **20**, 2, pp. 141–59.

WEBER, S.J. (1992) 'Playing their way to literacy', *Canadian Children*, **17**, 1, pp. 51–60.

WEBER, S.J. (1993) 'The narrative anecdote in teacher education', *Journal of Education for Teaching*, **19**, 1, pp. 71–82.

WEBER, S.J. and MITCHELL, C. (1995) *That's Funny, You Don't Look Like a Teacher! Interrogating Images and Identity in Popular Culture*, London: Falmer Press.

WEBER, S.J. and TARDIF, C. (1991) 'Assessing L2 competency in early immersion classrooms', *Canadian Modern Language Review*, **47**, 5, pp. 219–34.

WEBER, S.J. and TARDIF, C. (1987) 'An ethnography of French immersion kindergarten: Sense-making strategies in second language classrooms'. Paper presented to the 8th Second Language Research Forum, University of Hawaii at Manoa.

WEILER, K. (1992) 'Remembering and representing life choices: A critical perspective on teachers' oral history narratives', *Qualitative Studies in Education*, **3**, 1, pp. 39–50.

WHITMAN, W. (1936) *Leaves of Grass*, New York: Heritage Press.

WILLIS, P.E. (1977) *Learning to Labour: How Working Class Kids Get Working Class Jobs*, Farnborough, Engand: Saxon House.

WILLIS, S. (1991) *A Primer for Daily Life*, London and New York: Routledge.

WINEBURG, S.S. (1995) 'When good intentions aren't enough', in KLEINFELD, J.S. and YERIAN, S. (eds) *Gender Tales: Tensions in the Schools*, New York: St. Martin's Press, pp. 161–4.

YEATS, W.B. (1973) *Collected Poems*, New York: Macmillan.

ZANDY, J. (ed.) (1995) *Liberating Memory: Our Work and Our Working-class Consciousness*, New Brunswick, NJ: Rutgers University Press.

Subject Index

school photos and children's
    memories, 76–7
school portraits 75–81, 89, 134
in school year books 46, 77, 88, 94
stirring up memories, 98–102, 111
vernacular portraits, 77
see also photography; chapter 2
photography 195
    and colonization, 80, 122–3
    and identity
        cultural 106
        gender 92–3
        racial 102
        sexual 94
    and imagination and fantasy, 107–22
    and myth, 79–80
    and narrativisation, 106
    photo essays 99, 179
    photo projects, 105
    photo workshops for teachers 84–98
    picture day in school 85, 88–93, 96–8
    as a radical act, 111, 113–14
    in self-study
        see self-study
    see also memory work; photographs
playing school 10–11, 14–29
    commodification of 19–20, 25
    playing disruption 26
    playing work 26
    prompt 14–15
pleasure 145, 159, 161–3
Poitier, Sidney 167
Poppy 10
popular
    images 170–2, 187
    teacher 164, 167, 181, 184
    texts of teaching 182–3
popular culture 164, 170, 177, 183, 186–7
    high culture 178
    low culture 178
(post)colonial memory 71
power 21, 23, 54, 141, 161, 180, 185, 213
practicum 208
praxis 215
primary texts 172
Prime of Miss Jean Brodie (The) 3
professional
    development 186, 188, 215, 225
    growth 197, 199, 232

growth, personal 198
identity 170–1, 190
Prom Dress fantasy 117
prompts 2, 14–15
    artefacts of play 17
    differences 142
    localized and idiosyncratic 65
    movie 166
    objects 2, 15, 18, 20, 57, 65
    using 30, 36–7, 65
    writing memories 30
    see also memory work; photographs

race 178, 185, 213, 221, 225
rebellion 179
reel texts 166
reinvention 171, 214–15, 225, 231–2
    pedagogy of 8, 225
religion 213, 225
resistance 162, 215, 228, 230
Robert's pink sweater 138–9
romanticism 180, 182, 185, 187
*Romy and Michele's High School
    Reunion* 46
Rosa 154–5

Sam's memory 31–2
Sandra
    close reading of *Dangerous Minds*
        174–80
    photo essay 133–6, 159
    school photo 231
Sarafina 3, 167, 223, 224
scaffold of meaning 203
school
    bell 2
    cane 56–7
    images 7
    memories 3, 12, 218
    outside of school 3
    playing 10, 14–16, 18–25, 28
    reform 232
    rows of desks 56
    school-in-memory 41–2
school-house 2, 222
second draft 49–50, 53
self 8–9, 195, 201
    embodied 8
    hyphenated 231

Author Index

Allnutt, S. 118
Anderson, M. 119
Anstead, C. 58
Antze, P. 60
Aronowitz, S. 230
Ashton-Warner, S. 167–9
Atwood, M. 120
Axline, V.M. 170
Ayers, W. 225

Bailey, C. 54–5
Barreca, R. 145
Barthes, R. 125
Bartky, S.L. 122
Bartlett, F.C. 42
Beavin, J. 203
Benton, P. 25–6, 58, 62–6, 224
Boal, A. 113
Braithwaite, E.R. 165, 167, 174–80, 186
Britzman, D.P. 129, 157, 231
Bruner, J.S. 203
Brunner, D. 170, 184
Buckingham, D. 108, 192, 194–5
Bullough, R.V. Jr. 129, 225
Burnaford, G.E. 129, 170
Butler, F. 184

Chalfen, R. 79–80, 96
Chase, M. 221
Christian-Smith, L. 183
Clandinin, J. 225
Coetzee, J.M. 34, 56–7, 226
Cohn, M.M. 129
Cole, A. 225
Connelly, M.R. 225
Cooper, M. 180
Crawford, J. 25–6, 58, 62–6, 224
Crow, N.A. 129, 225

Dahl, R. 39–40
Davis, F. 126
De Lauretis, T. 182, 231
Delamont, S. 204
Denenholz Morse, D. 145
Denski, S. 215
Dewdney, A. 81, 106, 108
Doane, J. 221

Edwards, A.D. 204
Edwards, J.O. 59–60
Eicher, J.B. 127
Ellsworth, E. 201
Ewald, W. 108

Felski, R. 221
Finchler, J. 128
Fish, S. 227
Fiske, J. 180
Flax, J. 222, 224
Flugel, J.C. 151
Frame, J. 10–11
Frieden, S. 61

Garrett, A. 181
Gault, U. 25–6, 58, 62–6, 224
Gilligan, C. 28
Giroux, H.A. 129, 170, 184
Goffman, E. 127
Gold, J. 229
Goodlad, J. 230
Goodson, I. 57, 225
Gotfrit, I. 139
Grumet, M.R. 126, 143–5, 162

Hampl, P. 31, 34, 48–50, 73, 225
Hansen, A. 151
Harding, D.W. 220